Work Organisation in Practice

P-O Börnfelt

Work Organisation in Practice

From Taylorism to Sustainable Work Organisations

palgrave
macmillan

P-O Börnfelt
Göteborg, Sweden

ISBN 978-3-031-21666-4 ISBN 978-3-031-21667-1 (eBook)
https://doi.org/10.1007/978-3-031-21667-1

Translation from the Swedish language edition: "Arbetsorganisation i praktiken: En kritisk introduktion till arbetsorganisationsteori" by P-O Börnfelt, © P-O Börnfelt and SNS Förlag 2009. Published by SNS Förlag. All Rights Reserved.

Cover illustration: Busakorn Pongparnit-GettyImages

This Palgrave Macmillan imprint is published by the registered company Springer Nature Switzerland AG
The registered company address is: Gewerbestrasse 11, 6330 Cham, Switzerland

In memory of my parents Birgit and Per-Hugo.

Preface

The book is an introduction to work organisation. The reader is presented with an overview, based on research, of the development and diffusion of work organisation models used in practice from over a century ago onwards. The book was first published in Swedish in 2009 and then updated in 2018. This is the first edition in English. I have been using the book myself as a lecturer in Sweden. According to students, the book is easy to understand. The book can be used as an introduction at university level to work organisation in disciplines such as business administration, sociology, working life studies, organisational psychology and pedagogy. Other possible readers, other than university students, are managers, management consultants, HR personnel and union representatives.

Many people take the work organisation for granted and see it as an almost natural occurring phenomena and/or they think that there is only one way of organising a workplace. This is not the case at all. The work organisation is created by people and there are important decisions to be made when designing it. These decisions will have different effects on efficiency, innovation and workers' health. There is not one best model which fits all types of organisations and which optimises all aspects. However, a work organisation analyst should have knowledge about possible effects from different ways of designing work organisations. Bridge builders need education and training to be able to build sustainable bridges. The same goes for organisation builders. How to design work organisations that do not consume people resulting in unhealth, but instead create sustainable work organisations where healthy working conditions and efficiency are combined? I hope that this book can be used as an aid to critically reflect on the organisation of work.

The focus of my book is very practical; how work is organised in different tasks and how work is coordinated in different work organisation models. The critical perspective highlights working conditions, health and well-being, learning and development for workers, how workers are controlled in the different models, but also effects on efficiency, learning and innovation for the organisation. The book also critically examines the original literature behind models such as scientific management, the Toyota model and the related lean production, and New Public Management. The literature is examined by asking questions like; how do the authors come to their conclusions, what evidence do they present and what methods have they used? Are their conclusions plausible, are they in line with other researchers' results, and above all, what do critical authors say about these work organisation models? Furthermore, possible causes are discussed to why certain work organisation models are diffused globally, taking changes in the society into account.

I wrote the major part of this book in London while living there 2018–2021. I am grateful for the great company of the Greenwich writing group. We usually met once a week in a riverside pub in Greenwich, writing on our own stuff, had breaks and had a few pints together. Graham Archibald, one of the group members, helped me with language editing one of the first chapters, which went on peer review. Thank you for this and for your good ideas for improvement! I am also grateful for the help and support from Palgrave Macmillan. My editors Alec Selwyn and Lauren Dooley, editorial assistant, have given me valuable advice and feedback during the publishing journey.

Göteborg, Sweden P-O Börnfelt

About This Book

When I started teaching work organisation, I could not find a textbook which covered all the areas I wanted to include in my courses, or I was not satisfied with how the literature approached work organisation. That was the starting point to this book. Organisation research, which to a large extent is based on business administration, has since the 1960s distanced itself from the tangible work and the concrete organisation of work (Barley and Kunda, 2001; Härenstam et al. 2006). Organisation research has been more abstract and specialised. There are several organisation theory textbooks presenting theoretical perspectives on how to understand and study organisations such as Richard Scott's (2003) Organizations: Rational, natural, and open systems, Gareth Morgan's (2006) Images of organisation, Bolman and Deal's (2017) Reframing Organizations: Artistery, Choice and Leadership.

Paul Thompson and David McHugh (2009) are using a Labour process perspective in Work Organisations: A Critical Perspective. The book is very comprehensive and covers aspects such as organisation theory perspectives, power, control and resistance in organisations, gender, skill and knowledge. One book, which has got a lot in common with Thompson and McHugh, is Fiona Wilson's (2018) Organisational Behaviour and Work: A Critical Introduction. These books are, as I see it, on a more abstract theoretical level, structured in perspectives and functions in organisations. They do not, however, describe work organisation models on a concrete level.

In this book, organisation theories are presented, which have had influence on how work has been organised since the end of the nineteenth century. Some theories are whole work organisation models, that is they describe how work and the workplace are organised. Other theories cover only limited aspects of work organisation. The theories, however, have all been influential in the way work has been, or is organised. The models/theories have effects on overall efficiency and ability for innovation at the organisation level. From a worker perspective, research is presented about consequences for health, learning and competence development.

In the first chapter, organisation and work organisation are explained. The concept of work organisation, which is the focus of this book, is understood as division of labour into different tasks and the coordination of tasks. The coordination methods also have controlling functions. This structure, from the definition of work organisation, is used throughout the book to explain the work organisation models. The chapter also covers organisational objectives, efficiency, formal and informal organisation, a brief overview of some motivation theories and leadership styles. In the following chapters, work organisations models are presented, which have had influence over how work is organised. The order is more or less chronological. Scientific management and Fordism were developed around 1900 (Chapter 2), the bureaucratic organisation (Chapter 3) described by Max Weber in the same era. The development of the sociotechnical school (Chapter 4) started in the UK in the 1940s. During the same era, the development of the combined American-Japanese quality movement and process organisation started, which continued with lean production (Chapter 5). From the mid-1900s organisation, researchers started to be interested in change, learning and knowledge. In the 1990s this interest grew substantially with the concepts of learning organisations and knowledge management (Chapter 6). Three conflicting models have had impact on work organisation in the public sector. For a long time, bureaucracy was the model for organising the public sector. The professional organisation has also been influential. Since the 1980s, however, new public management has been the major model influencing the public sector. In Chapter 7, the latter two models, professional organisation and new public management, are presented. Lately also concepts such as network organisations and open innovation have been introduced. One example of network organising is the platform economy (Chapter 8). In Chapter 9, the consequences of the new work organisation models are discussed. The changes are described by highlighting changes in skills, work intensification, increasing pressure on workers and, as a consequence, increasing stress-related unhealth. Possible explanations are also put forward for why these new organisation models have been popular since the 1980s. In the last Chapter (10), the concept of sustainable organisation is presented. In the sustainable work organisation, a good work environment and efficiency are combined.

Contents

CHAPTER 1

Organisation and Work Organisation

Learning Objectives

This chapter should provide you with knowledge about:

- How we can understand organisations.
- A definition and explanation of work organisation.
- How work and work organisations can affect health and well-being.
- A number of motivation theories related to working life.
- Some of the reasons for the diffusion of certain organisation models and management concepts.

Introduction

Organisation and work organisation are two different concepts. This book is about work organisation, but in order to give context, the concept organisation is explained in the beginning of the chapter. Then the concept work organisation is presented and its basic components. The work organisation has consequences for skill development, health and motivation which also will be elaborated upon. Lastly, a few basic leadership styles will be introduced as leadership is part of a work organisation. The structure laid out in the chapter is used throughout the book.

The Organisation Society

There are many ways to explain the concept of organisation. Many definitions have however the following in common: '...social structures created by individuals to support the collaborative pursuit of specified goals.' (Scott, 1998,

P-O Börnfelt, *Work Organisation in Practice*,
https://doi.org/10.1007/978-3-031-21667-1_1

p. 10). Organisations have existed in all civilised societies historically, but it is from the start of the industrial society that we can talk about the organisation society. We can find organisations in areas such as the public authorities, defence, manufacturing, retail, wholesale, healthcare, sport, culture, religion, tourism, recreation and leisure activities. The number of organisations and their size have increased substantially over time.

Organisations can be described as having different elements. Scott (1998, pp. 17–23) refers to a model by Leavitt (1965) containing the elements: Technology, environment, participants, social structure and goals. All organisations use some kind of *technology* to process products or service. Technology is here understood as machines and equipment but also knowledge and skills of organisational members. Surrounding the organisation is the *environment*, which the organisation interacts with and is dependent on. In the environment there are for example suppliers, customers, laws and regulations, competitors, culture, technology and the labour market.

Participants are the individuals or social actors, such as owners and workers, that make contributions to the organisation. People in the organisation form a *social structure*, a pattern of relations. The social structure often is described as formal and informal organisation. The formal organisation is how the organisation is planned with different formal roles, positions, departments and how they should relate to each other and formal channels of communication. Another word, which is often used as a synonym to formal organisation, is organisation structure. Planned rules and policies are also part of the formal organisation. The informal organisation is what people actually do, who they cooperate with and communicate with. The well-known Hawthorne studies in the 1920- and 1930s highlighted the importance of the informal organisation. In the Hawthorne factory of the Western Electric Company outside Chicago, researchers found that workers communicated with people outside the formal communication channels. Workers also formed informal groups, which had their own group norms. The groups had developed norms about the quantity of products produced in a day, and the group could put up resistance towards changes that collided with the group norms. Also, various work roles had different status among workers. For instance, work, which was performed by men had a higher status compared to work performed by women (Roethlisberger & Dickson, 1939).

From a worker's perspective, the Norwegian sociologist Sverre Lysgaard (1961), has written about a similar informal organisation. He studied the worker collective in relation to the technical-economical system (more or less the management). The worker collective acted as a buffer against the unlimited demands of the technical-economical for profit maximization. By collaborating and acting as a collective, the workers could resist or decrease the demands from management, which otherwise could lead to de-humanizing effects.

Objectives is a central component in the organisation concept. Strategy is closely related to objectives and the terms are sometimes used interchangeably. The objectives of the organisation should tell you what type of business and how the organisation will achieve advantages in the market (Scott, 1998, chapter 11). It can be to have a low-cost strategy, have very special products or target a special group of customers (Porter, 1980). Objectives should, according to conventional authors, give the organisation and organisation members direction. According to Peter Drucker (1976) management by objectives should result in responsibility and commitment for self-control. The individual is expected to work towards the overall vision and objectives of the organisation using self-control.

Other organisation researchers, however, argue that new activities develop organically in the organisation independent of the objectives. Thereafter objectives are formulated, which legitimise the new activities. The conventional view is that top management formulate overall objectives. Middle managers then concretise and break down the goals at their levels. Studies have however shown that the reverse process is actually occurring. The process starts from below. New products or services are developed in development departments or elsewhere in the organisation and then receive support from middle managers (Scott, 1998, chapter 11).

The assumption that workers direct their energy towards official objectives formulated by management can also be strongly questioned. For instance, professionals like medical doctors and architects tend to be more interested in their job than the organisation they work in. Also, different groups and departments, like blue-collar workers and white-collar workers, a marketing department and a production department, tend to differ quite a lot in interest, focus and goals (Thompson & McHugh, 2002, pp. 8–10).

In order to perform well, organisations need to be effective and efficient. Otherwise they will not be profitable or, if they are a public organisation, will use more of tax-payers money than necessary. Effectiveness can be understood as being successful in achieving the objectives of the organisation. Organisations must produce products or services that are in demand from customers. In other words, effectiveness is about doing the right things. Efficiency is about organisations use their resources such labour and material well, without wasting any. Another way to describe efficiency is doing things in the right way (e.g. Drucker, 1963). The design of the work organisation will have an impact on efficiency. A good work organisation, designed for the task and for development and well-being for workers, will demonstrate good efficiency. However, effectiveness is of higher importance than efficiency. If the organisation is not effective, that is fails to produce products or services customers demand, it does not matter if the organisation uses its resources in an efficient way. Connected to efficiency is productivity. Productivity is often understood as number of products produced per time unit, for example number of cars produced per day. But to have high productivity does not necessarily lead to high efficiency. Also important is to make sure that the resources, like workers, are not exhausted. Thus, good working, and employment conditions will benefit a sustainable approach to an efficient organisation. Sustainable work organisations (Chapter 10) can be understood as the combination of a good working environment and high organisational efficiency. A good work environment, according to this view, results in healthier workers who develop and contribute to an efficient and successful organisation. Furthermore, a good work environment is seen as a precondition to an efficient, effective and competitive organisation (Docherty et al., 2002, chapter 1; Lindberg & Vingård, 2012, p. 40).

However, there are no simple answers how to design an organisation for optimal efficiency. Early organisation theorists, like Frederick Taylor (Chapter 2) and Henri Fayol (Chapter 3) assumed there is a single optimal organisation model for all types of organisations. This assumption, one best model for all, has however since a long time been abandoned among organisation theorists. In the 1960s the contingency theory was coined by Lawrence and Lorsch (1967). They concluded that the environment around the organisation affected what organisational structure would be better suited. A bureaucratic organisation (Chapter 3) can be efficient in a stable environment, where not many changes are taking place (like a government organisation). On the other hand, if the environment is characterised by uncertainty and change, for instance if the organisation is acting on a competitive market, there need to be more differentiation between organisational units, but also more integration and communication between the units. Two early theorists in the contingency tradition, Burns and Stalker (1961), make a fruitful distinction between mechanistic (see Chapter 3) and organic organisations. The latter organisations operate under highly uncertain conditions where innovation is essential for organisational survival, so these organisations develop an organic structure where work processes are informal and flexible (see Chapter 6).

Work

This book is about the organisation of work, and therefore it would be beneficial to explain the concept of work. The Swedish sociologist Jan Ch Karlsson (2017, p. 51) explains work as activities that are carried out in the sphere of necessity. Work is something we do to make a living. If we do the same activity in our leisure time it is not work. The most common form of work is to be an employee—employed by an employer. Another form of work is to be self-employed.

Work Organisation

The concept organisation comprises the whole coordinated system of for instance a company. The concept work organisation has a narrower meaning. An organisation often has several work organisations, especially if it is a big organisation. I am using Henry Mintzberg as a starting point for a definition of work organisation. 'Every organized human activity–from the making of pots to the placing a man on the moon–gives rise to two fundamental and opposing requirements: the *division of labor* into various tasks to be performed, and the *coordination* of these tasks to accomplish the activity.' (Mintzberg, 1983, p. 2). An organisation can have, and often have, different work organisations. The work organisation is different on the shopfloor compared for instance in the marketing department. The definition of work organisation used in this book is; *principles for dividing work into different tasks and for coordinating these tasks.*

In this book the work organisation models are described in their 'pure' forms, or what the German sociologist Max Weber (1864–1920) refers to as ideal types. These ideal types are seldom seen in practice. The organisation has, through history, adopted principles from several different work organisation models. How organisations organise work is therefore often a hybrid of different work organisation models.

Division of work and coordinating work can be done in different ways, which is shown in the different work organisation models. What decisions the organisation makes when dividing work into task and coordinating work will have great consequences for efficiency, worker well-being and opportunities for developing skills. Some of the fundamental theoretical frameworks this book builds upon is research on quality of work, such as Hacker, Volpert and Frese (Zacher & Frese, 2017), Gardell (1986), Lennerlöf (1986), and Karasek and Theorell (1990). The division of labour and coordination principles have a major impact on decision latitude which in turn affect possibility to develop skills and has consequences for health. Work with a high division of labour where workers are externally controlled is associated with de-skilling and health related problems. Also, in work with a high division of labour, people have a narrow decision latitude and only perform simple, repetitive and fragmented work tasks. There is no room for developing new skills. According to the action regulation theory, developed by Hacker and Volpert (Hacker, 2003; Zacher & Frese, 2017), this fragmented work is routinised and is merely carried out on the sensorimotor level. In order to develop new skills and knowledge people need to perform actions. Actions are goal-directed behaviour and requires that intellectual levels are active in order to analyse situations and evaluate action alternatives. Thus, decision latitude is necessary in order to decide how to carry out work tasks, but also to plan work and to evaluate the result of the final outcome. As Hacker put it: "…a task is considered *hierarchically* complete, when the mental regulation is not limited to automated processes, but requires controlled, i.e., knowledge-based, and moreover, intellectual control processes as well (Hacker, 2003, p. 112).

The Division of Work in Different Tasks

Work can be divided in different ways. It can be divided into smaller or larger tasks. On a societal level increased division of work results in people working in more specialised occupations and branches. An increased division of work at the workplace level leads to job content being divided into smaller tasks. An increased division of work results in people having narrower tasks which are easy to learn. The positive effect of increased division of work on productivity has for example been put forward by Adam Smith (1776) in the book *The Wealth of Nations*.[1] Smith used an example of the manufacture of pins where the work was divided into 18 different tasks, only one task for each worker. Smith presented three reasons why increased division of work results in higher productivity[2]:

1. Dexterity increases because the task is simple to perform and is repeated many times.
2. Time is saved because workers do not need to change between different tasks.
3. Improvements in machinery and innovations. Smith mentions that workers often find simpler and more efficient ways to perform work.

The increasing division in branches and occupations result in people becoming specialists who can perform their work more efficiently, which in turn leads to increased productivity in organisations and in society. Even if Smith was positive towards division of work, he also recognised it could have negative effects. Smith observed that the division of work has de-humanizing effects on workers. People do not get opportunity to use their intellectual and innovation abilities, which in turn results in they, in his vocabulary, becoming stupid and ignorant (Smith, 1776, Introduction and chapter 1). Other authors have further contributed to the notion of the degenerating effects on workers (see Chapter 2). If, on the contrary, the division of work decreases, this is usually described in two dimensions, horizontally and vertically. If the division of work decreases on the horizontal level, we talk about work enlargement. When the division of work decreases on the vertical level it is labelled work enrichment. Work enlargement is when a person performs more tasks of similar character. For instance, one worker performs only one task on the car assembly line. If the worker starts to rotate between different similar tasks on the assembly line, it is an example of work enlargement. The worker goes for example from only assembling the left door, to assembling the left door, boot, bonnet, front and front wing. Work enrichment is taking place if the worker on the assembly line also performs tasks on an intellectual level, with reference to aforementioned action regulation theory (e.g. Zacher & Frese, 2017), such as planning, clerical administration, communicating with customers, ordering materials and quality control. If a job is enriched it often results in the person having more control over work, whereby he or she can plan and decide how to perform work. A job, which is only increased on the vertical level, that is enriched, is specialised and the person would then be called a specialist or professional.

[1] The full title is: *An inquiry into the nature and causes of the wealth of nations.*

[2] Increased division of work is however not the only way to higher productivity, see for example Chapter 4 about sociotechnical work organisation. Another way is also to automate production.

In jobs, which are only enlarged, thus increased on the horizontal level, the worker will perform more different tasks of the same nature. He or she does not plan work or decide how to carry out work tasks, thus has no control over how work is performed (see for example Aronsson & Berglind, 1990, p. 77; Mintzberg, 1983, chapter 1; Lennerlöf, 1986, p. 32).

Coordination and Control

Like division of work, coordination can be achieved in different ways. All coordination methods also have controlling functions. Control can be understood as exercise influence on someone's actions or behaviour. In all social groups there is some kind of control. If there is no pattern in behaviour or norms you cannot talk about the existence of a social group. Control is a central aspect of management and organisational behaviour both in practice and in research. In management literature control is not so often mentioned explicitly. Instead, it is concealed under labels such as management, coordination and organisation structure. Control is carried out in many different ways and is integrated in many different aspects of an organisation such as hierarchy, technology, job descriptions, leadership, customers, colleagues, rules, policies, objectives and strategies. There are controlling methods in all models of work organisation, but they differ between the models (Scott, 1998, chapter 11; Thompson & McHugh, 2002, chapter 8).

Examples of coordination and controlling methods:

1. Direct supervision. Commands and instructions are given by a foreman or a supervisor.
2. Standardised work process is common in manufacturing. The task is standardised concerning tools to be used, and in what order work sequences are to be carried out (Mintzberg, 1983, chapter 1).
3. Mutual adjustment. Coordination by mutual adjustment is when several people are communicating informally to coordinate their work (Mintzberg, 1983, chapter 1). Mutual adjustment is the basic coordination method in self-directed working groups (see Chapter 4).
4. Formal work positions. Certain authority and responsibilities are tied to formal work positions. In the hierarchy managers have responsibility and authority over their subordinates.
5. Coordination through rules. In the bureaucracy the coordinating method is a system of rules. The administration is carried out using a system of rules.
6. Technological and physical coordination. The physical design or buildings, rooms and technology also coordinate and control behaviour. For example the assembly line in car manufacturing controls the pace of the workers in a very concrete way. Information technology is used to monitor and evaluate workers' behaviour. For example in call-centres, where workers are phoning up customers, their conversations are often

recorded in order to monitor behaviour towards customers and number of calls made. This can also be labelled visualisation, to visualise workers' work in order to control it (see Chapter 5).

7. Organisation culture. In latter decades organisation researchers and managers have started to be interested in organisation culture. The aim is to influence the norms and attitudes of workers. The idea is that if organisational members have the same norms and attitudes they can perform work in a similar way (e.g. Kunda, 1992).
8. Customers. If workers have customer contact, the customer also has a controlling function. The customer can give direct feedback to the worker or contact a manager about for example complaints (e.g. Normann, 1983).
9. Management by objectives. The top management define overall objectives for the organisation. Objectives should be distinct and clear. The different departments break down the objectives to more specific ones, but they must relate to the overall objective. Audits are carried out to control the results to find out if the objectives are met (e.g. Drucker, 1976).
10. Internal market or pseudo market. Workers and units can be labelled customers and suppliers. The internal customer is expected to control quality and delivery time from internal suppliers (see Chapter 5).

The division of work, how work is coordinated and other aspects of a work organisation has also got consequences for health. The work environment can be divided in a physical and a psychosocial one. The physical work environment is for instance related to physical work activities like heavy lifting, repetitive movement, but also noise, chemicals, air pollution and temperature. The psychosocial work environment includes all social relations on the workplace with colleagues, managers and customers, how work is organised and coordinated (Eriksson & Larsson, 2017).

An often used model to analyse the psychosocial work environment is the demand, control and social support model (Karasek & Theorell, 1990). The combination of high demands and low control is labelled strain and tends to activate stress mechanisms. The combination of high demands, low control and low social support, which is called iso-strain, tends to result in the highest risk to develop unhealthy stress reactions. High demand is when there is a high workload and work needs to be performed at high speed. Control has got two dimensions—decision authority and skill discretion. Low decision authority is when you have little or no influence on how to carry out work, for instance which work methods to use or in what order to carry out work tasks. Low skill discretion is when there are no or few opportunities to use skills and to learn new skills at work. These two dimensions go hand in hand, if a person has no or little decision authority there is very little room for using skills or developing new skills at work. Social support is about having opportunity of good cooperation and good relations with colleagues and managers. Low social support is for instance when work does not involve cooperation with colleagues or when relations with colleagues and/or managers are bad. The combination of high demands, low control and low social support tend to result in stress reactions. This in turn leads to higher risk of developing a number of stress related health problems such as sleeping problems, headache, back pain, stomach problems, depression, and cardiac diseases which is one of the most common causes of death. To have high social support can act as a buffer against negative stress reaction caused by high demands and low control. To have good relations with colleagues and managers can help workers to deal with high demand and low control. Good social support at work is, according to several studies, related to less sick leave, better mental health, less risk for back pain and cardiac deceases. Also, high control has similar positive health effects as high social support (Karasek & Theorell, 1990). Later overviews of research have by large confirmed these conclusions (Bowling et al., 2015; Lang et al., 2012; Nixon et al., 2011; Theorell et al., 2016).

High control also results in opportunities for using skills and to learn new skills, which thus leads to work enrichment (see above). People need to perform actions to develop new skills and knowledge. Actions are goal-directed and require that intellectual levels are active to analyse situations and evaluate action alternatives (Hacker, 2003, p. 112). The opposite is low control jobs where work is fragmented, routinised and repetitive and thus only performed on the sensorimotor level. In other words, these kinds of jobs require very limited intellectual activity and therefore limits learning at work. The combination high demand and high control is labelled active jobs. In Karasek and Theorell's original theory high control counteracts negative health effects from high demands, and also, this combination has been associated with triggering learning and skill development. However, these conclusions have been questioned. Stimulating, creative work with high decision authority and high cognitive demands can result in too high demands, which can have negative stress related effects. A complex work situation when people need to make many difficult decisions within limited time is one example on work situations that can cause stress related health problems (Waldenström & Härenstam, 2008).

Motivation

Motivation has, like control, been a central theme for managers and management research and is one of several factors which affects organisational performance. Work organisation models build on underlying assumptions about what is motivating workers. Some models differ widely on underlying assumptions about motivation, which will be elaborated upon in this section. How then can concept of motivation in working life be explained? People can be said to be motivated when they are prepared to put in extra effort to achieve certain goals (Thompson & McHugh, 2002, chapter 19).

Firstly, this section elaborates on what different assumptions management can have when managing in their type of work organisation. The work organisation is often taken for granted by managers and other employees. However, sometimes the work organisation has been designed in a deliberate way and certain principles have been pushed forward. *Secondly*, some research results will be presented on what conditions are favourable for work motivation and job satisfaction. There is a whole range of theories about human motivation. Only a brief overview of the most influential motivation theories related to work organisation, that is the division of work in different tasks and how work is coordinated, are presented here.

There is a dividing line between (a) seeing people as needing to be motivated or controlled at work and (b) seeing people as wanting to work as a starting-point. Douglas McGregor (1960/1987) addresses these two opposing views to understand human behaviour at work, and labels them theory X and theory Y. If a manager has a theory X view, he or she assumes that people are lazy, do not want to work and avoids work if possible. According to this view, people do not want to have responsibility and do not have ambitions. People want to be controlled and above else want to have security. Therefore, people need to be forced, controlled or threatened to work towards the objectives of the organisation. According to McGregor, classical management theory view humans according to theory X and this way of viewing people create problems for the organisation. Excessive control in theory X management makes people put up resistance and work against the objectives of the organisation.

Depending on conditions at the workplace work can be a source of satisfaction, which is carried out voluntarily, or as a source of dis-satisfaction, which is avoided if possible. Theory Z assumes that people do not avoid work. Physical and psychological effort is as natural as play and rest. People exercise self-control and self-governance towards the goals that he/she has motivation for. The most important driving forces are self-satisfaction and self-actualization. People accept and seek responsibility. In cases where people avoid responsibility and lack ambition it is a result of earlier experiences, like working in theory X oriented workplaces. Most people have the ability to solve problems and be creative. McGregor assumes that organisational and individual objectives can be integrated. Organisations need to create conditions, so individuals can achieve their objectives through aiming their efforts towards the organisational objectives.

Extrinsic Motivation

Extrinsically motivated behaviour is usually related to rewards or punishment, motivation factors that are instrumental and provided by external sources (Ryan & Deci, 2000). A manager who has a theory X view on organisation and workers, will allocate a lot of resources to control and finding different ways to motivate people through extrinsic motivation. The X manager assumes that people are motivated by command and control, detailed instructions and monetary rewards. Theory X management is connected to Taylorism, Fordism (Chapter 2) and bureaucratic work organisations (Chapter 3).

Intrinsic and Social Motivation

Intrinsic motivation is related to doing something that we find enjoyable or interesting (Ryan & Deci, 2000). The theory Y manager focuses on creating favourable conditions for learning and development. The manager assumes that workers are intrinsically motivated, that work itself can be motivating if it is skilled and workers are empowered to make decisions. Work enrichment (see above) is supposed to lead to intrinsic motivation and competence development. Work enlargement on its own does not have that effect. Social motivation is about motivation through social relations, support from colleagues and managers and sense of belonging to a group. The sociotechnical school (Chapter 4) and learning organisations (Chapter 6) build upon intrinsic and social motivation in their design of the work organisation.

There is research that explains intrinsic motivation in more depth suggesting that people have a natural desire to act competently. White (1959) refers to a number of studies in which humans and animals strive to interact with the environment in an efficient and competent way. Humans and many animals are curious about their environment and want to discover and find out about it if they get the opportunity. If you are able to control and change a part of your environment, you will experience satisfaction and your self-confidence will grow. In line with White, other studies show that people need to interact in an efficient way with their environment in order to grow and develop. In order to do that they need have control over a part of the environment, which is an essential condition for intrinsic motivation (Thylefors, 2006; Wilpert, 1998).

Decision authority and related concepts such as control and autonomy are central parts of influential theories about work enrichment and psychosocial work environment. Richard Hackman and Greg Oldham's theoretical framework (e.g. Hackman & Oldham, 1976), which builds upon Frederick Hertzberg's work, has been influential in motivation and work enrichment research. The job characteristics that are expected to contribute to motivation and performance are *skill variety*—the job requires the use of different skills, *task identity*—the job is made up of whole and meaningful piece of work, *task significance*—the job makes a contribution to the society and other people's life, *autonomy*—authority to make decisions at work, and *job feedback*—information about worker's performance is reported to workers. Many studies have been conducted using this model and the results support the model regarding the positive relation to motivation and job satisfaction, whereas the results regarding the relation to performance has been mixed (Oldham & Fried, 2016).

The components of the demand, control and social support model (Karasek & Theorell, 1990), presented above, have also been used to analyse motivation and job satisfaction. The control dimension is in line with autonomy and skill development in Hackman and Oldham's model. According to meta-analyses control/decision authority tends to foster engagement and higher job satisfaction (Nahrgang et al., 2011), high work demands are related to absenteeism and decrease in engagement and organisational commitment (Bowling et al., 2015; Nahrgang et al., 2011). Good social support from colleagues and managers, like control, tends to be beneficial for higher employee engagement (Nahrgang et al., 2011).

The concept of worker participation in decision making has been widely used in working life studies and is related to control, as participation in decision making presumes some degree of influence/control at work. Participation in decision-making has often been put forward to be important for intrinsic motivation. People tend to be motivated towards carrying out decisions when they have been taking part in the decision-making process. Participation has also, under certain conditions, been beneficial for productivity and quality. Together with employment security, opportunities for training, and a participative leadership style, participation can have positive effects on productivity and quality in the organisation (Strauss, 1998, chapter 6).

The so-called psychological contract is a theory that also affects motivation and employee engagement. The psychological contract is about what expectations the employer and worker have around the employment. The worker has expectation of what kind of efforts to put in and also what to receive back from the organisation. The expectations are not always conscious, but the worker will be aware of them if they are broken and this often makes the worker to react in some way. Expectations from a worker can be a certain level of compensation for work, development and career possibilities. Another example can be expectation to be treated in a fair way at the workplace. Workers' commitment and motivation can vary in the psychological contract. A breach of the psychological contract occurs when a worker finds that his or her expectations are not met regarding the employment. Overviews and meta-analyses show that workers often react by withdrawing commitment and engagement or ultimately, leave the employment (Allvin et al., 2006; Cantisano et al., 2008; Zhao et al., 2007).

Two examples are presented to illustrate what can be interpreted as broken psychological contracts. The first is from a Swedish manufacturing company. The blue-collar workers stopped handing in suggestions for improvement of the production system because they felt they were not treated in a fair and respectful way by management. Management ignored suggestions handed in by workers and did not show respect for their knowledge and skills (Forslund, 2002). At Mazda's car factory in the US the workers stopped doing kaizen[3]

[3] Continuous improvements of the production system (see Chapter 5).

activities because they found that it only intensified their work (Fucini & Fucini, 1990, p. 161).

Commitment is a concept related to motivation. Commitment can be understood as '…a force that binds an individual to a course of action of relevance to one or more targets.' (Meyer & Herscovitch, 2001, p. 301). People can be committed to different targets or objects, for example to organisations, to an occupation, a union. Organisational commitment means that workers identify with and are loyal to the organisation. Occupational commitment is about people who feel strongly for their occupation. For example, medical doctors are more engaged in their occupation compared to the organisation they work in. They have no problem to change organisation and are reluctant to engage in organisation activities such as meetings with administrative staff and other colleagues. They prefer to work independently without interference from others (Meyer & Herscovitch, 2001; Mintzberg, 1983, chapter 10).

Leadership—Autocratic, Democratic and Laissez-Faire

Managers are part of the coordination and control system in work organisations. Just like work organisations are different, leadership styles differ and have different consequences for health and motivation. One of the first models in leadership research builds upon three different leadership styles—autocratic, democratic and laissez-faire (Döös & Waldenström, 2008, p. 33). The model was developed by Lewin, Lippit and White (Lippit, 1940). Autocratic and democratic leadership are related to several work organisation models presented in this book. Autocratic leadership has often been associated with the classical organisation models like Taylorism, Fordism (Chapter 2) and the bureaucratic organisation (Chapter 3). Democratic leadership is in line with sociotechnical work organisation (Chapter 4) and learning organisations (Chapter 6). Laissez-faire leadership cannot be associated with a specific work organisation model.

The autocratic leader is in line with McGregor's theory X (see above). The autocratic leader takes all decisions and workers are expected to follow the decisions without argument. This leader closely controls and strives for loyal and obedient workers. The democratic leader is connected to McGregor's theory Z (see above), that is that people want responsibility, to perform well and develop. The democratic leader strives to take group decisions and to have good relations with workers. He or she shares information and asks for ideas and opinions from others. Critical viewpoints are asked for and are seen as necessary in order to develop the workplace. The democratic leader actively manages group processes, for example deals with conflicts and helps the group to take decisions. The laissez-faire leader is inactive and leaves everything to the workers. This leader has often low self-esteem, does not set any goals and does not give support to workers and does not help groups to take decisions (Bass & Bass, 2008, chapters 6 and 17).

Leadership is a factor which has substantial impact on organisational performance and workers' health and well-being. A democratic leadership style tends to have positive effects on health at the workplace. Many studies show that participation and influence in decision-making processes are beneficial for workers' health. The reverse conditions, low control, few possibilities to influence work and conditions at the workplace, combined with high demands leads to higher risk of developing stress-related problems like coronary diseases (e.g. Theorell, 2003). A meta-analysis on leadership and health shows that participation in decision-making through discussion between managers and workers have positive effects on workers' health. The risk decreases for developing coronary disease, taking sick leave and incurring hospital stays (Nyberg, 2008, pp. 73–178). Another meta-analysis, covering 162 studies about effects from rationalisations on workers' health, shows that downsizing the workforce or organisational change often leads to stress-related mental or physical problems for workers. The highest levels of problems are reported in cases when managers take all decisions without any say from workers in the change process. The study highlights that some factors counteract or eliminate the negative effects on health. Two of these factors are (1) when workers can give viewpoints and opinions on the way rationalisations are carried out. (2) A participative leadership characterized by transparency, dialogue and care about workers (Westgaard & Winkel, 2011).

Reasons for the Development and Diffusion of Work Organisation Models

Why are some work organisation models dispersed and others not? Several different reasons can be put forward and the question can also be analysed from different perspectives. Four complementary explanations are presented in this section: (1) Some work organisation models are given high status, (2) the labour market, (3) a neoliberal wave in the society, (4) a globalised economy and the growth of a global finance sector.

Some Work Organisation Models Are Perceived as Successful and Are Given High Status

A lot of people think that organisations rationally chose, what they perceive as, the most efficient work organisation model. This can be seen as a technical/rational perspective on how decisions are made. According to this perspective different options are compared using certain criteria, in this case, which models is the most efficient and thus can generate the highest profit for the owners of the company. An alternative perspective is the so-called institutional perspective. Certain values and aspects are perceived as high status and are interpreted as of a higher symbolic value than other options. For example, organisation concepts are interpreted as legitimate and are associated with success and scientific reasoning. These values are associated with success and development in the western society (Røvik, 1998, chapters 1–2). If we analyse the diffusion of lean production (Chapter 5), a popular contemporary model, both perspectives can be seen as valid at first glance. Lean production received a lot of attention after the publication of the book *The machine that changed the world* (Womack et al., 1990) where the authors presented the main results from a big study of car manufacturing from the high status American university MIT (legitimacy through science from an institutional perspective). According to the study Toyota had the most successful production system for manufacturing cars (argument from a technical/rational perspective). The authors named it lean production and argued: '… the whole world should adopt lean production, and as quickly as possible.' (ibid, p. 225). However, the assumption that lean production is the most efficient work organisation model have been questioned by several scholars (Chapter 5). It seems that the institutional perspective, rather than the technical/rational perspective, provides a more valid explanation to the diffusion of lean production and possibly management concepts in general.

The Labour Market

In times when employers experience difficulties recruiting and keeping staff, for example due to low unemployment level, employers tend to focus on creating better working conditions in order to attract people to their workplaces. Companies in Europe in the 1960s and 1970s had problems recruiting people (Chapter 4). There was high personnel turnover, conflicts with workers, growing protest against monotonous work and lack of influence for workers. These conditions laid the ground for workplace democracy projects and the more skilled work through the sociotechnical work organisation model (Karasek & Theorell, 1990, pp. 4–5; Schiller, 1988, chapters 1–2; Trist, 1981, chapter 1). A similar situation was seen in Japan during the 1990s onwards. There was high personnel turnover in Japanese car manufacturing plants, an aging population and a growing reluctance among young males to work on the assembly line. Toyota and other Japanese car manufacturers therefore changed their work organisations in order to create more attractive working conditions, with inspiration from Volvo's sociotechnical factories (Nohara, 1999, Monden, 2012, p. 438). Toyota has thus moved away from several lean principles, which were presented in the IMVP study by Womack et al. (1990).

A Neoliberal Wave in Politics, Society and Working Life

Since the 1980s roughly, the world has seen a neoliberal wave in politics, society and working life. 'Neoliberalism is a theory of political economic practises proposing that human well-being can best be advanced by the maximization of entrepreneurial freedoms within an institutional framework characterised by private property rights, individual liberty, unencumbered markets, and free trade.' (Harvey, 2007, p. 22). Financial markets have been deregulated globally. Many countries have reduced their welfare expenditure and weakened employment protections in line with neoliberal principles. Some governments, such as the USA, the UK and Australia, have from the 1980s made it more difficult for unions to take industrial action (Doellgast et al., 2021, pp. 364–366).

The development of neoliberalism is connected to Milton Friedman and the University of Chicago. The first attempt to practise neoliberal economy took place in Chile after the coup by Augusto Pinochet 1973 against the democratically elected left government led by Salvador Allende. The coup was supported by the US government and CIA. In order to counteract the recession at the time, economists from Chicago were summoned to reform the economy after the coup. Public assets were privatised, foreign investment and free trade were introduced, institutional 'restraints' were removed such as trade union power. This experiment set an example for changes in the US under Ronald Reagan's government and in the UK in the 1980s under Margaret Thatcher's government. Since then, neoliberalist ideas and principles have spread to many countries all over the world. The US dominated International Monetary Fund (IMF), the World Trade Organisation (WTO), the World Bank and organisations in the UN such as the World Health Organisation have all embraced neoliberalism and have promoted neoliberal principles to be diffused all over the world. According to David Harvey (2007, p. 23) 'Neoliberalism has, in short, become hegemonic as a mode of discourse and has pervasive effects on ways of thought and political-economic practises to the point where it has become incorporated in the common-sense way we interpret, live in, and understand the world.' One consequence of neoliberalism is that the gap between people with the highest income and those with the lowest income has increased dramatically in the world (Harvey, 2007; Navarro, 2007).

According to neoliberalism, the government should support unregulated markets and where there are no markets they should be created, for example in healthcare and education. Public assets and organisations are therefore privatised such as water and electricity supply, transportation, healthcare, education and pensions. Also, the labour market should be deregulated as much as possible, for example trade unions should be removed or their power substantially reduced. Furthermore, the expenditures of the welfare state should be reduced by decreasing the social welfare system such as sick leave pay and unemployment benefits (Harvey, 2007; Navarro, 2007).

Many countries have seen deregulation of markets, reduction of the welfare state, weakening of employee protection, privatisation and outsourcing of public services. Employers have gained more power as result of many countries have weakened employment protection. The financial markets have increased their expectations on short-term gains and higher demand on return on investment. The operators on the financial market invest in shares where they expect the highest profits in the future in the shortest time possible. Therefore, companies have incentive to create high short-term profits. These changes combined with weaker unions (see below) have laid the ground for growth of insecure work. Organisations are increasingly using subcontractors and employment agencies. Temporary workers are more easily made redundant and replaced. Their wages tend to be lower and the employer can put more pressure and demand higher output from temporary workers. In the rising Gig economy (see Chapter 8), the workers are not employed generally but contractors, who have to bear the costs for infrastructure, sick leave, holidays and insurance. They lack any kind of employment protection as they are not employed (Doellgast et al., 2021, pp. 364–366).

Neoliberalism has had a major influence on the way work is organised. The public sector in many countries have seen privatisation and competition introduced in healthcare, education etc. (Chapter 7). There has also been substantial downsizing in the public sector. Also, within organisations internal markets have been introduced, with the aid of NPM, TQM and lean production. According to NPM each department should be defined as a cost centre and be exposed to competition. If the department is not considered to be competitive in price and quality the function is outsourced to an external company. The internal market is also used as a control and coordination mechanism, where workers are expected to control each other as customers and suppliers. The internal customer is expected to control the quality of the service or product delivered by the internal supplier, and that it is delivered at the prescribed time.

With the neoliberal wave in society employee influence and trade union power have declined. The trade union density has decreased substantially in most countries in the world according to statistics from ILO covering 2000 to 2016/2017 (Visser, 2019). Examples from nine countries of union density changes from 1980 to 2013, reported by Anders Kjellberg (2017): The UK has declined from 52 to 26%, Australia from 49 to 17%, Germany from 35 to 18%, The Netherlands from 35 to 18%, the US from 23 to 11%, and France from 18 to 8%. Three Nordic countries, Finland, Sweden and Denmark stand out with a very high union density. Around 70% of the workforce are members in a trade union, but also Sweden and to some extent Denmark have seen some decline in union density. Sweden had 80% union density in 1980 and Denmark 75%.

Weaker unions have made it more difficult for unions to withstand impaired working conditions. As mentioned in Chapter 5, power loss of trade unions in North America, Mexico and in Europe has made it easier for employers to implement lean production (Berggren, 1992, chapter 2; Huxley, 2015), and digital Taylorism (Brown et al., 2011) often resulting in high surveillance, elaborate control systems and intensification of work.

A Globalised Economy and the Growth of a Global Finance Sector

People have traded with other parts of the world for thousands of years. In that sense a global economy is not new. However, the scale of the economy has increased. The trade between countries has increased substantially and national economies are increasingly integrated in a global market. Production, consumption, capital, work, raw material and management are taking place globally through a network of organisations (Chapter 8). Deregulations and removal of trade barriers such as tariffs have enabled increased trade and movement of capital. Since the General Agreement on Tariffs and Trade (GATT) was founded in 1946 the trend has been to remove trade barriers in the world. Especially the financial sector has seen a substantial deregulation. The restrictions on the movements of capital between countries have been removed. Multinational companies have also increased in size and nowadays compete with regional and national companies, which has led to increased competition. A faster diffusion of new technologies has also contributed to increased competition. Another new aspect is that activities and communication is taking place globally in real time with the aid of internet. Business projects take place in a global network of financial transactions, information, production sites, labour pools, markets and companies (Castells, 2000; Steger, 2020).

This new global network has had an effect on the distribution of power in society. The national states have lost power because large companies can move capital, production, capital on a global market and create value adding global networks. The market has gained power at the expense of national states and of democratic decision-making as it, to a large extent, takes place in national states. Especially the global financial market has had a major impact on the world economy and the society (Castells, 2000, 2008). The financial markets have increased their expectations on short-term gains and higher demand on return on investment. Also, companies to a higher degree finance their investments through the financial market rather than banks because they can obtain more capital faster through the financial market. The trade on stock markets have therefore increased substantially. The operators on the financial market invest in shares where they expect the highest profits in the future in the shortest time possible. Therefore, companies must take measures to create high short-term profits. Companies are therefore tempted to downsize their staff levels, sometimes with the aid of TBM or BPR (Chapter 5). From the 1990s downsizing is taking place in organisations both in bad and good times. The financial market's higher demand for short-term profit is a substantial driving force for downsizing. Furthermore, the management remuneration systems in companies are often tied to the economic result of the company. Often the share value is used as measurement of the economic result. The top management therefore receives higher remuneration when they downsize the organisation because the financial market tends to react positively on downsizing. Therefore, the share value often rises when organisations announce downsizing (Pfeffer, 2000; Schulz & Wiersema, 2018).

Increasing global competition between companies and demands from the financial market for higher profits drive outsourcing of production and service to low wage countries. In so-called Free Trade Zones (FTZ) or Free Ports in development, countries tax benefits are given and labour regulations are eased. FTZs have grown substantially over the last decades and companies often outsource production to suppliers in the FTZs (Kjellström et al., 2007; Schnall et al., 2016). Complex networks of suppliers form global supply chains. At the top of the supply chains are often powerful multinational companies. These lead companies can often decide the terms for the companies in the supply chain (Wright & Caine, 2015; Anner et al., 2020). Multinational companies can also execute influence over nations in terms of obtaining favourable legislation. Multinational companies might want to invest in nations that do not have strong unions and high labour standards. Nations then are tempted to compete with each other to give multinational companies the best deal with low taxes, low wages and mild labour condition laws, thus driving a 'race to the bottom' (Doellgast et al., 2021, pp. 373–374).

Global supply chains and global consultancy firms has a conforming effect on work organisation models. The increase in global connections and cooperation between companies through for example outsourcing makes it favourable to have common organisation models, administrative systems and technologies. Information technology also makes it easier to have standardised global administrative systems. Furthermore, international standards for accountancy are developed, which makes it easier for financial traders to compare the economic performance of firms in different parts of the world. Also, accounting and consulting firms are growing larger and are increasingly active globally, which supports the diffusion of standardised administrative systems. American companies dominate the consulting sector. Firms like Accenture, Mckinsey and the Boston Consulting Group have tens of thousands of employees and diffuse management trends worldwide. These consulting firms have a close relation with the prestige universities in Boston on the US east coast like Harvard and Massachusetts Institute of Technology (MIT). In Boston management concepts such as TBM, BPR, lean production and balanced scorecard have been created and diffused worldwide (Björkman, 2013).

Multinational corporations also have a conforming effect on work organisation. They often have a centralised decision and power structure. Their subsidiaries are often tightly controlled through policies and rules, for example about how to organise work and production systems (Morgan, 2006, chapter 9; von Otter, 2004, chapter 4).

Giant multinational corporations (MNC) account for over 70% of trade in the world. The largest MNCs have their headquarters either in the US, Europe, Japan, Mexico, China or other Asian countries. Some MNCs have higher annual sales than the gross national income of many countries. The MNCs are thus very powerful structures. The USA has the highest number of MNCs but China is closing in (Steger, 2020, pp. 54–55).

Summary

The number of organisations has increased and organisations have also become larger over time. Organisations are social structures with common goals. The concept work organisation is however narrower. The definition of work organisation used in this book is; ***principles for dividing work into different tasks and for coordinating these tasks.*** The work organisation has consequences for skill development, health and motivation. A low division o work—enriched work, is characterised by high control/worker decision authority to plan work and decide how to carry out work activities. Enriched work also involves opportunities to use skills and to learn new skills through work. Together with good social support from colleagues and managers this kind of job has benefits for health, learning and worker motivation.

The driving forces behind the diffusion of organisation models are:

- Some work organisation models are perceived as successful and are given high status.
- The labour market.
- A neoliberal wave in politics, society and working life.
- A globalised economy and the growth of a global finance sector.

Reflection Questions

1. How can the division of work affect individual learning, health and well-being?
2. What motivates you at work? What kind of work would you be happy with?
3. How would you prefer your manager to manage you and your colleagues? Can you give examples of bad leaders?

Bibliography

Allvin, M., Aronsson, G., Hagström, T., Johansson, G., & Lundberg, U. (2006). *Gränslöst arbete: Socialpsykologiska perspektiv på det nya arbetslivet*. Liber.

Anner, M., Fischer-Daly, M., & Maffie, M. (2020, October 14). Fissured employment and network bargaining: Emerging employment relations dynamics in a contingent world of work. *Industrial and Labor Relations Review*. https://journals.sagepub.com/doi/full/10.1177/0019793920964180

Aronsson, G., & Berglind, H. (1990). *Handling och handlingsutrymme*. Studentlitteratur.

Bass, B. M., & Bass, R. (2008). *The Bass handbook of leadership: Theory, research and managerial applications*. Free Press.

Berggren, C. (1992). *Alternatives to lean production: Work organization in the Swedish auto industry*. ILR Press.

Björkman, T. (2013). 3. Management: Still a fashion industry. In Å. Sandberg (Ed.), *Nordic Lights: Work, management and welfare in Scandinavia*. SNS Förlag.

Bowling, N. A., Alarcon, G. M., Bragg, C. B., & Hartman, M. J. (2015). A meta-analytic examination of the potential correlates and consequences of workload. *Work & Stress, 29*(2), 95–113.

Brown, P., Lauder, H., & Ashton, D. (2011). Digital taylorism. In *The global auction: The Broken promises of education, jobs and incomes* (Chapter 5). Oxford University Press.

Burns, T., & Stalker, G. M. (1961). *The management of innovation*. Tavistock.

Castells, M. (2000). Toward a sociology of the network society. *Contemporary Sociology, 29*(5), 693–699.

Castells, M. (2008). The new public sphere: Global civil society, communication networks, and global governance. *The Annals of the American Academy, AAPSS, 616*(March), 78–93.

Cantisano, G. T., Domínguez, F. M., & Depolo, M. (2008). Psychological contract breach and outcomes: Combining meta-analysis and structural equation models. *Psicothema, 20*(3), 487–496.

Docherty, P., Forslin, J., & Shani, A. B. (2002). *Creating sustainable work systems: Emergent perspectives and practise*. Routledge.

Doellgast, V., Wright, C. F., Lee Cooke, F., & Bamber, G. J. (2021). 15. Conclusions: Globalisation, crises and institutional responses. In G. J. Bamber, F. Lee Cooke, V. Doellgast, & C. F. Wright (Eds.), *International & comparative employment relations*. Sage.

Döös, M., & Waldenström, K. (2008). Alternativa former av ledarskap: En kunskap-söversikt om chefers ledarskap. In M. Döös & K. Waldenström (Eds.), *Chefsskapets former och resultat*. Vinnova.

Drucker, P. F. (1963, May). Managing for business effectiveness. *Harvard Business Review*.

Drucker, P. F. (1976). What results should you expect? A users' guide to MBO. *Public Administration Rewiew, 36*(1), 12–19.

Eriksson, B., & Larsson, P. (2017). 16. Våra arbetsmiljöer. In M. Bengtsson, & T. Berglund (Eds.), *Arbetslivet*. Studentlitteratur.

Forslund, M. (2002). *Det omöjliggjorda entreprenörskapet*. Växjö University Press.

Fucini, J. J., & Fucini, S. (1990). *Working for the Japanese*. The Free Press.

Gardell, B. (1986). *Arbetets organisation och människans natur: En forskningsöversikt om människans behov av att behärska tekniken*. Arbetsmiljöfonden.

Hacker, W. (2003). Action regulation theory: A practical tool for the design of modern work processes? *European Journal of Work and Organizational Psychology, 12*(2), 105–130.

Hackman, R., & Oldham, G. (1976). Motivation through the design of work: Test of a theory. *Organizational Behavior and Human Performance, 16*, 250–279.

Harvey, D. (2007). Neoliberalism as creative destruction. *The Annals of the American Academy, 610*(March), 21–44.

Huxley, C. (2015). Three decades of lean production: Practice, ideology, and resistance. *International Journal of Sociology, 45*(2), 133–151.

Karasek, R., & Theorell, T. (1990). *Healthy work: Stress, productivity and the reconstruction of working life*. Basic Books.

Karlsson, J. C. (2017). Arbetsbegreppet. In M. Bengtsson & T. Berglund (Eds.), *Arbetslivet* (Chapter 2). Studentlitteratur.

Kjellberg, A. (2017). Fack, arbetsgivare och industrial relations. In M. Bengtsson & T. Berglund (Eds.), *Arbetslivet*. Studentlitteratur.

Kjellström, T., Håkansta, C., & Hogstedt, C. (2007). Globalisation and public health. *Scandinavian Journal of Public Health, 35*(Suppl 70), 7–13.

Kunda, G. (1992). *Engineering culture: Control and commitment in a high-tech corporation*. Temple University Press.

Lang, J., Ochsmann, E., Kraus, T., & Lang, J. W. B. (2012). Psychosocial work stressors as antecedents of musculoskeletal problems: A systematic review and meta-analysis of stability-adjusted longitudinal studies. *Social Science & Medicine, 75*, 1163–1174.

Lawrence, P. R., & Lorsch, J. W. (1967). *Organization and environment*. Harvard Business School Press.

Leavitt, H. J. (1965). Applied organizational change in industry: Structural, technological and humanistic approaches. In J. G. March (Ed.), *Handbook of organizations*. Rand McNally.

Lennerlöf, L. (1986). *Kompetens eller hjälplöshet?: Om lärande i arbete: En forskningsöversikt*. Arbetarskyddsstyr.

Levinson, K. (2004). *Lokal partssamverkan: En undersökning av svenskt medbestämmande*. Arbetslivsinstitutet.

Lindberg, P., & Vingård, E. (2012). *Den goda arbetsmiljön och dess indikatorer: Kunskapsöversikt*. Arbetsmiljöverket, Rapport 2012:7.

Lippit, R. (1940). *An experimental study of the effect of democratic and authoritarian group atmosphere*. University of Ohio.

Lysgaard, S. (1961). *Arbeiderkollektivet: En studie i de underordnedes sosiologi*. Universitetsforlaget.

McGregor, D. (1987/1960). *The human side of enterprise*. Penguin Books Ltd.

Meyer, J. P., & Herscovitch, L. (2001). Commitment in the workplace: Toward a general model. *Human Resource Management Review, 11*(3), 299–326.

Mintzberg, H. (1983). *Structure in fives: Designing effective organizations*. Prentice-Hall.

Monden, Y. (2012). *Toyota production system: An integrated Approach to just-in-time* (4th ed.). CRC Press.

Morgan, G. (2006). *Images of organization*. Sage.

Nahrgang, J. D., Morgeson, F. P., & Hofmann, D. A. (2011). Safety at work: A meta-analytic investigation of the link between job demands, job resources, burnout, engagement, and safety outcomes. *Journal of Applied Psychology, 96*(1), 71–94.

Navarro, V. (2007). Neoliberalism as a class ideology; or, the political causes of the growth of inequalities. *International Journal of Health Services, 37*(1), 47–62.

Nixon, A. E., Mazzola, J. J., Bauer, J., Krueger, J. R., & Spector, P. E. (2011). Can work make you sick? A meta-analysis of the relationships between job stressors and physical symptoms. *Work & Stress, 25*(1), 1–22.

Nohara, H. (1999). The historic reversal of the division of labour? The second stage of the Toyota production system. In J.-P. Durand, P. Stewart, & J. J. Castillo (Eds.), *Teamwork in the automobile industry: Radical change or passing fashion?* Macmillan.

Noon, M., Blyton, P., & Morell, K. (2013). *The realities of work: Experiencing work and employment in contemporary society*. Palgrave Macmillan.

Normann, R. (1983). *Service management: Ledning och strategi i tjänsteproduktion*. LiberFörlag.

Nyberg, A. (2008). Det goda chefskapet: Organisatorisk effektivitet och anställdas hälsa. En kunskapsöversikt. In M. Döös & K. Waldenström (Eds.), *Chefskapets former och resultat* (Vol. 15). Vinnova.

Oldham, G., & Fried, Y. (2016). Job design research and theory: Past, present and future. *Organizational Behavior and Human Decision Processes, 136*, 20–35.

Otter, C. V. (2004). *Aktivt arbetsliv: Om dagens behov och framtidens möjligheter: En trendanalys*. Arbetslivsinstitutet.

Pfeffer, J. (2000). Flexibilitet på arbetsmarknaden: Vet företagen verkligen bäst? In L. Lennerlöf (Ed.), *Avveckla eller utveckla?: En antologi om verksamhetskonsekvenser i magra organisationer*. Rådet för arbetslivsforskning.

Porter, M. E. (1980). *Competetive strategy*. Free Press.

Roethlisberger, F. J., & Dickson, W. J. (1939). *Management and the worker*. Wiley.

Røvik, K. A. (1998). *Moderne organisasjoner: Trender i organisasjonstenkningen ved tusenårsskiftet*. Fagbokforlaget.

Ryan, R. M., & Deci, E. L. (2000). Intrinsic and extrinsic motivations: Classic definitions and new directions. *Contemporary Educational Psychology, 25*, 54–67.

Schiller, B. (1988). *"Det förödande 70-talet": SAF och medbestämmandet 1965–1982*. Arbetsmiljöfonden, Allmänna förl.

Schnall, P., Dobson, M., & Landsbergis, P. (2016). Globalization, work and cardiovascular desease. *International Journal of Health Services, 46*(4), 656–692.

Schulz, A.-C., & Wiersema, M. F. (2018). The impact of earnings expectations on corporate downsizing. *Strategic Management Journal, 39*, 2691–2702.

Scott, W. R. (1998). *Organizations: Rational, natural, and open systems*. Prentice Hall International.

Smith, A. (1776/2000). *The wealth of nations*. The Modern Library.

Standing, G. (2011). *The precariat: The new dangerous class*. Bloomsbury Academic.

Steger, M. B. (2020). *Globalization: A very short introduction*. Oxford University Press.

Strauss, G. (1998). Participation works—If conditions are appropriate. In F. Heller, E. Pusic, G. Strauss, & B. Wilpert (Eds.), *Organizational participation: Myth and reality*. Oxford University Press.

Theorell, T. (2003). *Är ökat inflytande på arbetsplatsen bra för folkhälsan? Kunskapssammanställning*. Statens folkhälsoinstitut.

Theorell, T., Jood, K., Slunga Järvholm, L., Vingård, E., Perk, J., Östergren, P. O., et al. (2016). A systematic review of studies in the contributions of the work environment to ischaemic heart disease development. *The European Journal of Public Health, 26*(3), 470–477.

Thompson, P., & McHugh, D. (2002). *Work organisations: A critical introduction*. Palgrave.

Thylefors, I. (2006). Arbets- och organisationspsykologi. In J. Holmer & B. Simonsson (Eds.), *Forskning om arbete*. Studentlitteratur.

Trist, E. (1981). *The evolution of socio-technical systems: A conceptual framework and an action research program*. Ontario Ministry of Labour.

Visser, J. (2019). *Trade unions in the balance* (ILO ACTRAV Working Paper). International Labour Organization.

Waldenström, K., & Härenstam, A. (2008). Does the job demand-control model correspond to externally assessed demands and control for both women and men? *Scandinavian Journal of Public Health, 36*(3), 242–249.

Westgaard, R. H., & Winkel, J. (2011). Occupational musculoskeletal and mental health: Significance of rationalization and opportunities to create sustainable production systems—A systematic review. *Applied Ergonomics, 42*, 261–296.

White, R. W. (1959). Motivation reconsidered. *Psychological Review, 66*(5), 297–333.

Wilpert, B. (1998). A view from psychology. In F. Heller, E. Pusic, G. Strauss, & B. Wilpert (Eds.), *Organizational participation: Myth and reality*. Oxford University Press.

Womack, J. P., Jones, D. T., & Roos, D. (1990). *The machine that changed the world: Based on the Massachusetts Institute of Technology 5-million-dollar 5-year study on the future of the automobile*. Rawson Associates.

Wright, C. F., & Kaine, S. (2015). Supply chains, production networks and the employment relationship. *Journal of Industrial Relations, 57*(4), 483–501.

Zacher, H., & Frese, M. (2017). Action regulation theory: Foundations, current knowledge, and future directions. In O. D. S., N. Anderson, V. Chockalingam, & K. S. Handan (Eds.), *Handbook of industrial work & organizational psychology, V3: Managerial psychology and organizational approaches*. Sage.

Zhao, H., Wayne, S. J., Glibkowski, B. C., & Bravo, J. (2007). The impact of psychological contract breach on work-related outcomes: A meta-analysis. *Personnel Psychology, 60*, 647–680.

CHAPTER 2

Taylorism and Fordism

Learning Objectives

This chapter should provide you with knowledge about:

- The fundamental change of work in Taylorism and Fordism compared with the artisan society.
- The power dimension in Taylorism, where workers lose power over how to perform work tasks and the de-skilling of work.
- The negative effects on health and well-being from Taylorism and Fordism and the causes for these effects.

Scientific Management

The Artisan Society

In the old artisan society, the craftsmen worked independently or like an apprentice. "Artisan is the kind of manufacturing where the production process and the end result are totally dependent on the craftsman's skills and knowledge, even if machines and technical aids are used (Parr, 1994, p. 1, writer's transl.).

Craftsmen belonged to a guild, which was a kind of association or brotherhood for merchants and craftsmen. Guilds have been present in Europe at least since early medieval times. Examples of crafts were tanners, shoemakers, weavers, bakers, fishmongers, goldsmiths, carpenters, butchers and saddlers. Guilds provided support to its members such as funerals, social solidarity,

P-O Börnfelt, *Work Organisation in Practice*,
https://doi.org/10.1007/978-3-031-21667-1_2

charity for poor people and members that have run into difficulties and could not care for themselves any longer. The guilds also dealt with disputes in their trade, had a controlling function of skills and quality among the craftsmen (the large majority were men). Control of quality and skills was partly managed through regulating apprenticeship, buy also through specification of materials such as leather and wood. Each craftsman also applied a marking to the product so that it could be identified. The guilds identified the skills needed to be a craftsman, who had the right to be a craftsman or a merchant, and also specified who had not got right to work as a craftsman or merchant. An apprentice worked for and was supervised by a master. After a number of years, the apprentice could be promoted to journeyman status but he would still have a placement with a master and was supervised by the master (Edgren, 2006; Keen, 2006).

Guilds have had a bad reputation and have often been seen as an old system preventing innovation, progress and prosperity. Examples of expressing such views were Adam Smith and the revolutionaries in France in the eighteenth century. Many countries in Europe therefore abolished the guilds in the eighteenth century. However, the reputation of the guilds have changed in recent years. Historians have shown that before the industrial revolution there was a long period of innovations in the preceding centuries. The guilds provided training in order to develop skilled craftsmen, which often was a long process of around ten years. Development of new types of clocks in the seventeenth century is one example of innovations. Also, the new technology was dispersed quickly in the trade, because there was no patent system. The clocks were copied by other clock makers within months. Also shipbuilding, mining, metal working and construction saw innovations, but it was impossible to pinpoint an individual inventor because the craftsmen worked together in large networks. The large majority of innovations were incremental which craftsmen discovered unintentionally when performing their work.

Different guilds also had coordinating functions in the economy. The tanners' and shoemakers' guilds in Bologna, for instance, negotiated prices and qualities of the hides that the tanners delivered to the shoemakers. These negotiated deals made it easier to form a chain of suppliers, thus a production network. It has been established that craftsmen were very mobile. The labour market for craftsmen was international. For instance, only 25 percent of 4 773 guild masters in Vienna in 1742 were born locally. A third of the masters were from other countries. The guilds often encouraged migration. This mobility was important for diffusion of skills, new products and new ways of working (Epstein & Prak, 2008).

Furthermore, skilled craftsmen were precursors to the engineer profession. Before the existence of engineers, craftsmen provided the development of new products and improvements of working methods. During the apprenticeship time the apprentices generally received education in mathematics, physics, geometry and work drawing. For example, in England in the mid 1800s there were around 1 200 technical schools and they had around 200 000 pupils.

What was even more important than theoretical education, was performing the occupation were the craftsmen applied theory and science in practical solutions, thereby developing their skills and products. Also, through many years of performing a craft occupation, the craftsman learned how to handle problems and situations which could occur, depending on for instance different materials, equipment and tools (Braverman, 1974, Chapter 1).

In the early industrial society, the craftmen performed their craft professions, but more and more in larger groups. Gradually the production moved into bigger workshops. The new larger workshops needed some kind of management and coordination of the work process. The employer strived to take that role as a capital owner. This was not, however, an obvious alternative at this time. The regulations from the guild age lived on for a relatively long time. It was also common that skilled workers hired their own help workers. As time went by, work was increasingly organised in a more structured and controlled way, such as regular working hours. Other control mechanisms were foremen who surveyed work and rules, for example smoking and talking was forbidden. Minimum levels for productivity were also common (Braverman, 1974, Chapter 2).

As factories grew larger and larger, company owners started to experiment with new methods for coordination and control of the work process. Military organisation with its focus on discipline was a popular model for organising the manufacturing industry. The first person who developed a systematic theory about the organisation of work was the American engineer Frederick Winslow Taylor (1856–1915). Taylor developed his theory scientific management at the end of the nineteenth century. It is often called Taylorism after its founder. The principles Taylor wrote about were known at this time, but Taylor was the first to compile them into a coherent theory (Braverman, 1974, Chapter 1). Taylorism has been very influential for how work is organised, even today. Also, office work has been affected through time and motion studies, standardised tasks and increased division of work (Braverman, 1974, Chapter 15). Taylor worked several years at Midvale Steel Company in the US where he started to develop his theory. He started as an ordinary worker. In eight years he advanced through the hierarchy up to chief engineer. Taylor continued to develop his theory at Betlehem Steel Company and then as a consultant (Taylor, 1947/1903, pp. ix–xi).

Taylor's main objective was to increase efficiency in the manufacturing industry. One big problem, according to Taylor, was that workers worked slowly and in different ways tried to avoid work. According to Taylor, there were two reasons for that, the first one was pure laziness, the other one informal agreements between workers. The latter Taylor labelled systematic soldiering. Workers often agreed upon a production level which they found reasonable. From the workers point of view, as it was a piecework, they did not want to increase the amount of work needed for pay. They were also afraid of increased productivity could lead to people being laid off. Workers who produced over the informal level were exposed to different kinds of group pressure.

Another reason for low efficiency, according to Taylor, was unsystematic and arbitrary work methods. The workers learned from each other and each worker decided for himself how to perform the work. The workers knew more about the production process than their supervisors and decided how to carry out work and how fast to run machines. If for example a new foreman came to their workplace and wanted to raise the work speed, the workers would resist that.

The Management Takes Control of the Work Process

Because of the reasons mentioned above, Taylor argued that the management needed to take control of the work process and obtain detailed knowledge of work methods. According to Taylor the management needed to take possession over the whole production process. It was not enough to control workers through rules and regulations, as long as the workers controlled the production process. The management should analyse work in detail and decide the optimal way to perform different work operations and then standardise them, so there would only be one 'right way' to work. The planning of work should be moved into planning departments and be performed by white-collar workers (Taylor, 1911).

Individually Organised Work

The informal agreements among workers were broken up by organising work individually as much as possible. Each worker was trained individually by a supervisor and worked without cooperating with any other people than their supervisors. The workers were observed and tested carefully and those who were up to standards were chosen. The workers who did not meet the requirements were either trained or dismissed.

In the piecework system Taylor used, the worker got a specific pay if he did a specific amount of work per day. If the worker did not reach the quantity of work, he got a reduced pay. The pay should be considerably higher (30–100%) after work had been reorganised according to Tayloristic principles, in order to gain acceptance from workers for the higher rate of work.

Taylor also emphasized the importance of creating 'friendly relations' (Ibid., p. 49) between management and workers in order to overcome antagonism. As previously mentioned, this was achieved by organising work individually, by instructing and carefully monitoring each worker. If cooperative relations were not created, scientific management would not work at all according to Taylor.

Taylor aimed to find the optimal work quantity which a worker could carry out daily without being harmed. In practice however, the work quantity was so high, that only a few workers had the strength and endurance to carry it out. In one example, where men loaded pig iron, only one of eight men had physical capability for Taylor's work pace. Before reorganising, each worker moved between 12 and 13 tons of pig iron a day, working in groups of 5 to 20 men. In Taylor's system each worker moved between 45 and 48 tons every day, which is about four times more than before. The pay for this work was $ 1.85 a day, which was 60 percent more than before. Every morning a worker received a piece of paper with the quantity of work carried out the previous day and the pay for that. The idea was that the quick feedback should be motivating. Each worker should be aware that if he did not achieve the goal for $ 1.85 another worker would replace him. An important part of the change process was for supervisors to talk to each worker about the advantages of the new way of working. The workers should learn to obey orders and be told that the white-collar workers from the planning department knew best how to perform work. If talk was not enough other methods were available before the last step, dismissal, (1) Reduce pay. (2) Suspension for shorter or longer periods. (3) Fines. (4) Warnings, which together could lead to any of the aforementioned measures. According to Taylor, one of the most important success factors was to obtain the attitude changes. A worker of the highest class (those who earned $ 1.85 a day) did not go slow or complain about the high rate of work. A worker should not see the employer as an opponent who wanted to exploit the worker as much as possible. Instead they should be seen as friends working side by side towards the same goal (Taylor, 1947/1903, pp. 49–56, 130–139, 196–197). One of the greatest advantages with the new work organisation, according to Taylor, was the lack of strikes (ibid., p. 69. Unions were hindering prosperity, Taylor argued. Unions should not interfere in questions of pay and working time. These issues were better judged by the experts in the company (ibid., pp. 186–187). When the organisation worked as planned, the workers would work together as a well-oiled machine (p. 120).

White-Collar Workers Planned the Work in Detail

Detailed planning was carried out by white-collar workers with different expert competences. The planning of work was far too complicated to be performed by workers, according to Taylor. Systematic time and emotion studies were carried out in order to design optimal tasks.

Different work methods were tried out in practice. Some of the best-suited workers were chosen and men from the planning department tried out what was the optimal work volume per day and how many and what length of breaks were needed. Equipment was tried out and deigned in an optimal way. One example is trying out different designs of shovels for different kind of material. The planners observed how the different workers performed their tasks and what equipment they used. Then they studied how long each work sequence took, and which way of working was the most efficient. One example was to try out a load of material on a shovel and the time for that. Unnecessary motions were removed. The planners combined the most efficient work methods with the most efficient tools and made a standard task. One example of time and motion studies was carried out by an apprentice to Taylor, Frank B. Gilbreth. He studied brick laying and reduced the number of motions from 18 to 5. Gilbreth also designed an adjustable table for putting bricks and mortar on, so the table would be on right level as the wall grows. A low paid worker placed the bricks in the right way on the table. The brick layer was taught how to use both his hands. With one hand he took the brick, with the other hand he put mortar on the wall. The productivity increased considerably with the new way of working, from 120 bricks per hour to 350 (Taylor, 1911).

From a Tayloristic point of view, there were however flaws to the early time and motion studies. The work process could only be studied in practice, when work was performed, and the measures generated were not very precise. Moreover, the method could only be used on some types of work. A more general method was needed. Gilbreth developed the system by setting standard times for different general body movements. These movements were not connected to specific types of work. They were basic movements and were called therblig, Gilbreth backwards. Examples are grasp, release, walk, sit, hold and kneel down. Each therblig was given a standard time. In later versions time is measured in time measurement units (TMU). There are about 28 TMU for a second. The system is labelled method, time and measurement (MTM). Planners can calculate how much working time and how many workers are needed. MTM experts emphasize another 'advantage'. Confrontations with workers are avoided using the MTM system. Workers are intimidated by close observation in traditional time and motion studies (Braverman, 1974, Chapter 8). The MTM system is still used today for planning work processes in manufacturing industry.

A consequence of a Tayloristic work organisation is thus increased division of labour and standardised work. One of Taylor's arguments for simple and standardised tasks is that the employer does not need to pay high wages because this kind of work does not require high-skilled workers (Taylor, 1947/1903, p. 105).

Control by Functional Leadership

Managers closely monitored and controlled to ensure that the workers used the standardised work methods. Taylor used so-called functional leadership, which means that each worker has several different leaders and these leaders are responsible for one specific function. One advantage with functional leadership is that the training time is shorter compared to a general leader. Taylor recommended eight different leadership roles. On the shopfloor there were four managers:

1. Gang bosses instructed the workers on how to use the machines in the most efficient way.
2. Speed bosses supervised that workers used machines in the correct speed and used other equipment in the most efficient way, according to the written instructions.
3. Inspectors were responsible for controlling both quality and work speed.
4. Repair bosses controlled that workers did maintenance on machines.

There were four managerial roles in the planning department:

1. Order of work and route clerks planned the work process, in what order to do the work and how the products should be moved.
2. Inspection card clerks gave written instruction to both managers and workers on the shopfloor. The instruction card gave information about what blueprint and what tools to use, exactly how to perform tasks, how long it should take and the pay providing the work was carried out within the specified time.
3. Time and cost clerks documented time and cost for the work and were responsible for calculating wages.
4. Shop disciplinarian. If workers did not obey orders, not did his/her duty, arrived late or were absent without approval the shop disciplinarian gave appropriate punishment (Taylor, 1947/1903, pp. 98–110).

Ford's Mass Production

Fordism is often understood, and somewhat simplified, by the application of Tayloristic principles in mass production with use of the assembly line (Björkman, 1996).

Fordism can be summarised as follows:

- Production of a few highly specialised products.
- Specialised machine equipment.
- Use of the assembly line where work thus is machine paced.
- Standardised tasks, which are repetitive and short-cycled[1] (often 1–2 minutes). There is minimal autonomy for workers.
- Strong hierarchy and functional organising. Planning, control and quality control is carried out in specialised units (Berggren, 1990, p. 44).

During the same period that Taylor developed scientific management, mass production was developed. Ford Motor Company is usually seen as the starting point, but according to Henry Ford himself, he got the idea from the meat

[1] A cycle time is the time it takes to perform at task, and then you repeat the task again and again. This kind of repetitive and short-cycled work is often called monotonous work.

industry in Chicago and Cincinnati. The meat industry used de-assembly lines when packing meat (Hounshell, 1984, p. 10). The mass production of cars however started at Ford with the T model, the T-Ford. Between 1908 to 1927 15 million T-Fords were manufactured (Ibid., p. 219). It is unclear to what extent scientific management was known at Ford, but as previously mentioned, the main principles were known at this time. According to Henry Ford himself they did not use Taylorism or any other management models. The work was mechanised as much as possible and the workers handled the machines. The work did not require any qualifications as the tasks were very simple and repetitive. The monotonous work caused a high turnover of workers and problems with recruiting new workers. In 1913 Ford had a turnover rate of 380 percent. At the end of 1913 a bonus was introduced for workers who had been employed more than three years. Only 640 out of 15 000 workers had been employed this long. Also, in 1913 the engineers started to experiment with an assembly line. In the beginning it was only a line, where the workers moved the cars manually. However, according to the engineers, problems arose because some workers worked too slow and some too fast. They then came up with the idea of fitting a chain to pull the line, so the line would have a constant pace. The line now forced the workers to work at the same pace. This principle was then used in all other work processes. It is not known whether time and motion studies were used at Ford. There was however a work standard department. Special tools were used in all parts of the production process. These were called 'farmer tools' because they were easy to use and did not require much time to learn (Hounshell, 1984, pp. 247–259, p. 221).

There were four different categories of foremen at Ford to control the production and the quality. All foremen had the authority to dismiss workers at their own will (Berggren, 1990, p. 39). Productivity increased considerably at the Highland Park factory. In 1925 the number of cars produced in a day was the same as was produced in a year when the T-Ford was introduced. The workers reacted strongly though towards the high work pace and the repetitive tasks. The high turnover rate is a sign of that. In the beginning people could switch to jobs in other companies, which still used more artisan work methods, but the Tayloristic and the Fordistic work organisation models spread more and more due to their gain in productivity. Soon workers had no other choice than this hard and monotonous work. After the first world war, and even more so after the second world war, the unions accepted the monotonous work in exchange for higher wages (Braverman, 1974, Chapter 5). Between the world wars Fordistic mass production was diffused in North America, partly by adding MTM. In Europe mass production was adapted to a large extent during the 1950s and 1960s. In the late 1960s and early 1970s there were revolts in Europe against the modern manufacturing work. This triggered an interest in alternative work organisation models such as the sociotechnical model in the UK and in Scandinavia in the 1970s, 1980s and 1990s (see Chapter 4). All in all though, Taylorism and Fordism remained as the main work organisation models used in manufacturing industry. In the 1980s the US started to adopt

Japanese organisation models, which were based on Fordism (see Chapter 6). This development continued in the 1990s with Europe as follower (Berggren, 1990).

Suggestion Schemes

Classical organisation models and tradition assume that there is a division of work between management and workers, where workers generally do not do problem solving and development tasks. These tasks are seen as belonging to the management domain. Suggestion schemes are however an exception from this rule. In Europe and North America, suggestion schemes were part of patriarchal management reforms. They expected they would boost working morale, commitment and that workers would be less interested in organising themselves in unions. The patriarchal strategy was criticised by Taylor who argued that efficiency could not be improved in this way. Instead efficiency should be improved by using a scientifically developed work organisation where management had full control of the work process. Taylor however emphasized that workers would be encouraged to take initiatives and come up with ideas.

The way suggestion schemes usually work is that one or several workers hand in suggestions for improvement to a committee, which evaluates them. Some kind of reward, usually financial, is handed out if the committee think it is a good suggestion. In the end of the nineteenth and the beginning of the twentieth century organised suggestion schemes were started to get used in Europe, North America and Japan (Dickinson, 1932; Hjelm, 1999, Chapter 2). Suggestions are often about improvements of efficiency like for example production methods and reducing waste, but also about improving products, and improvement of health and safety (Dickinson, 1932; Fägerborg, 1991, p. 388).

Critique of Taylorism and Fordism

In Taylor's time there was strong disagreement about management having single authority to design the work process. The strongest resistance against Taylorism came from the trade unions. They principally opposed that workers were deprived of their occupational skills and control over work (Braverman, 1974, Chapter 1). Also, politicians questioned Taylor's ideas. Taylor was called to testify for the special committee of the house of representatives about his work organisation model. The committee raised the question about the high work intensity (Taylor, 1947/1912, p. 124). The members of the committee questioned if workers could work a whole work life at this high work pace. They also raised concern about workers completely lacking control over the work process. The management alone decided and controlled the work process as well as the level of wages, which left no say for workers on working conditions (Ibid., pp. 144, 147, 164–167). The trade unions also lacked control in the companies using Scientific Management. Taylor could not, in his testimony, give one single example of negotiations between management and workers on wages, working conditions or tasks (Ibid., p. 49). The committee also highlighted the degraded work content, which made it cheaper for the employer to buy work. The degraded work resulted in reduced wages for many (Ibid., p. 154). They also asked questions about how people who were not 'first-class' workers should make a living. In Taylors work organisation only 'first-class' workers had a place. They were the only ones who had the strength and endurance to cope with the intensive work (Ibid., p. 175). The timekeeping of work was also criticised. The workers found that to be annoying and demeaning (Ibid., p. 167).

Taylorism has continued to be criticised for similar reason. One well-known critic is the American metal worker and editor Harry Braverman, who points out that work is degraded, above all because all intellectual work is taken away from the worker. Braverman points out the separation of the brain and the hand, planning and making, concept and execution, which has a dehumanising effect on work. Braverman argues that the worker is nearly reduced to an animal's level (Braverman, 1974, Chapter 2–4).

Alienation researchers such as Robert Blauner (1964, Chapter 2) points out that people tend to feel alienated by repetitive and fragmented work, where the worker has no power and is controlled by others. The worker is, in a sense, reduced to a cog in a machine. Blauner (1964, pp. 32–33) discusses four types of alienation: 1. Powerlessness, when a person is controlled by others or a system. 2. Meaninglessness, when the parts are separated from the whole, when a person's job is disconnected from a meaningful wider system and the goals of the organisation. 3. Isolation, when a person is not part of a social group. 4. Self-estrangement, a lack of connection between here and now and future considerations, but also when work is not connected to your identity and life outside work. Blauner compares four different jobs concerning division of labour. The alienated jobs are workers on the assembly line in a car factory and textile workers in the textile industry. As a contrast, he presents printers, which at that time still was a craft industry, and process operators in a chemical plant. These jobs are characterised by low division of labour. The process operators in the chemical plant work independently but also as a team. These jobs are highly skilled and the workers have a holistic understanding of the production process, which they need to have when problems occur in the production. The organisation is decentralised and the operators have a wide discretion how to carry out their work and work more or less without supervision. As it is a team organisation the operators have social support from each other (Blauner, 1964). This type of organisation is similar to the sociotechnical work organisation in Chapter 4.

There is also a lot of research about the negative consequences for health from Tayloristic work. Repetitive work, lack of control over work, no opportunities to use your skills and knowledge combined with high demands result in stress reactions. This in turn leads to higher risk of developing cardiac diseases, stomach problems and depression (Bowling et al., 2015; Karasek & Theorell, 1990, Theorell et al., 2016). There is also a higher risk for suicide. The results of surveys covering a vast number of people show that the risk for suicide is about the double for men who have monotonous, high strain jobs, have few opportunities to learn new things and who have little influence on planning their own work. For women the pattern is not as clear, but the tendency is the same (Lennerlöf, 1986). A manual, monotonous, high strain job, not surprisingly, also leads to musculoskeletal symptoms like back, neck and shoulder pain (Lang et al., 2012).

Learning and personal development is another area researchers have discussed. Studies indicate that long-term monotonous work inhibits intellectual development (Kohn, 1983). In many studies it is also concluded that a low degree of self-government and few opportunities to use your imagination clash against fundamental human needs such as self-esteem, need of variation and control over the environment (Gardell, 1986). People having that kind of work are at risk of developing learned helplessness or learned passivity, that is inability to take initiative to changes (Seligman, 1975; Gardell, 1986; Lennerlöf, 1986). Ability to take initiative and activity level tend to decrease and you learn to behave in a passive way. The explanation, put forward by quality of work researchers, is that in repetitive, low-skilled work people do almost not use any mental activities at all. This type of work is fragmented, that is the work is disconnected from any coherence. The individual is totally controlled by the environment, as for example at the assembly line, and has no opportunity to influence the content of the work (Frese, 1983).

Summary

In Taylorism the division of work changes in a fundamental way compared to earlier work organisations in manufacturing industry. Management takes control of the work process, plans the production and workers are degraded to only performing simple, standardised and repetitive tasks. For workers the work is de-skilled, compared to the earlier more artisan-like work, that is the work requires less skill and knowledge. The work is coordinated, through command and control by supervisors, standardised tasks and formal assignments. The same division of labour and coordination principles are used in Fordism. In Fordism the assembly line is added as a coordination/control principle, which controls the work pace in a very concrete way. Taylorism and Fordism led to a considerable increase in productivity but the negative effects for workers were numerous such as de-skilling, passivation, alienation and ill-health.

Reflection Questions

1. What personality do you think Frederick Taylor had?

2. At work, how would you feel being studied by a time and motion man with a clock?
3. Why do you think Taylorism and Fordism have been so influential as work organisation models?
4. How would you redesign a Fordistic work organisation to counteract the negative effects on health and wellbeing?

Bibliography

Berggren, C. (1990). *Det nya bilarbetet: Konkurrensen mellan olika produktionskoncept i svensk bilindustri 1970–1990*. Arkiv.

Björkman, T. (1996). The rationalisation movement in perspective and some ergonomic implications. *Applied Ergonomics, 27*(2), 111–117.

Blauner, R. (1964). *Alienation and freedom: The factory worker and his industry*. University of Chicago.

Bowling, N. A., Alarcon, G. M., Bragg, C. B., & Hartman, M. J. (2015). A meta-analytic examination of the potential correlates and consequences of workload. *Work & Stress, 29*(2), 95–113.

Braverman, H. (1974). *Work and Monopoly Capital: The degrading of work in the Twentieth Century*. Monthly Review Press.

Dickinson, Z. C. (1932). Suggestions from workers: Schemes and problems. *The Quartely Journal of Economics, 46*(4), 617–673.

Edgren, L. (2006). What did a guild do? Swedish guilds in the Eighteenth and early Ninteenth Century. In I. A. Gadd & P. Wallis (Eds.), *Guilds and association in Europe* (pp. 900–1900). Centre for Metropolitan History.

Epstein, S. R., & Prak, M. (2008). Introduction: Guilds, innovation, and the European Economy. In S. R. Epstein & M. Prak (Eds.), *Guilds, innovation, and the European Economy* (pp. 1400–1800). Cambridge University Press.

Fägerborg, E. (1991). Arbetarkreativitet inom modern processteknologi. Ett exempel från mejeriindustrin. In K. Båsk (Ed.), *Arbetarklassen i samhällets vardag: tredje nordiska arbetarkulturseminariet i Tammerfors, Finland 4.-6.september 1989 = The working class in the everyday life of society: 3rd Nordic seminar on working-class culture, Tampere, Finland, september 4–6, 1989*. Helsingfors: Sällskapet för forskning i arbetarrörelsens historia och arbetarkultur in cooperation with Museiverket and Folkkultursarkivet.

Frese, M. (1983). Fragmenterad handling och kontroll: två teman inom industriell psykopatologi. In G. Aronsson (Ed.), *Arbetets krav och mänsklig utveckling: Socialpsykologisk arbetslivsforskning*. Stockholm: Prisma.

Gardell, B. (1986). *Arbetets organisation och människans natur: En forskningsöversikt om människans behov av att behärska tekniken*. Arbetsmiljöfonden.

Hjelm, J. (1999). *Begåvningsreserven inom industrin: Förslagsverksamhet i Sverige under 1900-talet*. Arkiv.

Hounshell, D. A. (1984). *From the American system to mass production, 1800–1932: The development of manufacturing technology in the United States*. Johns Hopkins.

Karasek, R., & Theorell, T. (1990). *Healthy work: Stress, productivity and the reconstruction of working life*: Basic Books.

Keen, D. (2006). 1. English Urban Guilds, c.900–1300: The purposes and politics of association. In I. A. Gadd & P. Wallis (Eds.), *Guilds and association in Europe, 900–1900*. Centre for Metropolitan History, University of London.

Kohn, M. L. (1983). Arbetets komplicitet och den vuxna personligheten. In G. Aronsson (Ed.), *Arbetslivets krav och mänsklig utveckling*. Prisma.

Lang, J., Ochsmann, E., Kraus, T., & Lang, J. W. B. (2012). Psychosocial work stressors as antecedents of musculoskeletal problems: A systematic review and meta-analysis of stability-adjusted longitudinal studies. *Social Science & Medicine, 75*, 1163–1174.

Lennerlöf, L. (1986). *Kompetens eller hjälplöshet?: Om lärande i arbete: En forskningsöversikt*. Solna: Arbetarskyddsstyr.

Parr, M. (1994). *Det svenska skråväsendet: Hantverkets organisationshistoria i Sverige och Norrköping*. Stadsmuseet.

Seligman, M. E. P. (1975). *Helplessness: On depression, development, and death*. Freeman.

Taylor, F. W. (1911). *The principles of scientific management*. Harper & Brother.

Taylor, F. W. (1947/1903). Shop management. In *Scientific management*. Harper & Brothers.

Taylor, F. W. (1947/1912). Taylors's testimony before the special house committee. In *Scientific management*. Harper & Brothers.

Theorell, T., Jood, K., Slunga Järvholm, L., Vingård, E., Perk, J., Östergren, P. O., et al. (2016). A systematic review of studies in the contributions of the work environment to ischaemic heart disease development. *The European Journal of Public Health, 26*(3), 470–477.

CHAPTER 3

The Bureaucratic Organisation

Learning Objectives

This chapter should provide you with knowledge about:

- The function of a hierarchy and its effect on communication.
- The benefits of authorities in a welfare society which are coordinated by a system of rules.
- Under what circumstances a bureaucratic organisation can be efficient.
- The negative effects on innovation, learning and personal initiative from bureaucracies.

Introduction

Military organisation was a source of inspiration to Scientific Management and the same goes for the bureaucratic organisation. The same rationalisation and disciplining process, where people used like cogs in a machine, the German sociologist Max Weber (1922/1978) saw in public sector bureaucracies. An organisation for administrative work with a strong hierarchy, specialised work roles, which is coordinated mainly by a set of rules has been given several labels, but the most used is probably bureaucracy. Other labels are administrative organisation, mechanistic organisation and machine bureaucracy. Max Weber (1864–1920) described the development of bureaucratic organisations, which he above all saw in the public sector, but also in the church and in military organisations. Also private companies developed into bureaucracies when

P-O Börnfelt, *Work Organisation in Practice*,
https://doi.org/10.1007/978-3-031-21667-1_3

they grew larger. The bureaucratic organisation in the public sector is characterised by control by a set of rules and permanent employed highly qualified civil servants.

Bureau is French and means drawing desk. Cracy is derived from the Greek krati which means domination. So the bureaucracy can roughly be understood as authority through administrative units. With the help of Weber, the concept can be further defined. The central aspect of Weber's bureaucracy is rationality, which is reflected in:

1. Authority through professional knowledge.
2. Impartial administration of errands based on facts without any emotional considerations.
3. Administration is carried out by using a system of rules. To treat all people equally is the governing principle. Using one system of rules for all errands ensures that all errands are carried out in the same way, according to the rules (Weber, 1922/1978).

In order to understand what Weber meant by bureaucracy and the effects it has, a historical background is presented and an explanation of the rationalisation process, which Weber talked about. Weber studied the rationalisation process in society, which he saw as a general driving force in society independent of a capitalist or a socialist system. Weber understood the rationalisation process as a transformation in people's thinking, where magic, superstition and ignorance were replaced by systematic, scientific and technical thinking. People were more and more thinking in a rational way by using more precise abstract concepts and created theories and laws in order to understand the world. In order to control the environment people more and more started to calculate the practical outcome of different actions. The structural aspect of the rationalisation process is the bureaucratic organisation (Boglind et al., 1986, pp. 141–152).

The development of the capitalist system, where big companies started to emerge is also part of the explanation. Big companies needed a stable, strict and efficient administration (Weber, 1922/1978). The development of the bureaucracy was also fostered by the increased complexity in the welfare society that started to emerge. There were increasing need for social security, law and order. In democratic states judiciary and other public administration organisation grew and got more complex. Central principles in the welfare states were equality and social responsibility. In the old feudal society exercise of authority and administration were not carried out in an impartial way based on facts. One substantial reason for that was that the official was dependant on the prince's goodwill. To be an official was often a side-line occupation. No difference was being made between private and the official property. The administrative work was often carried out in the official's own home. The official often lacked education for the profession and received his/her position on arbitrary grounds, based on loyalty to the prince.[1]

The most important reason to the dissemination of bureaucracy was, according to Weber, the technical superiority of the bureaucracy compared to earlier work organisations. Weber resembled the bureaucracy with a machine, which works fast without friction. Personal engagement, goodwill and gratitude are in bureaucracy replaced by handling errands in an impartial way, based on facts and guided by a system or rules. Arbitrary treatment is in the bureaucracy replaced by the principle of equal treatment (Weber, 1922/1978).

Features of the Bureaucracy

Work in the bureaucracy is performed and coordinated by a set of general rules, for example laws or regulations. The official duties are performed by officials who have professional qualifications. The work requires a long and specialised education for example law studies, economy or business administration. Furthermore, there are also lower civil servants in the bureaucracy with less qualified jobs. Work in the bureaucracy is carried out by strictly and objectively following the rules without personal considerations. The managerial power, which is connected to the positions, is strictly confined by rules. The officials are organised in a hierarchy where the superior controls his/her subordinates. Decisions and messages are communicated by written documents.

The position of the official is independent, thus no other actors or organisations has authority to exert influence on it. Moreover, the position is often occupied for lifetime and it is difficult to dismiss the official because the independent position needs to be protected. Arbitrary reasons cannot be used for dismissal, serious proven misconduct is required. The position is full-time and there is a fixed salary based on position and number of years employed. The assets of the official and the bureau are separated. The official is expected to be loyal to his/her professional position, not as in the feudal society, loyal to a prince.

The official is appointed by a superior and the recruitment is carried out strictly based on formal qualifications. Advancement to higher positions in the hierarchy is also based on formal qualifications (Weber, 1922/1978).

Bureaucracies are often found in the public sector, as the handling of errands are based on the principle of equal treatment, which in turn is carried out with the use of a system of rules. In lawcourts the system of rules is made up of laws and other regulations. Other examples of bureaucracies are custom authorities and social welfare offices.

[1] Or as often is the case even today in many authoritarian hierarchical organisations, loyalty to managers and/or the organisation.

Bureaucracies are also found in areas where security is important such as airline companies. There are safety routines in order to avoid mistakes and if incidents occur there are routines for how to handle them. Furthermore, organisations which works with control, such as the police and prisons tend to develop bureaucracies (Mintzberg, 1983, pp. 174–175).

Strengths and Weaknesses Related to the Bureaucracy A Better Heading Would be: Some Dysfunctional Effects

Weber saw the bureaucracy as very efficient, but he also highlighted dysfunctional aspects. The control by rules tend to make the rules becoming ends in themselves by members or the organisation. The rules then become more important than more overall aims such as developing better welfare, or a more humane society. The bureaucracy resembles a machine, and this also have oppressive effects for organisational members (Boglind et al., 1986, pp. 141–152). According to Weber the individual bureaucrat is only a cog in a continuously growing mechanism, which essentially dictates a fixed march route for him. He is entrusted with specific tasks, and he cannot start or stop the mechanism (Weber, 1922/1978).

The control by rules leads to conformity where workers tend not to consider the special needs of different clients. The organisation cannot adopt to different situations due to the rigid way it is organised. Customers or clients of the organisation often experience that the workers in the bureaucracy cannot or do not want to help them, as the workers are strictly following the rules. The bureaucrat is treating the client as an impersonal errand and specific circumstances and needs are overlooked. The client can therefore experience the bureaucrat as arrogant and not caring (Merton, 1968, pp. 249–260).

Bureaucracies for Profit

Even if Weber included organisations for profit under the bureaucracy umbrella, he mostly studied public organisations. There are however some differences between private and public organisations, which have got bureaucratic features. In private bureaucracy like organisations the division of labour is often higher. Managers have also more power to execute command at will, so workers are more vulnerable. Authors have put different labels on bureaucracy like organisations such as mechanistic organisations (Burns and Stalker, 1961), formal organisations (Argyris and Schön, 1978), and machine bureaucracies (Mintzberg, 1983). One example of a bureaucracy like model in the private sector is Fayol's administrative theory.

Fayol's Administrative Theory

Henri Fayol (1841–1925) was a French head of a company in the mining industry. Fayol's theory highlights the managerial role and administrative routines for control and coordinate an organisation. His theory has been influential on organisation and management in practise.

Essential features of Fayol's theory are:

- High division of work. Like Taylor and Ford, Fayol favours increased specialisation (high degree of division of work). This is positive for precision and efficiency according to Fayol. Changing work assignments takes time and energy and it leads to productivity losses.
- Discipline. The management and workers should keep to their agreements and contracts. The agreements are aimed at fostering obedience, good behaviour, respect and high work ethic.
- Unity of command. Contrary to Taylor Fayol was in favour of every worker in the company should have only one supervisor. If not, it could jeopardise discipline and order. Furthermore, it can lead to irritation and conflicts.
- Formal communication. Communication should normally follow the line of command, vertically in the organisation. A worker should report only to his superior and so forth (Fayol, 1916/1949).

The Mechanistic Organisation

During the 1940s, 1950s and 1960s bureaucracies were studied extensively, which highlighted both advantages and disadvantages. Two British sociologists, Tom Burns and George Stalker (1961), carried out studies in 20 organisations in the UK. Organisation designers have much to learn from their findings even today. They found two organisation models, which had rather different features, the mechanistic and the organic organisation. According to the authors, the mechanistic organisation works well during a stable environment, where no major changes need to be made in the organisation. The mechanistic organisation has the following features:

- Specialised tasks and rules for how they should be carried out.
- Specified responsibility units, more or less de-coupled from the overall objectives of the organisation.
- Control and coordination of workers is carried out by their immediate superior. He or she makes decisions and give instructions to the workers.
- Communication flows vertically through the hierarchy.
- The essential knowledge in the organisation is placed at the top of the organisation. The hierarchy is thereby strengthened.
- Loyalty towards the organisation and obedience to managers is important for organisational membership.

- Specific and local knowledge is seen as more important compared to general and overall knowledge (Ibid., pp. 119–120).

Advantages and Disadvantages Related to Bureaucracy like Organisations

Some people find it safe and comfortable to have their own area of responsibility and specified tasks. They do not need to think about how to organise their work and they do not need to discuss and coordinate their work with others. Many studies have been conducted on job satisfaction and a common result is that even in repetitive work with low autonomy quite a number of people report high job satisfaction. A common explanation for these differences is that the socialisation process is influential, the values and attitudes we acquire through life, for instance through the socioeconomic class we are socialised in. Then there is a socialisation process taking place at work as well, for instance blue collar worker values tend to differ from white collar workers (E g. Berglund, 2017; Blauner, 1964).

As work in bureaucracy like organisations tend to be very prescribed for each work role, there is no room for workers to influence their work tasks. Thus control/decision authority is low which means a higher risk to develop stress related health problems such as sleeping problems, depression, back pain and cardiac deceases (Bowling et al., 2015; Karasek & Theorell, 1990; Lang et al., 2012; Nixon et al., 2011, Theorell et al., 2016).

Also, highly specified work assignments result in coordination problems if the environment around the organisation is unstable, for example a very competitive market or new technology developing. The more specified work assignments are the more managers need to have knowledge of what goes on in and outside the organisation. Managers need to create new positions, see to that workers do not have too big workload or too little to do. Managers also need to specify responsibility and authority for each position and manage communication channels. Specified work assignments also result in people tend to focus on his/her own responsibility area. All other issues are ignored, and problems and mistakes tend to be blamed on other people or departments. Errands and situations that is not covered by a responsibility area tend not be handled at all, or there will be lengthy discussion whose responsibility it is which will take time and energy. Relations between managers and between departments are characterised by rivalry. Departments are organised by function, which is labelled function organisation, that is there is for example one economy department, one marketing department, one HRM department and so on. Each department strives to receive as much resources as possible and tries to convince the management about the importance of their department. It is only the top management who has the overview and decide how to allocate the resources. The different departments only have knowledge about their own department. They view their own department as the most important one and fight for it to grow. This pattern results in the organisation tend not to focus on the essential factors for survival, such as having the right product or service, high quality and satisfied customers (Burns & Stalker, 1961, pp. 119–125).

In the mechanistic organisation nobody does anything else than what is specified in the work description, or instructions from their manager. The reason for that is work descriptions and direct supervision are the control and coordination mechanisms used in the mechanistic organisation. The function organisation makes the departments to focus on their own department only. In order to solve efficiency problems, managers tighten up responsibility areas even more, that is more of the same method. Furthermore, political conflicts tend to increase when major changes take place in the organisation's environment, for example the introduction of new technology or new competitors. The power and status structure is then threatened as well as managers spot opportunities for a advancement in the hierarchy. It can result in some managers become reluctant to advance in order to avoid political conflicts. There are often more changes on management positions taking place during such turbulent times (Ibid., pp. 126–132).

Hindrance for Learning and Development

Argyris and Schön have in different publications highlighted problems for learning and development in bureaucracy like organisations. In organisations where the work is highly specialised (high division of labour), power and knowledge are centralised, people can only use some of their skill and knowledge. This tendency is stronger the lower you go in the organisational hierarchy. Because bureaucracy like organisations strive for stability and continuity only small changes can be made in the organisation, which Argyris and Schön (1978) labels single-loop-learning. However, if there are a lot changes around the organisation, such as new technology developed by competitors, the organisation needs to create conditions for organisational members to make fundamental changes for the organisation to survive. A turbulent environment requires constant reflection and changes or status quo. Argyris and Schön use the term double-loop-learning for these fundamental changes. Double-loop-learning result in changes of organisational norms and assumptions, which in turn affect strategies and methods used (see Chapter 6). One example of double-loop-learning is when an organisation develops fundamentally new technology, for example from manufacturing mechanical calculators to electronic. There are however strong restraints for double-loop-learning in bureaucratic organisation, according to the authors, because the members of the organisation are using the so-called model I theory-in-use. A theory-in-use is the assumptions and values that are governing people's action. The model I theory-in-use hinders people to reflect over the values underpinning it, in turn hindering organisational learning (Argyris & Schön, 1978, pp. 60–64, 119–127).

The assumptions and values in model I are: '(1) be in unilateral control over others, (2) strive to win and minimize losing, (3) suppress negative feelings, and (4) act rationally...' (Argyris, 2004, pp. 8–9). Model I result in defensive routines which minimise reflection and inquiry. Examples of these defensive routines are distrust, competition, self-sealing, misunderstanding and action that prevent embarrassment. Due to the fact that the organisation is built upon distrust, the control of organisational members is high. People who express concerns about problems and miss conduct are punished. This result in people being afraid and people tend to take defensive attitudes. In order to avoid punishment from managers, workers only perform tasks according to job descriptions and protect their own area and the department. There is distrust and competition towards other departments. The answer from management is to increase control, which make problems even worse (Argyris & Schön, 1978, pp. 119–127). In chapter 6, model II is presented, which Argyris and Schön argue is beneficial for organisational learning.

Dependency

Bureaucratic organisations tend to create dependency on external structures such as rules, policies and instructions. Theories about dependency highlights that bureaucratic organisations result in decreased self-dependency and initiative taking. Heller (1998, p. 148) discusses, with reference to Mace, that lack of competence can lead to dependency. Heller also argue, with reference to Miller, that institutions can cause dependency. The individual gives up his/her autonomy and replaces it with support and protection from 'safe' external structures.

A German study, which is in line with dependency theories, is Frese et al. (1996). The authors use the concept personal initiative, which is about conduct in accordance with the vision of the organisation, has a long-term focus, is goal and action oriented, characterised by perseverance, is self-initiated and pro-active. In the former East Germany organisations had a lot in common with the bureaucracy with central planning and very little discretion for own initiatives. Due to fact there was no free market, organisations thereby lacked competition so there were few reasons to change the organisation. The managers were more risk avoiding compared to managers in West Germany. The workers had low control over work, low complexity in tasks and were closely controlled by their supervisors. The researchers tested the hypotheses that former East Germans would have less ability, compared to former West Germans to take initiative and instead prefer to be told what to do. The study gives support to the hypotheses. 13 percent of former East Germans, compared to 35 percent of former West Germans scored very high on initiative taking.

Summary

There is low division of work in public bureaucratic organisations for the higher civil servants. There are however often also low-skilled jobs in bureaucracy like organisations which have a higher division of work. The work in bureaucracies is coordinated by a system of rules which also is the foundation for the principle of equal treatment. Work is also coordinated by standardised skills through a common education (E g. legal studies), formal assignments, command and control by supervisors. There is a strong hierarchy where supervisors control their subordinates and workers report to their supervisor. The bureaucratic organisation can be efficient in a stable environment but has difficulties to adapt to a more changing environment due to its static structure. There are other set-backs such as suboptimization, lack of holistic understanding, dependence of rules and structures and few opportunities for workers to take initiative, learn and develop.

There might also be some health-related problems. As work is very prescribed, there is no room for workers to influence their work tasks. Thus control/decision authority is low which is related to a risk to develop stress related health problems such as depression and cardiac deceases.

Taylorism, Fordism, Fayol's administrative theory and the bureaucracy are often seen as the classical organisation models, which have strong hierarchy, supervisors control work and work roles are highly specified. In the next chapter the sociotechnical school is presented, which breaks with these three features.

Reflection Questions

1. Why has the metaphor "machine" been used to describe bureaucracies? In what way do the bureaucracy resemble a machine?
2. Some people prefer working in a bureaucracy. Would you like that, and if so, why?
3. Why do not bureaucracies always operate according to the plan?
4. What could be done to promote innovation
5. , critical thinking and personal initiative in bureaucracies?

Bibliography

Argyris, C. (2004). *Reasons and rationalizations: The limits to organizational knowledge*. Oxford University Press.

Argyris, C., & Schön, D. A. (1978). *Organizational learning: A theory of action perspective*. Addison-Wesley.

Berglund, T. (2017). 17. Attityder till arbete. In M. Bengtsson, & T. Berglund (Eds.), *Arbetslivet*. Studentlitteratur.

Blauner, R. (1964). *Alienation and freedom: The factory worker and his industry*. University of Chicago.

Boglind, A., Månson, P., & Lindskoug, K. (1986). *Kapital, rationalitet och social sammanhållning : en introduktion till Karl Marx', Max Webers och Émile Durkheims samhällsteorier*. Prisma.

Bowling, N. A., Alarcon, G. M., Bragg, C. B., & Hartman, M. J. (2015). A meta-analytic examination of the potential correlates and consequences of workload. *Work & Stress, 29*(2), 95–113.

Burns, T., & Stalker, G. M. (1961). *The management of innovation*. Tavistock.

Fayol, H. (1916/1949). *General and industrial management*. Pitman Publishing.

Frese, M., Kring, W., Soose, A., & Zempel, J. (1996). Personal initiative at work: Differences between East and West Germany. *Academy of Management Journal, 39*(1), 37–63.

Heller, F. A. (1998). Playing the Devil´s advocate: Limits to influence sharing in theory and practise. In F. Heller, E. Pusic, G. Strauss, & B. Wilpert (Eds.), *Organizational participation: Myth and reality*. Oxford University Press.

Karasek, R., & Theorell, T. (1990). *Healthy work: Stress, productivity and the reconstruction of working life*: Basic Books.

Lang, J., Ochsmann, E., Kraus, T., & Lang, J. W. B. (2012). Psychosocial work stressors as antecedents of musculoskeletal problems: A systematic review and meta-analysis of stability-adjusted longitudinal studies. *Social Science & Medicine, 75*, 1163–1174.

Merton, R. K. (1968). *Social theory and social structure*. Free press.

Mintzberg, H. (1983). *Structure in fives: Designing effective organizations*. Prentice-Hall.

Nixon, A. E., Mazzola, J. J., Bauer, J., Krueger, J. R., & Spector, P. E. (2011). Can work make you sick? A meta-analysis of the relationships between job stressors and physical symptoms. *Work & Stress, 25*(1), 1–22.

Theorell, T., Jood, K., Slunga Järvholm, L., Vingård, E., Perk, J., Östergren, P. O., et al. (2016). A systematic review of studies in the contributions of the work environment to ischaemic heart disease development. *The European Journal of Public Health, 26*(3), 470–477.

Weber, M. (1922/1978). *Economy and society: An outline of interpretative sociology*. University of California Press.

CHAPTER 4

The Sociotechnical School

Learning Objectives

This chapter should provide you with knowledge about:

- The connection between democratic processes in the society at large in the 1960s and 1970s and workplace democracy.
- How work is enlarged and enriched in the sociotechnical work organisation and the link to intrinsic motivation.
- How work is coordinated through a self-directed working group.
- Why the sociotechnical work organisation can benefit innovation.
- Why the sociotechnical work organisation can be beneficial for health and wellbeing.

The sociotechnical school has been influential in experiments with alternative work organisation models in Europe (Björkman, 1996). The sociotechnical school was developed at the Tavistock Institute of Human Relations in London. After the second world war, the institute took part in reconstructing the British coal mining industry. The aim was to find ways to organise work, which resulted in high productivity as well as humane working conditions. The government-owned coal mining company asked the institute for help. The company had problems with low productivity, high staff turnover, high absence and conflicts between workers and the employer. The researchers carried out studies in Yorkshire and found one coal mine where groups worked relatively independently with minimal control from supervisors. The workers rotated between tasks and the groups cooperated with each other. Work motivation was high, the absence was low, and accidents were rare. The workers

P-O Börnfelt, *Work Organisation in Practice*,
https://doi.org/10.1007/978-3-031-21667-1_4

had initiated this work organisation themselves and the site manager had contributed with the introduction of new technology.[1]

Before the change of the work organisation the work was more large-scale and mechanised using the so-called long wall method in the mine. The tasks were very narrow, and each worker had one own specific task to perform. The coordination and control were carried out by a foreman. The workers went back to an old method, before the mechanisation, where they worked independently in groups and took responsibility for the whole work (Trist, 1981).

Sociotechnical experiments were also carried out in the car manufacturing industry, the service sector in England, and the textile industry in India. The sociotechnical ideas were also taken up in Norway by Einar Thorsrud from the Technical University of Norway, in the 1960s who had contact with the Tavistock Institute. Norway's manufacturing industry had severe economic problems at this time. At about the same time the union started to demand increased influence at work. A number of development projects were started, but they did not get the dissemination they strived for (Trist, 1981).

The sociotechnical theory has developed in four different branches—one Scandinavian, one Dutch, one Australian and one North American (Eijnatten, Shani & Leary, 2008). In this book I am focusing on the classical theory, which derives from the Tavistock Institute in London and the first experiments in Norway in the 1960s. I am also referring to other authors, which is close to the foundations.

The Self-Directed Working Group

A basic assumption in the sociotechnical school is that democracy should not only exist in politics, but also in the workplace. Democracy works better if people get practise at the local level (Susman, 1976, pp. 39–43). The sociotechnical school focus on the work group level and how work is carried out. Worker influence at other levels such as representative democracy (i.e. having board representation) in companies has not been dealt with in sociotechnical theory (Trist, 1981, p. 22).

The self-directed working group is central in sociotechnical theory. According to Susman (1976, p. 91) the sociotechnical designer should limit planning to create organisational units and allocate material, personnel, technology, tools and to set standards on the products.

In the self-directed working group decisions are made about:

[1] Sociotechnical theory is based on a system view on organisations, where the technical system (machines and other equipment) is optimised together with the social system (workers). If they are well matched it is expected to result in both high efficiency and worker satisfaction. See for example Trist (1981) for a more in-depth presentation on the theoretical foundations.

- Group values. Members of a group decide what basic values should guide their activities (Susman, 1976, pp. 116–127; Thorsrud & Emery, 1969, p. 22).
- The production process: Coordination of work, allocation of resources to different places, changes of flow of resources in and out from the group (Susman, 1976, pp. 116–127), job design, division of work, work methods and work pace (Sandberg, 1982, p. 4). The group plans the work based on orders and can decide in what order to handle orders (Stymne, 1980). Objectives for productivity and quality are set by management but the group has got some authority to influence these. The management should give continuous feedback on the results (Thorsrud & Emery, 1969, pp. 21–23).
- Issues not directly related to production such as when to take breaks (Susman, 1976, pp. 116–127).
- Issues that facilitate self-direction. The group has authority on how to make decisions. Decisions can for example be made by voting, consensus or to appoint someone to take decisions. According to Susman democracy at the workplace is consistent with a democratic society, it prepares people for good citizenship and also provides training for a career in the organisation (Sandberg, 1982, p. 4; Susman, 1976, pp. 116–127).

Other characteristics are tasks organised in greater wholes, contrary to the fragmented Fordistic work. The group is responsible for an area, with different tasks forming a greater meaningful whole. Multi-skilling is strived for (Stymne, 1980; Trist, 1981, Chapter 1). The work should therefore demand a certain skill and knowledge level. The tasks should also have optimal variation. Too little variation can be tiresome and boring, too much variation can be inefficient because it will take too long time to master the working tasks. Work rotation and physical closeness between colleagues are strived for. It results in mutual understanding between workers who are dependent on each other. Indirect[2] tasks are also performed such as preparing work and service work. The work should be seen as contributing to a product, which is useful and of value for the customer (Thorsrud & Emery, 1969, pp. 21–23).

Sociotechnical theory builds on intrinsic motivation, that is that work itself is motivating when organised according to the aforementioned principles. The idea is that the enriched work leads to work satisfaction which in turn lead to engagement at work and for the organisation (E.g. Trist, 1981, p. 29, pp. 42–43).

[2] Direct work generally refers to the work, which adds direct value to the product. In this example the direct work is to build cars. Indirect work refers to task, which adds indirect value to the product. It can be for example planning, economy, ordering material and doing development activities.

In order to facilitate the group's self-determination other technical solutions are preferred than the assembly line, or the assembly line is modified by for example buffers[3] (Pruijt, 2003).

The leadership also changes in the sociotechnical work organisation. Traditional foremen are not used. Instead there are coaches of facilitators who are more equal discussion partners and give advice to the groups (Björkman, 1996; Trist, 1981, p. 41). Other specialists, such as production technicians become more like consultants to the groups. Specialists and groups work together to develop the technical system (Stymne, 1980).

Piece wages are abandoned in favour of permanent pay or competence-based pay. They both often are combined with some kind of group-based bonus system (Stymne, 1980; Trist, 1981, p. 41). At Volvo's Uddevalla factory, the pay was related to how large part of the car you could build (Pruijt, 2003).

Volvo's car manufacturing factories in Sweden were quite well-known examples of sociotechnical work organisation from mid-1970s to the beginning of the 1990s. According to Sandberg (1995, p. 87) in 1974 Volvo's new factory in Kalmar, Sweden was the first car manufacturing factory which broke away from Fordistic work organisation (often labelled post-fordism[4]). Volvo's Uddevalla factory has also quite often been mentioned as a post-fordist example. In Sandberg (1995) the Uddevalla model is labelled enriching production. At the Uddevalla factory, they used the holistic principle to build the whole or a large part of the car yourself, and that workers should understand the whole production process. The assembly of the car was carried out on wagons, which the workers had control over, so they could move them when they wanted to. The group's tasks were planning the work, assembly, control and adjustments. The factory was organised in six workshops, each having eight working groups. Each group had 8–10 assembly workers and each group built a whole car. The cycle time for each worker was around two hours. In theory a worker could build a whole car him/herself even if it seldom happened (Boglind, 2013; Ellegård et al., 1989). The group also worked with economy, quality and maintenance (often labelled as indirect tasks). The aim was to rotate these tasks every month. The production targets depended on the number of workers in a team (Berggren, 1992, pp. 161–162).

The Kalmar factory and the Uddevalla factory, which only were assembly plants, were closed down in 1994 and 1993 respectively. Both the top management and the unions came to the same conclusion, to keep the Torslanda factory (which used the traditional assembly line) because it was a whole factory (body, painting and assembly work-shops), also it did not use it's

[3] On a car assembly line, the line can be divided in sections. Between the sections a number of cars can be placed acting as buffers, in order not to stop the whole line if there are delays.

[4] Post-fordism means after fordism. Post-fordism breaks with the main principles in fordism such as repetitive, fragmented work and management power over the work process. A synonym is post-taylorism (Noon et al., 2013; Pruijt, 2000).

full capacity. When it comes to productivity, both Kalmar and Uddevalla had higher productivity during their last years compared to Torslanda, but still not better than the best Volvo factory in Ghent, which used the assembly line (Boglind, 2013).

Research from Chalmers University in Gothenburg, Sweden explain why group-based parallel production (as used in Uddevalla) can result in higher productivity compared to assembly line production. The assembly line always has production losses, which are due to waiting times, even if it is to a certain extent possible to reduce these by using buffers between line sections. Parallel group production is more flexible due to the fact that workers do not need to wait for the previous work station to finish, as on the assembly line. It is also easier to coordinate a smaller group compared to a large assembly line production made up of several hundred workers, which also results in less production losses (Blomquist et al., 2013).

Empowerment and the Work Environment

Supporters of sociotechnical theory argue it is better suited to cope with a changing and turbulent environment compared to bureaucratic and Tayloristic organisations. The sociotechnical organisation is more flexible and can adapt to changes in demand from customers, deliveries from suppliers and technology. Workers are empowered to take decisions and can therefore adopt to changes in circumstances. One explanation of empowerment from a sociotechnical perspective is shared responsibility between managers and workers. It means that all members of the organisation can be leaders and followers, and that these roles can shift (Taylor & Felten, 1993, pp. 6–7).

In the US the term Quality of Working Life programs was often used when changing organisations in a sociotechnical direction (Karasek & Theorell, 1990, pp. 179–187). 'Sociotechnical systems methods provide organizations and job design techniques that provide employees with greater control over their work, greater quality of working life through feelings of personal competence, a central place in the product stream, and a sense of the social relevance of that product.' (Taylor & Felten, 1993, pp. 126–127).

The sociotechnical work organisation has several characteristics of a good work environment set out in the first chapter. The self-directed working group provides opportunities for social support, decision authority and opportunities for using skills and learning new skills.

These conditions are, according to several studies, related to less sick leave, better mental health, less risk for back pain and cardiac deceases (Bowling et al., 2015; Karasek & Theorell, 1990; Lang et al., 2012; Nixon et al., 2011; Theorell et al., 2016).

Workers Participating in Development Work

One effect from sociotechnical projects in England, Norway and Sweden was that workers participated more in troubleshooting and handling problems in the production system (Sandberg, 1982, pp. 196–197). In a sociotechnical work organisation design and development of work methods should be included in the group's work. This work enrichment results in intrinsic motivation according to Niepce and Molleman (1998).

A couple of examples illuminate how workers can participate in change and development activities at their workplaces. In 1992 a kaizen[5] program was introduced at the Volvo Uddevalla factory, which worked well according to Berggren (1994). The workers reported they got support from management and carried through improvements in the groups. When changing car models, workers themselves reorganised their workplace after studied instructions. As the workers built a large part of the car themselves, they developed a holistic understanding of car manufacturing, which helped them to analyse where problems could arise when starting to build a new model. Another effect was productive discussions between workers and production technicians about work methods (Berggren, 1994). Another example from the Uddevalla factory shows how the workers discovered a tube, which touched the fuel tank. This could risk shaving a hole in the tank. Neither the engineers or the workers at the Torslanda plant had discovered this. The workers at Uddevalla factory built the car in functional wholes and thereby got a holistic understanding of the construction of the vehicle. At the Torslanda factory the fragmented and short-cycled work hindered the workers from making such discoveries. The workers at the Uddevalla factory came up with a temporary solution and reported back to the construction department, which then developed a permanent solution to the problem.

Gardell and Svensson (1981) tell the story about development of self-directed working groups at the Swedish ticket machine manufacturing company Almex in the 1970s. The management and the union cooperated in changing the work organisation in a more democratic direction. Self-directed working groups were introduced and the foreman role was removed. The initiative to the change the work organisation was taken by the blue-collar workers and their union. According to managers at Almex, workers took more initiative after the change regarding troubleshooting and making improvements of administration and the production system. One department developed a test program together with designers to control the quality of the products. Other initiatives were simplifications of routines and administrative work.

[5] Kaizen means continuous improvement work, see chapter 5.

The Diffusion of the Sociotechnical Work Organisation

Protests

In the 1960s and 1970s there were growing protest against authoritarian structures in society and there were increasing demands for industrial democracy. There were demonstrations and wild strikes in several countries in Europe. Workers and unions demanded better working conditions, increased influence and co-determination. Also, employer's associations felt a pressure to democratise working life. Companies had problems with recruiting people, work dissatisfaction, high personnel turnover and conflicts with workers. (Karasek & Theorell, 1990, pp. 4–5; Schiller, 1988, Chapter 1–2; Trist, 1981, Chapter 1).

Experiments

As mentioned previously, the sociotechnical ideas spread from the UK to Norway in the 1960s. The experiments in Norway did not get any widespread diffusion. However, the experiments in Norway created interest in Sweden towards the end of the 1960s from the trade unions and employers' associations. Work redesign projects started in many different industries. In Sweden between 500 and 1000 experiments were carried out up to 1973 (Trist, 1981, p. 26). From an employer point of view the sociotechnical work organisation was seen a way to solve problems such as strikes, high personnel turnover and problems of recruiting. The sociotechnical work organisation was thought to result in work satisfaction, which would lead to higher motivation. The self-directed working groups were also more flexible, which together with the higher motivation would lead to higher productivity. The employers were also influenced by the political climate during the 1960s and 1970s. Political parties worked actively to improve working conditions through legislation and funding of development projects. For unions the sociotechnical work organisation provided better working conditions, influence, competence development and more interesting work.

The ideas also spread to the US in the 1960s where Lou Davis and colleagues started the Quality of Working Life (QWL) movement. The number of companies in North America with participative work organisations grew substantially from the 1980s. Examples are General Motors, Procter and Gamble, Gaines Pet Food and Shell Canada's Sarnia plant. However, the overall diffusion in the US has been very limited. In West Germany the long-lasting Humanisation of Working Life Program started in the 1970s (Karasek & Theorell, 1990, p. 4, Chapter 7 and 8). In Sweden, government-funded development programmes continued in the 1980s and 1990s. Swedish work-life development was internationally well-known during this time and attracted attention from researchers, industrial leaders and unions. The most comprehensive development programme was the Working Life Fond 1990–1995, where around 25 000 workplaces took part (Björkman, 2013). An evaluation of the project showed increased productivity and improvements in health and safety as a result of changing the work organisation. Also, in the other Nordic countries Norway, Denmark and Finland work development programmes have been launched. In Denmark and Finland there have been initiatives to form learning oriented forms of work organisations. In Denmark this work was not research led but took place in regional industrial networks throughout the 1990s. Finland also use regional networks of organisations, researcher and regional actors. In 2007 the number of development projects was about 1000, which included around 200 000 workplaces. Norway, and especially Sweden, were at the forefront of work organisation development from the 1960s onwards, but roughly after the millennium shift Denmark and especially Finland are the most active among the Nordic countries (Gustavsen, 2007). In line with the aforementioned evaluation of the Working Life Fond in Sweden, several overviews of QWL development projects show positive results such as increased productivity and quality, cost reductions, better health and safety (Karasek & Theorell, 1990, p. 181).

The diffusion of the sociotechnical work organisation model is difficult to map. Studies in Sweden however indicate an increased number of workplaces with decentralised decision-making. A survey in 1991 about 'new management', interviewing managers in Sweden showed only 6% of the workplaces had a decentralised work organisation. Three questions were related to this area:

- Decisions concerning tasks are to some extent taken by workers themselves.
- Decisions on how to perform tasks are to some extent taken by workers themselves.
- Differences between blue- and white-collar workers are reduced (Edling & Sandberg, 2013, p. 396).

In 2002 the study was replicated and the number of workplaces having a decentralised work organisation had then increased to 23% (Eriksson & Karlsson, 2013, p. 375). A comparison of the private sector in 15 EU countries showed that the Netherlands and the Nordic countries have the highest share of work with high levels of autonomy, task complexity and problem solving (year 2000). In these countries firms also tend to be more active in innovation work within the organisation (Arundel et al., 2007).

However, since the 1990s other work organisation models such as Lean production have been influential, which is reflected in more monotonous work and high pressure (see Chapters 5 and 8). Public statistics from Sweden describe a negative trend regarding strain at work (high demand combined with low control). From 1989 to 2015 the number of people who report high strain has increased, from 15 to 20% for men, from 20 to 35% for women.

Working life researchers point out that there has been a fairly limited diffusion of the sociotechnical model and that organisations often return to the traditional mindset of hierarchy and control. The traditional hierarchical view of the organisation with centralised power is difficult to challenge. Many managers do not feel comfortable sharing power with subordinates. Middle managers also often resist decision-making being decentralised. Managers might see this as losing power and tend to resist their role being changed to a support role. Also, the finance sector, when considering which companies to invest in, often prefer short-termed profit gains instead of more long-termed investments in human resources (Karasek & Theorell, 1990, Chapter 7; Riegler, 2008). In North America the interest in QWL programmes has also declined from the 1990s with the rise of a neoliberal agenda and the lean wave (Huxley, 2015).

Critique of the Sociotechnical Work Organisation

One problem with self-directed working groups is the tendency of group pressure against persons who do not work according to the group norms (Gardell, 1983, p. 363).

The work is not standardised as in Taylorism and this has been criticised from an organisational learning point of view. Adler and Cole (1993) pointed out that the Uddevalla factory did not have beneficial conditions for organisational learning[6] due to the work not being standardised and documented. Then it is difficult to diffuse efficient methods in the organisation.

The interest in workplace democracy and employee influence triggered experimentation with flatter organisations in the 1970s and 1980s, which implied middle managers and foremen being removed. According to some studies workers did not experience having more control over their work. The sick leave did not decrease either. Töres Theorell (2006, Chapter 6) discuss possible reasons. One reason can be that workers might not get enough support to handle their increased discretion, for example by lack of sufficient training. Lack of support, high demands at work and a high workload can lead to long working hours and frustration over not mastering your job. You can then experience the situation as uncontrollable (low control).

[6] Organisational learning is here understood as the diffusion of "best practise" routines and work methods in the organisation. Read more about organisational learning in chapter 6.

Summary

The work in the sociotechnical school is characterised by low division of labour. The work is both enlarged and enriched compared to Taylorism and Fordism. The work is coordinated by the self-directed work group. The foremen are replaced by coaches or facilitators, in line with a democratic leadership style, who give support and feedback to the groups. Enrichment, empowerment and a holistic understanding of the work support intrinsic motivation. As a result, workers tend to feel more responsibility and take more initiative in making changes at the workplace. These work characteristics are also in line with healthy working conditions, for instance better mental health and less risk to develop stress related health problems such as cardiac deceases. However, high demands of productivity can lead to peer pressure in the group. Workers can also feel frustration if they are not prepared and trained for self-direction and more skilled work.

Reflection Questions

1. What do you think are the reasons for the rather limited diffusion of sociotechnical organising?
2. Would you like to have more responsibility and authority at work (compared to e.g. the bureaucracy) and take group decisions about how to organise your work?
3. What advantages and disadvantages could there be with self-directed working groups? Try to distinguish between the individual, group and organisational level.
4. What are possible advantages and disadvantages with developing the skills and a holistic understanding of, for instance building a large part of a car yourself? Try to distinguish between the individual, group and organisational level.

Bibliography

Adler, P. S., & Cole, R. E. (1993). Designed for learning: A tale of two auto plants. *Sloan Management Review, 34*(3).

Arundel, A., Lorenz, E., Lundvall, B-Å., L., & Valeyre, A. (2007). How Europe's economies learn: A comparison of work organization and innovation mode for the EU-15. *Industrial and Corporate Change, 16*(6), 1175–1210.

Berggren, C. (1992). *Alternatives to lean production: Work organization in the Swedish auto industry*. ILR Press.

Berggren, C. (1994). NUMMI vs. Uddevalla. *Sloan Management Review, 35*(2), 37.

Björkman, T. (1996). The Rationalisation Movement in perspective and some ergonomic implications. *Applied Ergonomics, 27*(2), 111–117.

Björkman, T. (2013). Management: Still a fashion industry. In Å. Sandberg (Ed.), *Nordic lights: Work, management and welfare in Scandinavia*. SNS Förlag.

Blomquist, B., Engström, T., Jonsson, D., & Medbo, L. (2013). Assembly systems and work in the Swedish automotive industry. In Å. Sandberg (Ed.), *Nordic lights: Work, management and welfare in Scandinavia*. SNS Förlag.

Boglind, A. (2013). Volvo and a Swedish organisation and management model. In Å. Sandberg (Ed.), *Nordic lights: Work, management and welfare in Scandinavia*. SNS Förlag.

Bowling, N. A., Alarcon, G. M., Bragg, C. B., & Hartman, M. J. (2015). A meta-analytic examination of the potential correlates and consequences of workload. *Work & Stress, 29*(2), 95–113.

Edling, C., & Sandberg, Å. (2013). New management and good work? A Swedish experience. In Å. Sandberg (Ed.), *Nordic lights: Work, management and welfare in Scandinavia*. SNS Förlag.

Eijnatten, F. M., Shani, A. B., & Leary, M. M. (2008). Socio-technical systems: Designing and managing sustainable organizations. In T. G. Cummings (Ed.), *Handbook of organizational development*. Sage.

Ellegård, K., Nilsson, L., Engström, T., & Arbetsmiljöfonden. (1989). *Principer och realiteter vid förnyelse av industriellt arbete: Projekteringen av Volvos bilfabrik i Uddevalla: Sammanfattning av forskningsprojektet "Dokumentation av utvecklingsprocessen för Volvos Uddevallafabrik, 1985–1988"*. Arbetsmiljöfonden.

Eriksson, B., & Karlsson, J. C. (2013). Flexibility in practise. In Å. Sandberg (Ed.), *Nordic lights: Work, management and welfare in Scandinavia*. SNS Förlag.

Gardell, B. (1983). Worker participation and autonomy: A multi-level approach to democracy at the work place. In C. Crouch & F. A. Heller (Eds.), *Organizational democracy & political processes*. John Wiley & Sons Ltd.

Gardell, B., & Svensson, L. (1981). *Medbestämmande och självstyre: En lokal facklig strategi för demokratisering av arbetsplatsen*. Prisma/Arbetslivscentrum.

Gustavsen, B. (2007). Work organization and 'The Scandinavian Model.' *Economic and Industrial Democracy, 28*(4), 650–671.

Huxley, C. (2015). Three decades of lean production: Practice, ideology, and resistance. *International Journal of Sociology, 45*(2), 133–151.

Karasek, R., & Theorell, T. (1990). *Healthy work: Stress*. Basic Books.

Lang, J., Ochsmann, E., Kraus, T., & Lang, J. W. B. (2012). Psychosocial work stressors as antecedents of musculoskeletal problems: A systematic review and meta-analysis of stability-adjusted longitudinal studies. *Social Science & Medicine, 75*, 1163–1174.

Niepce, W., & Molleman, E. (1998). Work design issues in lean production from a sociotechnical systems perspective: Neo-Taylorism or the next step in sociotechnical design? *Human Relations, 51*(3), 259–287.

Nixon, A. E., Mazzola, J. J., Bauer, J., Krueger, J. R., & Spector, P. E. (2011). Can work make you sick? A meta-analysis of the relationships between job stressors and physical symptoms. *Work & Stress, 25*(1), 1–22.

Noon, M., Blyton, P., & Morell, K. (2013). *The realities of work: Experiencing work and employment in contemporary society*. Palgrave Macmillan.

Pruijt, H. (2000). Repainting, modifying, smashing Taylorism. *Journal of Organizational Change Management, 13*(5), 439–451.

Pruijt, H. (2003). Teams between Neo-Taylorism and Anti-Taylorism. *Economic and Industrial Democracy, 24*(1), 77–101.

Riegler, C. H. (2008). Why is learning from national working life programmes not a matter of course? *International Journal of Action Research, 4*(1+2), 90–113.

Sandberg, T. (1982). *Work organization and autonomous groups*. LiberFörlag.

Sandberg, Å. (1995). *Enriching production: Perspectives on Volvo's Uddevalla plant as an alternative to lean production*. Avebury.

Schiller, B. (1988). *"Det förödande 70-talet": SAF och medbestämmandet 1965–1982*. Arbetsmiljöfonden, Allmänna förl.

Stymne, B. (1980). Design principles for a participative organization of work. Some conclusions from the URAF experiments. *Economic and Industrial Democracy, 1*, 197–224.

Susman, G. I. (1976). *Autonomy at work: A sociotechnical analysis of participative management*. Praeger Publishers.

Taylor, J. C., & Felten, D. F. (1993). *Performance by design: Sociotechnical systems in North America*. Prentice-Hall.

Theorell, T. (2006). *I spåren av 90-talet*. Karolinska institutet, University Press.

Theorell, T., Jood, K., Slunga Järvholm, L., Vingård, E., Perk, J., Östergren, P. O., & Hall, C. (2016). A systematic review of studies in the contributions of the work environment to ischaemic heart disease development. *The European Journal of Public Health, 26*(3), 470–477.

Thorsrud, E., & Emery, F. E. (1969). *Medinflytande och engagemang i arbetet: Norska försök med självstyrande arbetsgrupper*. Utvecklingsrådet för samarbetsfrågor.

Trist, E. (1981). *The evolution of socio-technical systems: A conceptual framework and an action research program*. Ontario Ministry of Labour.

CHAPTER 5

Total Quality Management (TQM) and Process Organisation

Learning Objectives

This chapter should provide you with knowledge about:

- The main ideas of process organisation.
- Why there are dividing views between commentators over the effects of lean production for workers.
- The principles of lean production, based on the Toyota model.
- The (actual) negative effects from lean production for health and well-being.
- Changes of the Toyota work organisation model.

Quality for the Customer

After World War II the economies of South East Asia grew substantially, and western companies experienced increased competition from South East Asian companies. During the decline in the western economies in the 1980s the successful Japanese companies became a source of inspiration for the west. Western companies have tried to copy, what they view to be successful concepts such as quality circles, kaizen, total quality management (TQM) and lean production. In this section the quality movement is presented, that is the concepts, which emphasises that quality should be a responsibility for all employees in the organisation as well as creating value for the customer. The quality movement has got one overall idea for all kinds of organisations—to satisfy the customer. Even within the organisation, people and departments are divided in suppliers and customers, which forms an internal market, sometimes called a pseudo market. Organisational members are not referred to as

P-O Börnfelt, *Work Organisation in Practice*,
https://doi.org/10.1007/978-3-031-21667-1_5

colleagues but as intra suppliers and intra customers (Dotchin & Oakland, 1992; Hasselbladh, 2002). Most of the principles presented here are also used in lean production (see next section). During a number of decades there have been a diffusion of ideas between the US and Japan. The direction of the diffusion has changed during periods. First, principles for quality control spread from the US to Japan. In the so-called quality movement focus changed from productivity to satisfying the customer by above all focus on quality. Quality should be everybody's responsibility and only processes, which add value to the customer should be used in the organisation (Axelsson & Bergman, 1999). The American Edward Deming is probably the most influential person for the quality movement. During the 1940s and 1950s he developed the idea of the customer in the centre, the statistical method and the so-called PDCA cycle. The PDCA cycle has got four steps: (1) Plan and think before you do something (plan). (2) Carry through what you have planned (do). (3) Reflect over and evaluate what you have done (check, study). (4) Learn from your experiences and implement what works well (act). The US was not ready for Deming's ideas. He went to Japan where his ideas were well received. Two other Americans, Joseph Juran and Armand Feigenbaum, also helped to develop quality control as a management concept in Japan. Juran introduced the pareto principle, which would be a basic quality tool. According to the pareto principle a problem will often be caused by a few important factors which must be addressed. Other more trivial factors can be ignored. Feigenbaum, who was production manager at General Electric in the 1950s and 1960s, argued that a durable improvement work can only be achieved if the company has got a participative atmosphere. According to Feigenbaum quality was everybody's responsibility and he introduced the concept total quality control (TQC). Quality control was now no longer only a responsibility for production technicians. TQC did not only focus on quality control in the production process. The whole process, from construction to delivery should be controlled for quality (Axelsson & Bergman, 1999; Dotchin & Oakland, 1992; Hasselbladh & Lundgren, 2002, p. 44).

During the 1950s and 1960s total quality management (TQM) became the general concept used for management and techniques focusing quality (Hasselbladh & Lundgren, 2002). According to Deming (1994) the management should facilitate communication between workers and between departments. Each department should take responsibility for the success of the whole organisation, and not only optimise their own department. Furthermore, workers should be given opportunities to use their imagination, develop their skills and feel pride at work.

Kaizen is Japanese for improvements in small steps but is often translated as continuous improvements. Japanese companies started to use kaizen after World War II and over time it got integrated in TQM. All members of the organisation are expected to perform kaizen. Improvements can for example be made in the production system, delivery system and work operations (Nilsson, 1999). Kaizen is mostly focused on continuous small changes that can be made easily by a group or workers, as opposed to more comprehensive changes that include the whole organisation (e.g. Imai, 1986).

TQM is not only used in manufacturing industry, but also in other sectors such as the healthcare sector. The customer, in the healthcare sector the patient, should have the opportunity to choose between caretakers (Bejerot, 2008, p. 145). Models, such as the EFQM Model, have been developed to help organisations to introduce TQM. The EFQM Model—the European for Quality Management Excellence Model, has been used since the early 1990s to help organisations to organise and evaluate according to TQM principles, and it is widespread and accepted according to van Shoten et al. (2016).

The Quality Standard ISO 9000

ISO 9000 is usually associated with TQM but has got other origins than TQM. It was developed from quality standards in the US military and Nato. ISO 9000 stipulates standards for the organisation's quality systems and is based on written routines for operations. The organisation decides how to design the routines. EU has actively promoted ISO 9000 since the end of the 1980s and it is widely disseminated in Europe. An external inspector certifies the organisation if it follows the routines it has written down. The organisation should also evaluate and adjust its routines and make sure that they are followed. A study in the US stated that it took on average 15 months to get certified and the cost were substantial. As the routines should be written down a certification requires a lot of documentation. ISO 9000 does not give any instructions or advice on the quality of the product or the provided service. An organisation can produce a product no one is buying and even so will be certified. There is an evident risk that the organisations energy will focus on developing and following rules. Just as the bureaucracy, ISO 9000, has been criticised from TQM supporters among others for being rigid and static (Mendel, 2006).

Cutting Down Process Time

In several contemporary organisation models one of the major goals is to cut down on process time, or in other words lead time, for example from order to delivery of a product. Instead of organising in functions these models strive to organise in processes. The following organisation models are process oriented: Lean production, time based management (TBM) and business process reengineering (BPR). Sometimes process management is used as an overall concept (Bélanger et al., 1999). Like the quality movement, process organising has its roots from North American and Japanese management. One example of how organisations can organise in processes is presented by Ashkenas (1995) in the book *The Boundaryless Organization*. First you need to identify the central processes. Common processes in a manufacturing company are product development, dealing with customer orders, buying and ordering products and services from suppliers and dealing with complaints from customers. When the central processes have been identified, process managers are appointed. Their responsibility is to make sure that the process runs as smoothly and quickly as possible. The process manager summons the people from the different function that are part of the process. The group map the process, identifies problems which slows the process and discuss solutions. When the process runs efficiently teams are organised which have representatives from all the functions that affect the process. The teams set targets for their processes and follow them up.

The major part of the chapter is about lean production because it is a whole work organisation model and it is a concept that is widely used in today's working life.

Lean Production

Lean production was promoted by the American research programme International Motor Vehicle Programme (Womack et al., 1990). The research programme IMVP at MIT (Massachusetts Institute of Technology), which was carried out 1985–1990, compared efficiency between car manufacturers. The researchers put forward Toyota as the best organisation for building vehicles. The principles of lean production are therefore based on the work organisation Toyota had in the 1980s and the descriptions, laid out in this chapter, are therefore from that period. Examples are also taken from other Japanese companies, which have similar work organisations. Lean production, as the name suggests, is above all characterised by the strive to eliminate unnecessary resources, or waste. Lean production is based on Fordistic principles with the assembly line and repetitive and short-cycled tasks. A distinctive difference however is that there are no buffers along the assembly line, as this would be seen as waste from a lean point of view. In lean production a continuous flow of components is strived for. The components should arrive just-in-time (JIT), that is exactly when the next task is due to be carried out. Just like in Taylorism and Fordism it is the management who plans the work, and workers carry out the standardised tasks. Workers, however, have responsibility to carry out continuous improvement work, unlike in Taylorism and Fordism (Monden, 1994). Synonyms to lean production are neo-taylorism, neo-fordism, high-fordism, toyotism and JIT-system. The two first concepts point at lean production builds on and is developed from Taylorism and Fordism. Lean production does not depart from the most central principle in Taylorism, the separation between planning and the execution. The management plan the production and the workers carry out standardised tasks (Monden, 1994, chapter 10; Noon et al., 2013, chapter 6; Pruijt, 2000).

Lean production seems to be widely disseminated in manufacturing industry. Also, it is spreading to other sectors, such as the public sector. Industryweek reported from a survey in 2007, that almost 70% of 433 manufacturing companies in the US used lean production (Blanchard, 2007). A survey by consultants in Europe in 2008 indicated that 57% of 771 organisations (manufacturing, administration and public) used lean production and another 20% were considering it. In manufacturing 69% of the companies replied they are using lean production, whereas 40% of administration and public organisations replied yes (ACE, 2008). Lean is implemented in various sectors under concepts such as lean management, lean healthcare, lean office and lean banking (see for example Sederblad, 2013; Wittrock, 2015). Furthermore, the way managers, organisations and researchers understand and define lean differ widely. For example, in the healthcare sector managers and even researchers might say they use lean in a hospital, but in reality organisations, especially in the healthcare sector often only use only one or two lean principles such as kaizen and value stream mapping (VSM) (see for example Sederblad, 2013). Below the lean principles are presented, but first some words about the debates between researchers about lean, where the contrasting views and different ways to understand lean will be evident.

Criticism of Lean Production

The conclusions from the IMVP study and other studies, which describe lean production in positive terms have been heavily criticised from many authors. The results from the IMVP study about the differences in efficiency between car factories have been questioned. Williams et al. (1992) argue, after a thorough analysis of the results from the IMVP programme, that it lacks empirical evidence for the conclusions made about the differences in efficiency between car factories in Japan and other countries. Berggren (1992, p. 4) delivers the same critique and adds that the same goes from the conclusions from the IMVP programme about good working conditions.

Womack et al. (1990) do not present any empirical evidence for their statements about good working conditions. Two overview studies about health effects by lean production show on the contrary negative effects on workers' health. The first overview (Landsbergis et al., 1999), covers studies of lean manufacturing companies, most of them in North America. It reveals high stress levels caused by high work pace, repetitive work and few breaks. Due to the high workload older workers are more affected. Moreover, when the companies recruit they also select young and strong individuals. Older or weaker persons are ruled out. The second overview (Toivanen & Landsbergis, 2013) more or less confirms the results in the first overview. Lean work organisations are often related to low control and intensified work (high demand). This kind of work, low control/decision authority and high demands corresponds well with research about the psychosocial work environment, that is—higher risk for stress related unhealth such as sleeping problems, stomach problems, sleeping problems, back pain, headache and cardiac deceases (Bowling et al., 2015; Karasek & Theorell, 1990; Lang et al., 2012; Nixon et al., 2011; Theorell et al., 2016).

Advocates of lean production often argue that lean production results in up-skilling for workers (e.g. MacDuffie, 1995). Womack et al. (1990, p. 102) wrote that the manual work would soon be automatized. At the end of 1990s:

> lean-assembly plants will be populated almost entirely by highly skilled problem solvers who's task will be to think continually of ways to make the system run more smoothly and productively. (p. 102)

We know now this did not happen. Womack's thesis about up-skilling also depart from Toyota's own principles. According to Toyota it is more flexible to hold on to manual work because it is easier to re-organise the production system. Toyota only automatize when there are very strong reasons for it. They do not want to invest in machinery, which they later discover they will not need (Monden, 1994, pp. 181–182). Companies using the Toyota work organisation therefore keep the repetitive, short-cycled work. The top management at Toyota and several management researchers argue that the philosophy at Toyota is based on humanity and respect for people (Monden, 1994; Pil & Fujimoto, 2007) and focus on good health and safety. Lean production has been labelled democratic Taylorism by Adler and Cole (1993) because, according to the authors, the workers analyse and design their own tasks. Furthermore, they argue that the work is very motivating because there are a lot of opportunities for learning through the continuous improvement activities (Adler, 1993; Adler & Cole, 1993). According to MacDuffie (1995), lean production has high commitment HRM-policies, and highly motivated workers solve problems visualised in the JIT-system. These studies, which describe the lean workplace in positive terms, are to a large extent based on interviews with managers or questionnaires addressed to managers. There are however many studies, which have more appropriate research designs for studying actual working conditions, workers experience of work and the effect lean work has on workers. The picture of lean production that emerge from these studies is strikingly different. As an introduction two of these studies are presented and in then follows a systematic presentation and analysis of several of these studies.

Satoshi Kamata, a freelance journalist, worked as a temporary worker for six months in 1972–1973 at the Toyota assembly line. Kamata (1983) describes the harsh working conditions. Injuries were common (pp. 72 and 107), for example crushed fingers and most workers had stomach problems. Managers sometimes held meetings with the workers about the importance of safety, but according to Kamata, the real problems; the high work speed and the stress were not addressed. If you got injured management made it appear as you were to blame and that you made things difficult for you colleagues. A worker got his finger cut off in a machine. A foreman made a speech to staff afterwards:

> There's no point in blaming anyone for what happened. But be careful, otherwise you inconvenience the others. They'll have to do your job as well as their own. (Kamata, p. 109)

According to Kamata, the high work pace was evidently the reason for the accident. The foreman says that the worker will not get any reprimands because he quickly apologised to the section manager instead of complaining. If you fell ill it was very likely you lost your job. One example was a man who fell on the floor because he was feeling ill. He got sacked due to this. The foreman told him:

> Once you fall, you can't work any more. (pp. 124–125)

A lot of workers quit their jobs because of the inhumane workplace. Only 30% of the temporary workers finished their contracts (p. 172).

30 years after Kamata's study the American researcher Darius Mehri (2006) presents a surprisingly similar picture from a supplier in the Toyota network. Mehri worked as an engineer at the large Toyota supplier 1996–1999. The company had adopted the Toyota model so well that Toyota sent employees to be trained there. Mehri made observations and conducted 75 interviews with workers, engineers and union representatives. The study shows that what managers told workers was very different from how managers actually acted in reality. For example, managers talked a lot about safety at work, but not much was done to improve safety on the shopfloor in practise. Managers informed about risks but the very high work pace, which was the major cause for accidents, was not addressed. One aspect of lean production is to minimise the floor areas, which result in lack of space along the assembly lines. Along with inferior safety on tools, low quality on safety equipment and long work shifts these factors result in injuries being common. Examples are lethal accidents, cut off fingers, high blood pressure and hearing problems. Around 50% of workers at Toyota and their suppliers had some kind of work-related health problems. If someone got injured managers got upset and made it appear as it was the worker's fault, exactly what Kamata reported 30 years earlier (Mehri, 2006).

The Principles of Lean Production

In the introduction the advocators picture of lean production was presented, which could be labelled the rhetorical picture as it is not grounded in meticulous research of the workplace. In order to give a more valid picture of lean production the descriptions below are taken from studies which are carried out at the workplace by using observations but also interviews with workers. Also, some studies from advocates of lean production are used as these studies are more valid compared to the previous presented, provide detailed descriptions and revealing details about the work organisation. The lean principals presented below are: Eliminate surplus, low-skilled work, just-in-time, technological control, team organisation, direct supervision, internal market, visual control, emotions as motivation method, continuous improvement, commitment, management by stress, manipulation, and hostility towards trade unions.

Eliminate Surplus

Toyota production system (TPS) is thoroughly described by Yasuhiro Monden (1994, 1998, 2012). The main focus in TPS is to reduce costs by eliminating surplus. There are four categories of surplus, or waste that TPS strives to reduce:

1. Production resources: Workers, inventories, equipment and machines;
2. Over production: Results in a stock of unsold products, which leads to;
3. Items in stock which leads to building warehouses and recruiting staff to handle them which leads to;
4. Unnecessary investments (Monden, 1994, p. 2).

Taiichi Ohno (1988b) is often seen as the founder of the production system at Toyota. He has been chief engineer and later became CEO at Toyota. According to Ohno (p. ix) TPS can be summarised in one sentence: 'Make only what you need, in the quantity you need, when you need it.'

Muda in Japanese means waste. Management aim to eliminate waiting time; muda, that is time when workers are not active. Workers should be active 60 seconds every minute (Monden, 1994, p. 180). According to Monden the aim is not to work harder, but to remove unnecessary movements:

> Standard operations are aimed at using a minimum number of workers for production. The first goal of standard operations is to achieve high productivity through strenuous work. Strenuous work at Toyota, however, does not mean forcing the workers to work very hard; instead, it means working efficiently without any wasteful motions. (p. 145)

According to Ohno (1988b, p. 31) lean management is about trimming away fat so the ideal weight is achieved. You should not however cut away productive meat, only fat. The road to profit is through improving efficiency by cutting costs. 'This does not mean making a profit by driving workers like slaves or by underpaying them' (p. 57). Later in the book Ohno contradicts himself:

> When you establish standard times, leave no breaks at all for workers to attend to personal hygiene. Some people argue that this departs too much from reality, and they insist on figuring in time for trips to the bathroom or for setup

changes. But this is where managers can be really very sneaky. If people have to go to the bathroom, they say, stop the line and go. (p. 152)

Low-Skilled Work

Japanese car manufacturers have different strategies when it comes to production technology. Companies like Honda, Nissan and Mazda have higher degree of automatization in the production. As previously mentioned at Toyota the line of argument is that automatization can reduce the flexibility to decrease employees (Monden, 1994, pp. 181–182). A later study (Åhlström, 1999a, p. 25) also shows a low degree of automatization at Toyota. According to Åhlström, at Toyota they argue machines and the maintenance of them cost more than to use workers. Mitsubishi has a different strategy. They have a high degree of automatization because they want to decrease repetitive and stressful work according to Rognes (1999, p. 13).

The direct work at Toyota is short-cycled (around one minute) and repetitive. The workers should be multi-skilled, that is be able to perform different standardised tasks. According to Womack et al. (1990, p. 99) the workers are also responsible for indirect tasks such as simple machine repairs, quality control, ordering material and keeping tidy. Åhlström (1999a, pp. 22–29) reports from Toyota's Takaoka factory that workers have few indirect tasks. All planning of the work is performed by white-collar workers in a planning department. When Saab Automobile implemented a lean work organisation in the end of the 1980s the administrative task in the teams decreased considerably (Stjernberg, 1993, pp. 177–178).

Just-In-Time

Toyota production system is based on Taylorism and the Fordistic assembly line system (Monden, 1994, p. 1). The assembly line at Toyota (1980s) has not, like the traditional Fordistic assembly line, got any buffer zones. The production is characterised by just-in-time (JIT), that is production or delivery of the right quantities of products at the right moment, when they are needed. When it comes to inventories the JIT principle is not used in a consistent way. There are warehouses for inventories. The production process is however organised according to the JIT-principle. A system of so-called kanban cards controls the number of products ordered and produced. The number of kanban cards should be as low as possible, so inventory levels are minimised. Thereby workers cannot hide behind a buffer stock. They are forced to constant activity, so the following stations receive their deliveries. When there are problems in the JIT-system these are visualised because the whole process (e.g. an assembly line) comes to a halt. This pressure is built into the system by purpose (Monden, 1994, pp. 5–6, 24–27).

The quality concept is used to sell the concept to the workers. Workers often resist increased production because they are afraid, they need to do more work according to the Japanese consultant Imai (1986, chapter 3). However, nobody can say no to quality. Without referring to improved quality control it would have been impossible to implement concepts like Toyota's kanban system according to Imai (1986, chapter 3).

Technological Control

The assembly line is the most striking example of technological control in Fordism and in Lean production. The assembly line controls the work pace in a very concrete way (e.g. Durand, 2001, pp. 98–99). Together with the kanban system it ensures that all workers have the same work pace.

There are two methods to make sure that only perfect products are forwarded to the next step in the production process within the time limit; people or automatic functions (labelled autonomation). All employees have authority to stop the assembly line if there is a problem (see below). One example of autonomation is a carpet beside the assembly line. If the worker exceeds the cycle time he/she steps om the carpet, a lamp lights and the line stops automatically (Monden, 1994, pp. 227–229).

Team Organisation

According to Womack et al. (1990, pp. 56–57) the workers are organised in teams. The team is responsible for a part of the assembly line.

However, Toyota is not explicitly using the team concept. Group organisation is seen as natural and taken for granted. The team concept was introduced first in the middle of the 1980s when Toyota together with GM started the NUMMI factory in Fremont, California. The team concept was used in order to give positive sport associations (Adler et al., 1998, pp. 132–133). The groups at Toyota are supervised by under foremen (hancho). According to Berggren (1992, pp. 32–35) the foreman (kumicho) has a very strong position. The kumichu coordinates work, chooses work methods and cycle times, evaluates workers and their attitudes. The kumichu is often also union representative. Workers in Japanese companies are expected to use un-paid time for preparations, kaizen activities, training and work-related social activities (Berggren, 1992, pp. 32–35).

There is no extra staff who can replace absent workers. The teamleader can however replace a worker when needed. Lack of replacement staff results in intensified work for those who turn up for work. The system thereby creates a pressure on the workers not to let their colleagues down. Those who are present tend to blame their hard work on the absent colleagues. Parker and Slaughter (1988, p. 22) report from the NUMMI factory:

> Because the jobs are already hard, survival and self-preservation produce enormous peer pressure against absenteeism. Several workers interviewed at NUMMI commented that they would like to have people who were absent too much removed from their group.

Graham (1995, p. 99) also reports group pressure from Subaru-Isuzo. The management did not do anything about unfriendly behaviour in the teams and sometimes even encouraged it. Group pressure is common in all Japanese or Japanese American car manufacturing companies in the US (Kenney & Florida, 1995).

Because the strive to keep resources at a minimum absence is frowned upon in Japanese companies. At NUMMI workers are disciplined after having three absences in three months. At Toyota three absences in a year is seen as problematic and five absences as serious (Kenney & Florida, 1995).

Direct Supervision

The traditional supervision is also used as a coordination and control method. Foremen should always make sure workers follow the standardised work operations (Monden, 1994, p. 158). Kumicho, the foreman, coordinates work, make decisions about work methods and cycle times, evaluates workers' performance and attitudes. The setting of wage rates and career advancement are based on the foreman's evaluation of each individual (Berggren, 1992, pp. 32–35; Pardi, 2007).

Ohno (1988b) provides an example of direct supervision at Toyota. Discipline is generated by yelling at an individual in front of others in order to create fear and a sense of shame.

> When I get mad at a supervisor in the workplace, the workers naturally feel sympathy for their boss who is getting yelled at. That makes both supervisor and subordinates more apt to be careful. The message would not be as effective if I were to take a supervisor aside to vent my anger. (p. 113)

Internal Market

As in TQM internal markets are used also in manufacturing work organisations. According to Imai (1986, chapter 3) the next receiver in the production process is customer. Workers should make sure that their customer is satisfied with what is delivered. Garrahan and Stewart (1992) carried out an interview study with 20 workers at Nissan's factory in Sunderland (UK). They describe the internal market at Nissan where workers are defined as suppliers and customers to each other (p. 64). The internal customer should check the quality on the product from the internal supplier. Nissan has a special procedure for this purpose, a so-called neighbour check. Employees should report errors they discover on the product. The error is traced to the specific worker and each worker is evaluated regarding number of errors (Chapter 4).

Visual Control

To visualise problems is a control principle used in lean production in different ways. In the JIT-system problems are visualised because the whole production process comes to a halt if there is a stop, because there are no buffers in the process (Monden, 1994, pp. 27, 233). If a worker finishes his/her task before the next task can be started, the worker should stand still in order to visualise the unproductive time (pp. 180–182). It is equally important to visualise departments, which never have any problems. This means they have too much resources (muda). All work should be visible and who is responsible when a problem arises. Every workstation has got a panel of lamps, which shows green (ok), yellow (require assistance) and red (has stopped the line). If a worker has stopped the line there is a tendency to put the blame on the worker (Berggren, 1992, pp. 46–47). The managers at Toyota use 'management by walking around' to visually inspect if workers are following the standardised tasks, which are displayed at each workstation (Ohno, 1988a, p. 98).

Visualisation can be interpreted and understood through the disciplinarian concept panopticism (Foucault, 1977, chapter 3.3). The concept is derived from the English philosopher Jeremy Bentham's (1748–1832) prison Panopticon, which has a tower in the middle surrounded by the prison cells. The guards in the tower can see all the prisoners in their cells at all times. The prisoners however cannot see the guards and thereby do not know when they are being observed. The disciplinary power is exercised through the prisoner is aware he/she can be surveilled at any time but do not know when. According to Foucault panopticism is a disciplinary power mechanism that has spread in society. It is for example used to control workers. It uses the physical room and has a direct influence on people. The worker in a JIT-process knows he/she will be identified if he/she causes a delay. It is the awareness of being observed and knowing he/she will be uncomfortably exposed if doing a mistake that make up panopticism. Objectives and key performance indicators are also displayed on so-called Andon boards in the workshop. They display productivity goals, number of produced cars, machinery faults, staff absence and need for overtime (Womack et al., 1990, p. 99). Wilkinson et al. (1995) visited 22 Japanese factories in Wales. 19 of them had information boards, which displayed objectives, results and quality defects for each team. In the Nissan factory in Sunderland absence statistics is also displayed (Niepce & Molleman, 1998). The management confront the teams with these results and compare each team with the other teams.

Using Emotions to Motivate and Control

Japanese management also use emotions as a strategy to motivate and control workers. Competition is one such method used both between individuals and groups. Workers are evaluated individually and compared with other workers. Individual pay is used to support the competition (Kumazawa, 1996, p. 2). As mentioned above, display boards with objectives, results and so on are often put up for each team in the work-shop, which can be used to compare teams. To further spur competition between individuals and between groups improvement suggestions are also displayed (Imai, 1986, chapter 1).

Shame and pride are other emotions used to control workers. One example is taking a picture of an untidy workspace, put up the picture on a board so workers can see. The idea is that the workers then should feel ashamed. The next step is to do 5S-work (see below), basically to clean and put things in order. Then a new picture is taken and put up on the board with comments.

The workers should then feel pride (Monden, 2012, pp. 217–218). According to Mehri (2006) managers often bully workers, who break norms or rules, in front of other people so that they should feel ashamed (see also the example below by Ohno).

The visual control, mentioned above, is also built on shame. The worker does not want to be seen as the cause of a disruption of the line. If a worker pulls the cord because of a problem on the assembly line, he/she tends to feel like an inferior worker (see for example Durand, 2001, pp. 98–99; Kamata, 1983; Pardi, 2005a, 2005b; Parker & Slaughter, 1988). An example from Subaru in the US shows how it works (Graham, 1995, p. 113). When a worker pulls the cord a lamp starts to blink and the team's music will be heard from the loudspeakers. The foreman then comes running. The team-members say that this is stressful. They are afraid to be seen as incompetent. There is an IT-system that registers the amount of times the cord is pulled and where. If a team has had a lot of stops, this is addressed in a team-meeting by the foreman, which deter other teams as well.

Continuous Improvement in Quality Control Circles

In Japan suggestion schemes started in the 1930s and the first quality control circles started in the beginning of the 1960s. The quality control circles aim to solve problems in the production and make improvements of it. The development of quality control circles in Japan reached a peak at the end of the 1980s. Since then the interest has declined. One reason is that cooperation between development and production has increased. Another reason is the number of permanently employees has decreased in Japan. It is hard to motivate temporary workers to engage themselves in unpaid improvement work. In 1980 65% of the big companies (more than 5000 employees) and less than 20% of the small companies (less than 300 employees) in Japan had introduced quality control circles (Nilsson, 1999).

During the 1970s and the 1980s the successful Japanese companies received attention in North America and western Europe. It was their achievements in efficiency and quality that impressed. Quality control circles were introduced in the US and in western Europe in the 1970s, but the diffusion speeded up in the 1980s. Due to the negative connotations control was removed in the US and the term quality circles was used. However, many companies found it difficult to get the quality control circles to work over a longer period of time. The reasons were overestimation of short-term profits, resistance from managers, lack of support from the top management, lack of training for workers and bad relations between workers and the management (Bengtson & Sandberg, 1987, pp. 36–37).

Some workers in Japanese companies take part in quality control circles. However, the major part of analysis, planning and changes of the production system in Japanese manufacturing companies are carried out by foremen and production technicians. The workers role is often restricted only to learn and carry out new standardised tasks (Monden, 1994, chapter 10; Nilsson, 1999, pp. 14–15). At Toyota a quality control circle (QC) is often made up by the work team, working to come up with solutions to quality problems. The aims are to create a sense of responsibility, to save costs, contribute to competence development and to create opportunity for each worker to be accepted and respected (Monden, 1994, p. 193). At Toyota the suggestions are evaluated by committees. Monetary rewards are usually given to the whole group to be used for a group activity (Monden, 1994, chapter 12). An improvement tool connected to the Toyota model is 5 S: es. It should be used by the teams to eliminate surplus, improve quality and reduce costs.

The five S: es are:

1. Seiri—to separate necessary resources from unnecessary and eliminate the latter.
2. Seiton—to organise material and equipment in suitable order so they can be easily found.
3. Seiso—to keep tidiness. Dirt can otherwise cause machine problems.
4. Seiketsu—to always keep the above three points in mind.
5. Shitsuke—to make sure workers always are following the rules.

Berggren (1992, pp. 32–35) report that workers in Japanese manufacturing industry (1980s) are expected to take part in QCs in unpaid time. Managers say it is voluntary to participate in QCs but in reality, it is mandatory. Participation in QCs is used in appraisal of workers. Those who participate actively get promoted and those who do not are severely disciplined (e.g. Bengtson & Sandberg, 1987, pp. 11–12; Chikudate & Alpaslan, 2018). The management set up objectives for the QCs for how many suggestions are expected from them. Also foremen are appraised on the number of suggestions their team has come up with. To spur competition between individuals and between teams the suggestions are often displayed on boards (Heller, 1998, p. 174; Imai, 1986, chapter 1).

Studies at Toyotas factories in the 1990s showed that the factories use different approaches. According to Åhlström (1999a) at the Takaoka factory, the classical example of Toyota production system, all workers are involved in QCs at paid overtime. Since 1951 they have also a suggestion scheme where 99% of the suggestions are implemented. On average every worker hand in 14 suggestions a year. Most of the suggestions are very small. First the teamleader evaluates the suggestions and gives rewards up to 1000 yen.[1] The rest of the suggestions are evaluated higher up in the hierarchy. These suggestions can be rewarded with 500 up to 200,000 yen. In one year less than ten suggestions are rewarded with 100,000 yen. In the QCs the suggestions are discussed. The foreman listens to the workers and then decides how to implement the suggestions. Of the Toyota factories Åhlström and his colleagues visited, Takaoka was

[1] £5.50 or €8.40 in 1999.

the only factory which involved all workers in QCs (Åhlström, 1999a, pp. 22–29). In the newest of the Toyota factories, the Kyushu plant, only 50 people participate in QCs and there is also a suggestion scheme (Åhlström, 1999b, pp. 46–52).

There are several examples of dissatisfaction and resistance against participating in kaizen activities when workers find they are not treated well. Workers find that kaizen work result in intensifying work such as at the Mazda factory in the US (Fucini & Fucini, 1990, p. 161). The workers at Mazda have also at times boycotted the suggestion scheme because they have been dissatisfied with the company policies (Kenney & Florida, 1995). At Subaru-Isuzu Automotive (Graham, 1995, p. 43) workers were dissatisfied because they did not get any feedback on the suggestions they handed in. Also, according to the management, decisions about kaizen should be taken in consensus. In reality, the decisions were taken in favour of the management and they decided the agenda (Graham, 1995, p. 106). The repetitive and monotonous work, lack of influence at the workplace and hard control tend to be demotivating. These working conditions can result in workers not engaging in kaizen activities (Börnfelt, 2006).

Commitment

According to Japanese corporate culture you do not only work in an organisation, you belong to the organisation. The organisation is basically seen as a family (Fucini & Fucini, 1990, pp. 104–107). There are no job descriptions for permanent employees in Japanese companies. Maximal commitment is expected (Berggren, 1992, pp. 34–35). As previously mentioned, meetings, preparations, kaizen activities, training and cleaning of the work-space are often carried out outside regular paid work. These are 'voluntary activities' but workers are expected to be so committed so they carry them out anyway (Berggren, 1992, pp. 34–35; Fucini & Fucini, 1990, pp. 104–107; Garrahan & Stewart, 1992, p. 110). Workers at Toyota and other Japanese companies work long hours because full commitment and self-sacrifice is expected from them. A father of an 30 year old quality control engineer who died in 2008 of karoshi (sudden death caused by extreme stress) in a Toyota factory accepted the death of his own son and saw it as self-sacrifice to Toyota, commenting: 'active participation is a necessity…the virtues of unlimited patience and endurance are integral parts of what it means to be a Toyota employee' (Chikudate & Alpaslan, 2018, p. 74).

Management by Stress

The JIT-system has been named management by stress by Parker and Slaughter (1988, chapter 3). The continuous hunt for muda (waste, surplus) in the JIT-system, above all waiting time results in intensified work. The aim is to eliminate all waiting time, which otherwise could be an opportunity for the worker to catch breath. The JIT-system visualises all problems, due to the fact that one stop somewhere makes the whole production process to stop, because there are no buffers of products in the system. The workers are supposed to solve problems to make the production process running again, which can be very stressful.

At the assembly line at Toyota every worker can stop the line by pulling a cord, if problems arise. The other members of the team should help if someone is delayed in performing their task (Ohno, 1988b, p. 25). Studies at Toyota in the UK and France provide examples on how it can be in practise. If a worker pulls the cord a yellow lamp starts to blink (the line is still running) and the teamleader arrives. The teamleader pulls the cord again, and the light is off. Either they manage to solve the problem or the teamleader continuous into the next work station which happens often (even if this not allowed) to fix the problem at the car. If the teamleader does not pull the cord the line will come to a halt and the groupleader will arrive to see what has happened. Every worker is controlled on both productivity and quality errors. The workers are evaluated in relation to productivity and quality objectives which creates a lot of pressure because the workers are forced to choose between these contradictory goals[2] (Pardi, 2007).

Manipulation

Advocates of lean production often describe the working conditions in positive terms (e.g. Womack et al., 1990, p. 102). They write about the importance of respect for people, self-control, open communication, trust between managers and workers (Monden, 1994, pp. 3, 185, 216). The contrast with reality is however striking. The reality on the shopfloor is monotonous, intensive work under hard pressure (e.g. Fucini & Fucini, 1990; Graham, 1995; Kamata, 1983). Furthermore, advocates of lean production even put in writing that some aspects of the reality must be concealed from workers. Positive terms are used to portray lean work in attractive light, for example lean is not about working harder, it is about working smarter (Monden, 1994, p. 185).

Hostile Attitude Towards Trade Unions

Japanese companies tend to avoid trade unions or minimise their activities also when Japanese companies establish abroad (Huxley, 2015; Kumazawa, 1996, p. 2). After the second world war trade unions were legalised in Japan. Democratic trade unions, often quite militant, were formed and made some progress after strikes in 1946 regarding for example employment security. In some companies unions even gained power on the shopfloor. The employers did not tolerate this and counter attacked with several years of conflicts. In the early 1950s most militant unions were broken by the employers and replaced with more compliant unions integrated with the companies. This labour relations system gives the employers considerable power superiority and unions

[2] If a worker causes a delay by fixing a problem, so the quality will be up to standard, this will reduce productivity (the number of cars produced per time unit). If on the other side, the worker chose not to deal with the problem, the quality will suffer.

only play a minor role. So week, or rather totally integrated unions, provided employers with freedom to design organisations at their own will. This historical background explains why lean production emerged with its many control mechanisms and the high pressure on workers, due to defeated unions, which otherwise could have worked for more humane working conditions. The weakening trade unions in North America and in Europe has provided a fertile ground for lean production (Berggren, 1992; chapter 2; Huxley, 2015).

Some Lean Production Effects

Lean principles can result both in positive and negative effects, but it also depends on which context they are implemented in. Studies of change programs (Brännmark & Eklund, 2013) with the aim of implementing lean in Swedish manufacturing companies show improved orderliness, improved safety in the production and possibilities for workers to influence through kaizen. However, also from this study workers report intensified work and stress.

According to Dellve et al. (2013) value stream mapping (VSM) is used in Swedish healthcare. Using VSM the processes in the organisation are mapped and unnecessary activities and waiting times are eliminated. Effects from VSM and kaizen are decreased waiting time for patients, increased throughput of patients, improved healthcare quality and reduced costs for healthcare organisations. Standardisation of routine operations has also led to increased productivity. However, attempts to standardise more complicated healthcare processes have proved more problematic, as flexibility is needed to tackle different circumstances and differences in patient's needs.

A Swedish study on product development showed negative effects on innovation from decreased throughput time. The demands on the product development engineers were both to be innovative and decrease the time for product development. Some engineers resisted, a second group of engineers opted for more simple solutions and a third group took on more work than they could handle (Lovén, 2013).

Lean Production Principles in Summary

Eliminate Surplus

The overall aim in Toyota production system is to reduce costs by eliminating surplus overall. The strive is to reduce production resources, surplus production, parts in store and unnecessary investments. For workers elimination of waiting time is the most concrete aspect, which intensify work.

Division of Labour—Low-Skilled Work

The tasks are standardised like in Taylorism and Fordism. The direct work at Toyota is short-cycled (around one minute) and repetitive. The workers sometimes also perform indirect tasks such as simple machine repairs, quality control, kaizen, ordering material and keeping tidy. The indirect work should be categorised as a fairly light form of work enrichment.

Several Different Coordination and Control Mechanisms
The management talk about respect for people and lean is all about working smarter. The rhetoric is used as manipulation, to conceal the fact that work is monotonous and intensified and many control mechanisms are used. These coordination and control mechanisms are:

- Just-in-time processes. The production is characterised by just-in-time (JIT), production or delivery of parts just when they are needed. The traditional assembly line is used, as in Fordism. Unlike Fordism there are no buffer zones between workstations in order to have a continuous process flow. Kanban cards limit the number of parts being delivered to a workstation. It is thereby not possible for workers to build up a buffer in order to have a small pause.
- Technological control. The JIT flow made up of the assembly line and kanban cards controls the work pace.
- Team organisation and direct supervision. The team is responsible for a part of the assembly line and is supervised by a foreman/teamleader. The foreman should always make sure workers are following the standardised work operations. He/she manages the division of work, decide work methods and cycle times, evaluate workers' performance and attitudes. The foreman also replaces absent workers. There is no extra staff who can replace absent workers, other than the foreman. The system thereby builds up group pressure which is increased by the intensified work. If workers are absent, they are often disciplined by the management. The company is basically seen as a family. Workers not only work at a company, they belong to a company and are expected to do for example kaizen work at unpaid time.
- Internal market. The relations between workers should be like suppliers and customers. The next step in the production process is customer.
- Visual control. To visualise problems and people who cause these is a control principle used in lean production. In the JIT-system problems are visualised on the assembly line, because there are no buffers of parts in the process. Thus if there is a stop anywhere the whole process comes to a halt. Also objectives and results are visualised on Andon boards in the work-shop.
- Emotions as a motivation method. Workers' emotions, as for example shame and pride, are used as a motivation and control method. One example is to take pictures of untidy places and put the pictures on boards in order for workers to feel ashamed. Another example is when workers need to pull the cord to stop the line and thereby stop the JIT-flow, getting attention as to be the cause of the stoppage.

Continuous Improvement Work and Commitment
Some workers at Toyota take part in quality control circles (QC). A QC is a small group of workers who work together to solve quality problems. The aims are to create a sense of responsibility, to save costs, competence development and to create opportunity for each worker to be accepted and respected. A QC is most often made up of the work team and their foreman. Managers say it is voluntary to participate in QCs but in reality, it is mandatory (when they are used). Participating in QC are said to be 'voluntary activities' but workers are expected to be so committed so they carry them out anyway. The management sets target for the number of suggestions expected. Moreover, workers and foremen are evaluated on the number of suggestions. Small rewards are given the group for suggestions and not taking part in kaizen is disciplined be the management.

Management by Stress
The JIT-system, a continuous flow of products, aims to eliminate all waiting time and visualise all problems. If there is a stop somewhere in the production process the whole process stops, because there are no buffers of products in the system. The workers are supposed to solve problems to make the production process running again, which can be very stressful. The managers and advocates of lean production tries to cover up the reality of lean production by using rhetoric. They talk about the importance of safety at work, respect for people, open communication, and trust between managers and workers. The reality is however striking. The work on the shopfloor is monotonous, hard and intensive. Accidents and other work-related health problems are common.

Hostile Attitude Against Trade Unions
In Japan most trade unions are weak or integrated in companies, which go back to conflicts in the 1940s and 1950s where employers won over the unions in many companies. Japanese companies tend to avoid trade unions or minimise their activities also when Japanese companies establish abroad.

A Comparison Between Lean Production and the Sociotechnical School

The differences between the two work organisation models can be highlighted by using the sociologist Jürgen Habermas's (1994) action typology, which in turn is built on Max Weber's work. An actor uses instrumentally rational action when he/she uses other people only to achieve his/her own goals. Other actors are only seen as means to achieve one's own goals such as winning or making a profit. Value-rational action, on the other hand, is based on beliefs in certain ethical or religious values. These values are seen as ends in themselves and are used as a moral compass guiding action. Lean production uses the Fordistic assembly line and the traditional direct supervision by foremen.

Furthermore, it adds a range of other coordination and control mechanisms in order to fully control workers behaviour and attitudes. The worker is here reduced to a subordinate object who is expected to give up his/her free will and instead belong to a company and make full sacrifice to the company. The workers participate in kaizen activities because they have to, otherwise they are disciplined. The company can consequently be said to act according to instrumentally rational action where other actors are just means used to obtain, in this example, the goals of the company—highest possible productivity, quality and profit.

The sociotechnical school however combines instrumentally rational action with value-rational action. It both strives for a profitable organisation, and put forward democratic and humanistic values such as self-actualization and empowerment as important to strive for. Even if the autonomous work group, following instrumentally rationality is seen as a means to achieve profit, it is at the same time seen as having a value in itself. Autonomous working groups, where workers participate in decision-making in a democratic way is seen as consistent with a democratic society and it prepares people for good citizenship. The sociotechnical work organisation empower workers by giving them a relatively high degree of autonomy and highly skilled work. The foreman is replaced by a facilitator who gives support to the group. The workers run their department relatively independently and as a result of the empowerment they engage in developing their workplace and the production system.

Shifts of Work Organisation Models

Changes happening in the society (macro level) have of course effects on organisations (meso level) in different ways. When for example there is low unemployment in the society, organisations have to work harder to attract people to work for them. During the 1960s and 1970s in Sweden the manufacturing industry experienced problems with dissatisfaction from workers concerning lack of influence, strikes, high personnel turnover and difficulties for companies to recruit (e.g. Björkman & Lundqvist, 1981). The interest therefore grew stronger for the sociotechnical work organisation, because it could provide a more interesting and humane work combined with more influence for workers. Many companies therefore tried this new alternative way or organising work, introducing self-directed working groups, as presented in the previous chapter. During the 1990s however, the unemployment increased, so it was again easier for companies to recruit and the interest from management to humanise work thereby decreased. At the same time competition from Japan increased and companies wanted to know about the success factors. Lean production thereby became a source of inspiration for the how to organise manufacturing work in Europe and North America. Lean is also spreading to other sectors such as healthcare, public administration and banking. As presented above lean production tend to result in more repetitive work, intensified work and increased stress levels.

The concept of digital Taylorism (Brown et al., 2011) has recently been used to describe work organisations in the service sector with many similarities to lean production, which use IT to manage and control work and workers. As in Taylorism and in lean production work is broken down in smaller components, that is an increase in the division of labour. The work components are then standardised and digitalised. The standardisation builds upon the exception principle. All routine errands are standardised, for instance when we contact call centres or customer service, we are met with standardised options, pressing numbers and only if we do not have a standardised errand we will be forwarded to a person. Also knowledge work is increasingly standardised, by breaking down work processes in smaller parts and standardising these work tasks, for instance in banks and insurance companies. The driving force for digital Taylorism, according to Brown et al. (2011), is to cut costs but also for top management to gain more control over operations and workers. The control aspect of digital Taylorism is becoming more and more apparent. Companies are increasingly using IT for surveillance and control of workers. To monitor workers by using IT is just another method to visualise workers behaviour, thus using the previously mentioned visualisation mechanism for control. Employers are increasingly monitoring e-mails, worker's internet browser history, how much and when workers are typing on their computers. Wearable devices are also used to monitor the location and movements of workers within the workplace and webcams on work computers are used to monitor workers mood. These control mechanisms will be described more in depth in Chapter 8 (Brown et al., 2011; TUC, 2018).

While many organisations in the world is occupied implementing lean production, or similar variants such as digital Taylorism, Toyota and other companies in Japan have changed their work organisation with inspiration from the sociotechnical school (Chapter 4). The background is Japan's aging population, a growing reluctance among young males to work on the assembly line and high personnel turnover in Japanese car manufacturing plants. The companies are therefore making efforts to attract female and older workers to their plants (Monden, 2012, p. 438; Nohara, 1999). There are thereby similarities to the conditions in the society, which laid the ground for the sociotechnical experiments in Scandinavia during the 1960s and 1970s.

Both Toyota and Nissan changed their work organisations in the middle of the 1990s in order to create more attractive working conditions. One of the inspiration sources has been Volvo's sociotechnical factories (Moldaschl & Weber, 1998). The same goes for Honda's new factory according to Benders (1996). Toyota has moved away from several lean principles, which were presented in the IMVP study (Womack et al., 1990). According to Nohara (1999) Toyota used the Volvo Uddevalla factory as a source of inspiration to implement a more humane work organisation. In two factories, Kyushu and Tahara, assembly plant 4, Toyota introduced shorter sections of assembly lines with buffer zones between them. As a consequence, the workers no longer have to put up with the pressure of stopping the whole process when a problem arises. On the assembly line there are wagons, which has adjustable speed and height. More ergonomic tools are introduced, and dangerous tasks are automatized. The workshop is also brighter, cleaner and more quiet. Furthermore, work is organised in functional wholes, which a team is responsible for and therefore workers have opportunity to create a holistic understanding of the function as they rotate between the different tasks in the function. The work intensity is however still high and work enrichment has not been achieved according to Nohara. In the fourth edition of Toyota Production Systems Monden (2012, chapter 28) reports all Toyota's factories now have implemented the aforementioned work organisation. Studies at Toyota in the UK (2001) and in France (2003) show the same development. The assembly line has been divided in sections with buffer zones in between according to Pardi (2007).

The JIT principle is one of the basic principles of lean production put forward in Womack et al. (1990) and Liker (2004) in the widely distributed book The Toyota Way. Strangely enough Liker did not acknowledge the changes that have taken place at Toyota in his book. The fact that Toyota has introduced mini lines with buffer zones in between means that Toyota has abandoned the JIT principle in the assembly line, that is the uninterrupted flow of products. To conclude, Toyota has partly abandoned what Womack et al. (1990) described as lean production.

Even if lean production is the most popular work organisation model in manufacturing industry today it is not always implemented in its pure form. Sociotechnical principles are sometimes mixed with lean principles forming a hybrid organisation. Schuman (1998) describes such a model in German car manufacturing industry, the structurally innovative model, which has self-directed groups. Also in Sweden there are examples of hybrid forms at Volvo Cars (Brulin et al., 2005; Ohlsson, 2003) and Parker Hannifin (Börnfelt, 2006). Lean principles are short-cycled, standardised tasks, kaizen and JIT. They are, in these organisations, combined with sociotechnical principles such as self-directed groups and work enrichment in the form of indirect roles such as economy, ordering material and production planning.

In the following sections two other concepts, which also have American/Japanese origins, are presented: Time based management (TBM) and business process reengineering (BPR). They have, just like lean production, the overall aim to organise in processes and to make the processes as effective as possible.

Time Based Management

Time based management (TBM) is a management concept, which is developed by The Boston Consulting Group (Stalk & Hout, 1990). TBM is only presented as an outline because it is not really a work organisation model. It is however worth mentioning as it is a part of the management trend to focus on processes. Cutting throughput times reduce costs for the organisation and the customer benefits from shorter time between order and delivery. Japan is highlighted as an example to learn from when it comes to create speedy processes. Japanese companies are said to be fast to develop new products, produce products and deliver them to customers. Processes are shortened by first mapping the process and analysing where there are bottlenecks. Often time can be saved by eliminating waiting times. One example of using TBM is Asea Brown Boveri (ABB) in their project T-50. The object in the project was to reduce throughput time, from order to delivery, by 50%, which they succeeded with between 1991 and 1993 (Björkman, 2003).

The next section is about business process engineering (BPR), which has a lot in common with TBM but also is dealing with the work organisation, which is radically changed. It has also been used more than TBM. For these reasons I will deal more in-depth with BPR in the next section.

Business Process Reengineering

Compared to kaizen business process reengineering (BPR) is a more radical model for change in organisations. According to Wilkinson and Willmott (1995) advocates of BPR criticize TQM, which is using kaizen, for preserving existing structures. TQM preserves bureaucratic structures where departments act without collaboration. BPR aims to break down the existing function structure and rebuild the organisation into processes. According to Björkman (2003, p. 71) BPR was one of the most popular management concepts in the western world from 1993 and a few years onwards, but it is not widely used today. The founder of BPR, Michael Hammer, has background as professor in computer science at MIT. That can, according Björkman, explain his machine-like view on organisational change. In BPR the starting point is that the whole value adding work process is ineffective. The structure of the organisation is completely changed and everything that does not add value to the product or the service is eliminated. The new processes should be as simple as possible. The changes are initiated, planned and managed by the top management. The role of the top management is also to convince organisational members that the change is necessary for the survival of the organisation and to break down resistance from workers and middle managers. The function organisation, often the starting point, is transformed to a process organisation with a customer focused culture. Some departments disappear or are radically transformed, which result in conflicts and anxiety among workers. According to Hammer and Champy (1995) managers need to be endurable and manage the change process in a forceful and aggressive way. The management appoints process owners and form reengineering teams who are going to carry through the change work.

The work is changed to be more skilled. Workers get more responsibility and authority. The division of labour is decreased with the aim to create a work content which forms a meaningful wholeness (similar as in sociotechnical work). If it is not possible to design work for one person which he/she can manage and have an overview over, a team will be formed with all the competences needed in the work process. Before the change people would have been sitting in different departments, as in a function organisation which results in coordination problems. The individuals in the new teams become generalists, contrary to the specialist roles they had in the old organisation. All people in the team learn all the tasks in a process to a basic level. The team is responsible and has authority to make sure the customer receives the product or service which is demanded. Because the team is working independently, direct supervision is not needed any longer. The team control and manages its own activities. Different tasks are carried out simultaneously if possible. When developing new products, the design of the product is coordinated with the manufacturing process in order for the product to be manufactured efficiently. The manager role changes from supervision to facilitation. Managers become coaches, giving advice, helping the teams to solve problems. An important task for managers is to change the culture in the organisation to be customer focused. The teams should only work with processes, which adds value to the customer. The organisation is more decentralised than before with fewer layers of managers because there is no need for so much supervision and coordination by managers anymore. The team handle most of the communication and coordination with the rest of the organisation.

According to Hammer and Champy a process can be speeded up ten times after it has been reengineered. The reengineering has however often failed in many companies, which have tried to implement it. Hammer and Champy themselves estimate that 50–70% of the attempts to reorganise using BPR methods do not achieve their objectives. The reasons, according to Hammer and Champy, managers are not acting forcefully enough, the reorganisation is not going all the way, lack of resources and change processes are terminated due to resistance from staff (Hammer & Champy, 1995).

Critique

Change programs inspired from TBM or BPR often result in major lay-offs, so-called downsizing. Studies in the US in the end of the 1980s showed that 80–85% of companies had used downsizing. People who become employed as a consequence from downsizing have a higher risk of physical and psychological ill-health. The remaining people in the organisation often experience anxiety, decreased trust and loyalty towards the organisation. Other consequences are increased conflicts and resistance to changes (Jackson et al., 2000), intensified work, stress and longer working days (Arnetz & Skärstrand, 2000). Even two of the most prominent authors on BPR, Hammer and Champy, argue that downsizing often has been too radical and human aspects have been neglected (Mumford, 1997).

Summary

In total quality management (TQM) it is a responsibility for all workers in the organisation to focus on creating value for the customer. The quality movement has got one overall idea for all kinds of organisations—to satisfy the customer. To satisfy the customer is also emphasised in time based management (TBM), business process reengineering (BPR) and lean production. People and departments are, in TQM and lean production, divided in suppliers and customers, which forms a so-called internal market. In order to overcome lack of communication, coordination and focus on creating value for the organisation and the customer, process organisation has been introduced as a remedy. Instead of organising in functions, the organisation is centred around its processes. Only activities, which adds value to the customer should remain in the processes and the throughput time should be shortened as much as possible in order to save costs. Lean production, TBM and BPR are process oriented organisation models.

Lean production builds on the Fordistic assembly line system but without buffers. The work is, like in Taylorism and Fordism, characterised by a high division of labour. There are sometimes minor indirect work roles such as quality checking and kaizen activities, but these must be regarded as very light job enrichment. The coordinating/controlling methods are the assembly line, the just-in-time (JIT) principle, team organisation combined with a highly demanding culture focused on sacrifices for the company, internal market, command and control by supervisors, visualisation, management by feelings such as shame and pride. The JIT-principle combined with limited recourses such as staff, and a sophisticated system of control mechanisms put a lot of pressure on workers. Lean production has, as a consequence, been criticised for high levels of stress and work-related ill-health.

Business process reengineering (BPR) is a very radical model for change in organisations. The traditional function organisation, which is often the starting point, is broken down and people are instead relocated in process teams. The individuals become generalists, contrary to the specialist roles they had in the old organisation. All people in the self-directed team learn all the tasks in a process to a basic level. The change process most often includes downsizing, which combined with high demands on the teams, often creates a stressful work situation. There also tend to be a lot of conflicts, resistance from workers and many change projects fail to achieve their objectives as a result.

Increased Focus on Change and Learning

In Taylorism and Fordism employers only wanted workers to perform standardised tasks in a disciplined way. In the bureaucracy workers were expected to follow a set of rules when performing their duties. The demands on workers in these classic work organisation models were thus limited to learn ready-made knowledge, which other have developed. Later work organisation models however strive to make use of the whole person at work, that is also his/her intellectual and creative abilities. The demands thereby increase on people, at the same time as opportunities for people to develop their competence increases. In sociotechnical work organisation workers have freedom and resources to change their workplace. In lean production the management expect workers to participate in change work (kaizen). In BPR workers have responsibility to give the service and products demanded by the customers and have authority to take necessary actions. There is thus a trend in organisation theory to focus change, learning and knowledge. Organisation researchers have studied how to design learning organisations, which both have beneficial conditions for workers and the organisation to learn and develop. Other scholars have focused their attention how to best control and disseminate knowledge in the organisation. Learning and knowledge have been put forward as important for the survival and success of organisations. The next chapter will deal with these matters.

Group Exercise—Organising Work in Restaurants
You are owners of an Italian style restaurant chain and are planning to open two new restaurants with around 30 employees in each. You have recently studied work organisation and decide to try new ways of organising in order to boost performance. In restaurant A you decide to use sociotechnical organisation principles and in restaurant B lean production principles. Discuss how you would divide work in different work tasks and how to coordinate/control the work process in the two restaurants. Also, discuss how the two restaurants may differ on productivity, quality, innovation ability and worker's health.

Reflection Questions

1. Why has lean production become so popular as a work organisation model?
2. Is lean production built on intrinsic or extrinsic motivation? Discuss a few examples.
3. What could be possible advantages and disadvantages with the just-in-time system for workers, the organisation and unions?
4. Visualisation is a control method used in lean production. Can you give some examples how it is used in working life and in the society at large? What are the effects on people and the society?

Bibliography

Adler, P. S. (1993). Time-and-motion regained. *Harvard Business Review, 71*(1), 97–109.

Adler, P. S., & Cole, R. E. (1993). Designed for learning: A tale of two auto plants. *Sloan Management Review, 34*(3).

Adler, P. S., Goldoftas, B., & Levine, D. I. (1998). Stability and change at NUMMI. In R. Boyer, E. Charron, U. Jurgens, & S. Tolliday (Eds.), *Between imitation and innovation: The transfer and hybridization of productive models in the international automobile industry*. Oxford University Press.

ACE. (2008). *Operational and Lean Management Survey 2008*. https://consultus.se/wp-content/uploads/ace-2008.pdf. Accessed September 19, 2022.

Åhlström, P. (1999a). Toyota Kyushu. In C. Karlsson (Ed.), *Japanese production management in sunrise or sunset*. Economic Research Institute Stockholm School of Economics (Ekonomiska forskningsinstitutet vid Handelshögsk.) (EFI).

Åhlström, P. (1999b). Toyota Takaoka. In C. Karlsson (Ed.), *Japanese production management in sunrise or sunset*. Economic Research Institute Stockholm School of Economics (Ekonomiska forskningsinstitutet vid Handelshögsk.) (EFI).

Arnetz, B., & Skärstrand, E. (2000). Arbetsmiljö- och hälsoaspekter av processer relaterade till magra organisationer. In K. Barklöf (Ed.), *Smärtgränsen?: En antologi om hälsokonsekvenser i magra organisationer*. Rådet för arbetslivsforskning.

Ashkenas, R. N. (1995). *The boundaryless organization: Breaking the chains of Organizational structure*. Jossey Bass Inc.

Axelsson, J. R. C., & Bergman, B. (1999). Att bygga och riva pyramider - offensiv kvalitets- och arbetsutveckling. In T. Nilsson (Ed.), *Ständig förbättring*. Arbetslivsinstitutet.

Bejerot, E. (2008). Kapitel 8. Patienten i centrum – ett tvingande styrningsideal. In H. Hasselbladh, E. Bejerot, & R. Å. Gustafsson (Eds.), *Borton new public management*. Academia Adacta.

Bélanger, J., Berggren, C., Björkman, T., & Köhler, C. (1999). *Being local worldwide: ABB and the challenge of global management*. Cornell University Press.

Benders, J. (1996). "Leaving Lean? Recent changes in the production organization of some japanese car plants". *Economic and Industrial Democracy, 17*(1), 9–38.

Bengtson, G., & Sandberg, Å. (1987). *Kvalitetscirklar: en översikt om bakgrund och erfarenheter: Arbetsrapport*. Sociologiska inst. Uppsala univ; Programomr. 3 Arbetslivscentrum.

Berggren, C. (1992). *Alternatives to lean production: Work organization in the Swedish auto industry*. ILR Press.

Björkman, T. (2003). "Management"—En modeindustri. In Å. Sandberg (Ed.), *Ledning för alla?: perspektivbrytningar i arbetsliv och företagsledning*. SNS.

Björkman, T., & Lundqvist, K. (1981). *Från MAX till PIA: Reformstrategier inom arbetsmiljöområdet*. Arkiv för studier i arbetarrörelsens historia.

Blanchard, D. (2007, October). Lean, green and low cost. *IndustryWeek*, 37–39.

Brulin, G., Hammarström, O., & Nilsson, T. (2005). *Between "lean and mean" and "lean and healthy" production—The auto assembly at Volvo and Saab* (Unpublished report). Arbetslivsinstitutet.

Börnfelt, P.-O. (2006). *Förändringskompetens på industrigolvet: Kontinuerligt förändringsarbete i gränslandet mellan lean production och socioteknisk arbetsorganisation*. Arbetslivsinstitutet.

Bowling, N. A., Alarcon, G. M., Bragg, C. B., & Hartman, M. J. (2015). A meta-analytic examination of the potential correlates and consequences of workload. *Work & Stress, 29*(2), 95–113.

Brännmark, M., & Eklund, J. (2013). Leaninspirerade förändringar och personalens upplevelser. In P. Sederblad (Ed.), *Lean i arbetslivet*. Liber.

Brown, P., Lauder, H., & Ashton, D. (2011). Digital Taylorism. In *The global auction: The broken promises of education, jobs and incomes* (Chapter 5). Oxford University Press.

Chikudate, N., & Alpaslan, C. M. (2018). The curse of the #1 carmaker: Toyota's crisis. *Critical Perspectives on International Business, 14*(1), 66–82.

Dellve, L., Eriksson, A., Fredman, M., & Kullén Engström, A. (2013). Lean i hälso- och sjukvården. In P. Sederblad (Ed.), *Lean i arbetslivet*. Liber.

Deming, W. E. (1994). *The new economics for industry, government, education* (2nd ed.). Center for Advanced Engineering Study, Massachusetts Institute of Technology.

Dotchin, J. A., & Oakland, J. S. (1992). Theories and concepts in total quality management. *Total Quality Management, 3*(2), 133–145.

Durand, J.-P. (2001). New models of production and constrained participation in France. In S. Jefferys, F. M. Beyer, & C. Thörnqvist (Eds.), *European working lives: Continuities and change in management and industrial relations in France, Scandinavia and the UK*. Edward Elgar.

Foucault, M. (1977). *Discipline and punish: The birth of the prison*. Allen Lane.

Fucini, J. J., & Fucini, S. (1990). *Working for the Japanese*. The Free Press.

Garrahan, P., & Stewart, P. (1992). *The Nissan enigma: Flexibility at work in a local economy*. Mansell.

Graham, L. (1995). *On the line at Subaru-Isuzu: The Japanese model and the American worker*. ILR Press.

Habermas, J. (1994). *The theory of communicative action*. Beacon Press.

Hammer, M., & Champy, J. (1995). *Reengineering the corporation: A manifesto for business revolution*. Brealey.

Hasselbladh, H. (2002). Kvalitetsrörelsen – konsekvenser för individ, organisation och samhälle. In E. Bejerot & H. Hasselbladh (Eds.), *Kvalitet utan gränser: En kritisk belysning av kvalitetsstyrning*. Academia Adacta.

Hasselbladh, H., & Lundgren, R. (2002). Kvalitetsrörelsen i Sverige. In E. Bejerot & H. Hasselbladh (Eds.), *Kvalitet utan gränser: En kritisk belysning av kvalitetsstyrning*. Academia Adacta.

Heller, F. A. (1998). Playing the devil's advocate: Limits to influence sharing in theory and practise. In F. Heller, E. Pusic, G. Strauss, & B. Wilpert (Eds.), *Organizational participation: Myth and reality*. Oxford University Press.

Huxley, C. (2015). Three decades of lean production: Practice, ideology, and resistance. *International Journal of Sociology, 45*(2), 133–151.

Imai, M. (1986). *Kaizen: The key to Japan's competive success*. Kaizen Institute.

Jackson, P., R, Brenner, S.-O., & Johansson, C., R. (2000). Downsizing och magra organisationer – en litteraturöversikt över psykologiska reaktioner. In K. Barklöf (Ed.), *Smärtgränsen?: En antologi om hälsokonsekvenser i magra organisationer*. Rådet för arbetslivsforskning.

Kamata, S. (1983). *Japan in the passing lane: An insider's account of life in a Japanese auto factory*. Pantheon Books.

Karasek, R., & Theorell, T. (1990). *Healthy work: Stress, productivity and the reconstruction of working life*. Basic Books.

Kenney, M., & Florida, R. (1995). The transfer of Japanese management styles in two US transplant industries: Autos and electronics. *Journal of Management Studies, 32*(6), 89–102.

Kumazawa, M. (1996). *Portraits of the Japanese workplace: Labor movements, workers, and managers*. Westview Press.

Landsbergis, P. A., Cahill, J., & Schnall, P. (1999). The impact of lean production and related new systems of work organization on worker health. *Journal of Occupational Health Psychology, 4*(2), 108–130.

Lang, J., Ochsmann, E., Kraus, T., & Lang, J. W. B. (2012). Psychosocial work stressors as antecedents of musculoskeletal problems: A systematic review and meta-analysis of stability-adjusted longitudinal studies. *Social Science & Medicine, 75*, 1163–1174.

Liker, J. K. (2004). *The Toyota way: 14 management principles from the world's greatest manufacturer*. McGraw-Hill.

Lovén, E. (2013). Kreativitet, innovation och lean. In P. Sederblad (Ed.), *Lean i arbetslivet*. Liber.

MacDuffie, J. P. (1995). Human resource bundles and manufacturing performance: Organizational logic and flexible production systems in the world auto industry. *Industrial and Labor Relations Review, 48*(2), 197–221.

Mehri, D. (2006, May). The darker side of lean: An insider's perspective on the realities of the Toyota production system. *Academy of Management Perspectives, 20*, 21–42.

Mendel, P. (2006). The making and expansion of international management standards: The global diffusion of ISO 9000 quality management certificates. In G. S. Drori, J. W. Meyer, & H. Hwang (Eds.), *Globalization and organization: World society and organizational change*. Oxford University Press.

Moldaschl, M., & Weber, W. (1998). The "three waves" of industrial group work: Historical reflections on current research on group work. *Human Relations, 51*(3), 347–388.

Monden, Y. (1994). *Toyota production system: An integrated approach to just-in-time* (2nd ed.). Chapman & Hall.

Monden, Y. (1998). *Toyota production system: An integrated approach to just-in-time* (3rd ed.). Engineering & Management.

Monden, Y. (2012). *Toyota production system: An integrated approach to just-in-time* (4th ed.). CRC Press.

Mumford, E. (1997). The reality of participative systems design: Contributing to stability in a rocking boat. *Information Systems Journal, 7*(4), 309–322.

Niepce, W., & Molleman, E. (1998). Work design issues in lean production from a sociotechnical systems perspective: Neo-Taylorism or the next step in sociotechnical design? *Human Relations, 51*(3), 259–287.

Nilsson, T. (1999). Ständiga förbättringar—inledning. In T. Nilsson (Ed.), *Ständig förbättring*. Arbetslivsinstitutet.

Nohara, H. (1999). The historic reversal of the division of labour? The second stage of the Toyota production system. In J.-P. Durand, P. Stewart, & J. J. Castillo (Eds.), *Teamwork in the automobile industry: Radical change or passing fashion?* Macmillan.

Noon, M., Blyton, P., & Morell, K. (2013). *The realities of work: Experiencing work and employment in contemporary society*. Palgrave Macmillan.

Nixon, A. E., Mazzola, J. J., Bauer, J., Krueger, J. R., & Spector, P. E. (2011). Can work make you sick? A meta-analysis of the relationships between job stressors and physical symptoms. *Work & Stress, 25*(1), 1–22.

Ohlsson, B. (2003). *Arbetet på Torslandaverken: En berättelse om ett göteborgskt kulturarv*. Göteborgska tidsspeglar.

Ohno, T. (1988a). *Just-in-time for today and tomorrow*. Productivity Press.

Ohno, T. (1988b). *Workplace management*. Productivity Press.

Pardi, T. (2005a). *Beyond empowerment and management by stress: Technical viability and social sustainability of teamwork in the Toyota Production System*. Paper presented at the International Workshop on Teamworking (IWOT 9), Lissabon.

Pardi, T. (2005b). Where did it go wrong?: Hybridization and crises of Toyota motor manufacturing. *International Sociology, 20*(1), 93–118.

Pardi, T. (2007). Redefining the Toyota production system: The European side of the story. *New Technology Work and Employment, 22*(1), 2–20.

Parker, M., & Slaughter, J. (1988). *Choosing sides: Unions and the team concept*. South End Press.

Pil, F. K., & Fujimoto, T. (2007). Lean and reflective production: The dynamic nature of production models. *International Journal of Production Research, 45*(16), 3741–3761.

Pruijt, H. (2000). Repainting, modifying, smashing Taylorism. *Journal of Organizational Change Management, 13*(5), 439–451.

Rognes, J. (1999). Company visit to Mitsubishi Motors. In C. Karlsson (Ed.), *Japanese production management in sunrise or sunset* (pp. [6], 104, [105]). Economic Research Institute Stockholm School of Economics (Ekonomiska forskningsinstitutet vid Handelshögsk.) (EFI).

Schuman, M. (1998). New concepts of production and productivity. *Economic and Industrial Democracy, 19*(1), 17–32.

Sederblad, P. (2013). *Lean i arbetslivet*. Liber.

Stalk, G., & Hout, T. M. (1990). *Competing against time: How time-based competition is reshaping global markets*. Free Press and Collier Macmillan.

Stjernberg, T. (1993). *Organisationsideal: Livskraft och spridning: Dialog, humanitet, inflytande, konkurrens, livskvalitet, produktivitet, samarbete: Ett 20-årigt perspektiv*. Norstedts juridik: Fritze distributör.

Theorell, T., Jood, K., Slunga Järvholm, L., Vingård, E., Perk, J., Östergren, P. O., et al. (2016). A systematic review of studies in the contributions of the work environment to ischaemic heart disease development. *The European Journal of Public Health, 26*(3), 470–477.

Toivanen, S., & Landsbergis, P. (2013). Lean och arbetstagarnas hälsa. In P. Sederblad (Ed.), *Lean i arbetslivet*. Liber.

TUC. (2018). *I'll be watching you*. https://www.tuc.org.uk/research-analysis/reports/i'll-be-watching-you. Accessed September 19, 2022.

van Shoten, S., De Blok, C., Spreeuwenberg, P., Groenewegen, P., & Wagner, C. (2016). The EFQM model as a framework for total quality management in healthcare: Results of a longitudinal quantitative study. *International Journal of Operations & Production Management, 36*(8), 901–922.

Wilkinson, A., & Willmott, H. (1995). Introduction. In A. Wilkinson & H. Willmott (Eds.), *Making quality critical: New perspectives on organizational change* (pp. xii, 247). Routledge.

Wilkinson, B., Morris, J., & Munday, M. (1995). The iron fist in the velvet glove: Management and organization in japanese manufacturing transplants in Wales. *Journal of Management Studies, 32*(6), 819–830.

Williams, K., Colin, H., Williams, J., Cutler, T., Adcroft, A., & Johal, S. (1992). Against lean production. *Economy and Society, 21*(3), 321–354.

Wittrock, C. (2015). Reembedding lean: The Japanese cultural and religious context of a world changing management concept. *International Journal of Sociology, 45*(2), 95–111.

Womack, J. P., Jones, D. T., & Roos, D. (1990). *The machine that changed the world: Based on the Massachusetts Institute of Technology 5-million-dollar 5-year study on the future of the automobile*. Rawson Associates.

CHAPTER 6

Organising for Change, Learning and Knowledge

Learning Objectives

This chapter should provide you with knowledge about:

- The main principles for how to organise for innovation, exemplified in the organic organisation, the learning organisation and project organising.
- The kinship between the organic organisation and the learning organisation and how they differ from knowledge management.
- In what sense organisations can learn.
- How learning organisations can be both good and bad for health and wellbeing.

During the last 6–7 decades organisation theorists have, increasingly talked about the importance of change, learning and knowledge. Many texts have been written about organisational change, learning organisations, project organising and knowledge management which the chapter covers. There is a lot of research about organisational change, see for example the doctoral dissertation by Nonås (2005) for an overview. In many studies it has been said that organisations have to make changes in order to respond to changes which is taking place outside the organisation. Changes are happening for example at competitors, customers preferences, technology, laws and regulations. Companies must respond to more rapid changes and increased competition on a global market. Studies show, however, that many organisational change programmes fail. In general, major radical changes are more difficult to carry out then minor, continuous changes of routines and procedures. Research

P-O Börnfelt, *Work Organisation in Practice*,
https://doi.org/10.1007/978-3-031-21667-1_6

differ between two different change strategies, the plan strategy and the process strategy. There have been given different labels from various authors, but these are the two most common strategies for organisational change. In the plan strategy, a major radical change is carried out in pre-planned phases. The change is planned and carried out by the management, who also define visions and objectives (E g. as in BPR in the previous chapter). In the process strategy, there is a wide participation by workers and the change process develops organically. The change process is managed by a facilitator who help staff to interpret the need of change, and together with the staff develop a vision and objectives. In the process strategy change is carried out continuously by modifying procedures and work routines.

Overall, research show that the process strategy, or a combination with the plan strategy, has been most successful. Important success factors seem to be to clarify why change is needed, worker influence and participation in developing visions and taking part in carrying out the changes, to combine advantages for the organisation as well as for workers, and a concrete connection to workers' tasks. Staff participation results in opportunities to exchange experiences and ideas and is therefore positive for competence development. Participation also has a positive effect on motivation because people feel they can influence the change process (Nonås, 2005, pp. 1–41). Worker participation in decision-making is also a central component in the organic and in the learning organisation, which are presented in the following. In the process strategy change is continuous and is taking place organically, which also is in line with the organic and the learning organisation. There is also a connection the concept change competence, that is an individual or a group has competence to carry through changes of their work and the workplace (see below).

The Organic Organisation

Burns and Stalker (1961) carried out case studies in the UK and found major differences how companies organised their work. In, what they labelled, mechanistic organisations departments had very specialised functions, workers had specialised roles and work descriptions. Work is coordinated by managers and a formal hierarchy. The mechanistic organisation works well during stable conditions, when only minor changes need to be made in the organisation (Read more about the mechanistic organisation in Chapter 3).

The organic organisation is more appropriate when the environment around the organisation is more turbulent, that is more changes are taking place among competitors, technology and customers preferences. Unforeseen events often occur and the organisation must be prepared to respond to these. The mechanistic organisation cannot deal with such changing circumstances due to its rigid structure. The organic organisation is more flexible and has the following features:

- Workers cooperate and use their special competences to achieve the overall objectives of the organisation.
- Tasks are developed and decided depending on circumstances and the situation in the organisation at the moment.
- Adjustments and re-definition of tasks are decided together with colleagues. People discuss what needs to be done to solve problems and handle different situation.
- Responsibility areas and authority are rather unclear. It is seen as more important to take responsibility for the overall running of the organisation.
- The major coordination and control mechanism is to develop common views on values and objectives. People develop a common view on the focus of the organisation, taking the organisation's environment into account.
- All knowledge is not located at the top of the organisation, instead it is spread in different informally developed centres and groups. The knowledge is used to act directly in the organisation.
- Organisational members are communicating horizontally rather than vertically in the organisation. The communication is characterised by information, consultation and discussion rather than orders and instruction.
- Commitment to the overall purpose of the organisation is valued higher than loyalty and obedience.
- Status is acquired through knowledge and skills which are important for the survival of the organisation.

Relations in the organic organisation are characterised by cooperation and relative equality. Few managers have titles and people are communicating by informal talk. Managers tolerate questioning and open discussions with workers. Coordination between managers is mostly taking place through meetings where decisions are made how to handle new situations and how work is going to be divided. The extensive communication result in diffusion of knowledge about the organisation and its environment, which in turn help people to take beneficial decisions for the whole organisation (ibid., pp. 85, 90–91).

Major changes take place in different ways in the mechanistic and in the organic organisation. In the mechanistic organisation the existing structure is transformed, for example a new department is created, or a department is increased in size in order to handle a new situation. Burns and Stalker saw in connection with the changes political conflicts between departments, which they explained was a result of the function organisation. The changes were seen as a threat to the existing power structure. In the organic organisation changes affected the whole organisation and everybody's tasks. Here, there were also discussions and conflicts about how to handle the new situation. The members of the organisation were however aware that changes were necessary (Burns & Stalker, 1961, pp. 8–9).

The Learning Organisation

Learning organisations can be said to be a reaction against the dysfunctional aspects of Tayloristic and bureaucratic organisations (see Chapter 3). Some of the more influential sources of inspiration to theories of learning organisation have been Kurt Lewin's work on leadership styles—autocratic, laisses-faire and democratic leadership, Burns and Stalker's (1961) distinction between mechanistic and organic organisations, Reg Revan's theories about action learning groups, McGregor's theory X and Y, and the sociotechnical school (Garrat, 1995).

The interest in learning organisation and organisational learning started to grow in the 1980s but in the 1990s the amount of literature exploded (Maier et al., 2001, p. 14). Two overviews of the literature are Dierkes et al. (2001) and Easterby-Smith and Lyles (2003a). The concept organisational learning is used by researchers aiming at understanding learning processes in organisations and generating theories. The concept learning organisation is predominantly used by practitioners. It has a normative focus, to create or improve the learning organisation (Easterby-Smith & Lyles, 2003b).

Scholars who have laid the foundation to theories about organisational learning are Cyert and March (1963) and above all Argyris and Schön (1978), see for instance Easterby-Smith and Lyles (2003b). There is a big interest for the concept in working life. Top management often talk about their organisation as a learning organisation. However, if you look closer how organisations actually are designed, these theories have a more limited diffusion (Pawlowsky et al., 2001, p. 775).

The Features of the Learning Organisation

Authors have described learning organisations in many different ways. Here a summary is presented on features which several theories have in common. Pedler et al., (1991, p. 1) use the following definition:

> A Learning Company is an organization that facilitates the learning of all its members *and* continuously transforms itself.

The top management is initiating and creating the learning organisation. They initiate organisational culture change projects with the aim to create a learning culture where workers are empowered and intrinsically motivated. The management develops a vision, a common identity and/or shared mental models for the members of the organisation. Cooperation based on trust is emphasised in the organisation rather than competition, and conflicts should be used constructively (Scarbrough & Swan, 2003, pp. 501–503).

Organisational Structure

Work roles and departments are loosely structured and can be changed easily, which provide opportunities for development and experimenting. The structure can be changed in order to respond to needs in the organisation and changes taking place outside the organisation (Pedler et al., 1991, p. 22).

A learning organisation tend to be less hierarchical and has fewer management levels than traditional organisations (Coopey, 1995; Örtenbland, 2004).

Another structural feature is learning forums, that is planned events where people meet, exchange ideas and reflect over how the organisation can develop and be more successful.

Organisational Culture

An essential aspect of the learning organisation is to facilitate learning processes by developing a creative culture where people and the organisation can develop (Scarbrough & Swan, 2003, pp. 501–503).

A learning culture is characterised by:

- People are open to each other. They make their intentions explicit and share knowledge. The culture is tolerant to mistakes.
- There is a curious attitude, people ask open questions, gather information and analyse problems.
- People are prestigeless and have no problems to admit that other's ideas and interpretations can be better.
- Responsibility for one's own actions and people change their behaviour as a result of experiences.
- Task orientation. Discussions are factual without taking personal interests and status into consideration.
- Equality. Communication is taking place irrespective of position and status. Participation is strived for. Responsibility and authority are delegated and shared.
- Commitment to learning which will benefit the organisation (Friedman et al., 2001).

A company that has many features of a learning organisation is Google. The company is considered to be one of the most innovative companies in the world and is continuously innovating technology, products and services (Finkle, 2012; Steiber & Alänge, 2013). The founders of Google had a bold vision to change the world, to organise the world's information and make it accessible universally. They also wanted to create the best company to work for (Steiber & Alänge, 2013). Google has a flat and loose structure with few managers. Most employees work in self-directed teams made up of three to four engineers with a leader (Finkle, 2012). According to Steiber and Alänge (2013), the leaders should trust and support empowered employees in the innovation process. People are free to move between teams according to their interest and they often work in several teams. There is an intranet where a lot of knowledge sharing takes place. All projects are displayed at the intranet and the teams communicate with each other about their progress or if they need help with their project from other engineers. The Google culture is influenced by academic freedom and critical thinking, and the Silicon Valley culture of thinking big, openness and sharing ideas. The two founders of Google, Sergei Brin and Larry Page, met at Stanford university 1995 where they were PhD students in computer engineering. The strived to create a democratic culture in their company, as in academia where open critical discussions prevail and where authority and position is not important for decision-making. Employees are encouraged to question old ways of doing things and come up with new ideas. According to Brin and Page innovations are fostered by questioning taken-for-granted assumptions and old paradigms. Furthermore, 20% of their time, employees are free to explore and develop their own ideas, which has led to several innovations. This free time, sometimes labelled organisational slack,[1] is valuable as it provides workers with time away from the demands of daily operations in order to reflect and explore new opportunities. The reward system based on bonuses and financial awards also supports innovation. Moreover, Google provides a lot of free perks to employees such as gyms, yoga classes, gourmet food, laundry service, and healthcare service (Finkle, 2012).

However, cracks in the Google facade have started to emerge. There have been reports about silencing critics, harassments and unlawful firing of employees for union activity. In 2018 Google workers around the world made a series of walk outs in protest of inequality and sexual misconduct against women. The workers that participated in the walkouts left a note on their desks saying: "I'm not at my desk because I'm walking out with other Googlers and contractors to protest sexual harassment, misconduct, lack of transparency, and a workplace culture that's not working for everyone" (BBC, 2018).

In 2020 the US National Labor Relations Board filed a complaint that employees were fired in 2019 for attempting to form a labour union. One of the employees named in the complaint said according to the BBC: "Employees who speak out on ethical issues, harassment, discrimination and all these matters are no longer really welcome at Google in the way they used to be."

> I think it is part of a shift in culture there. (BBC, 2020)

In the beginning of 2021 over 200 workers formed a union for Google workers, the Alphabet Workers Union, The Guardian reports. The union aims to work for fair pay, against abuse and discrimination. The union is open to all workers, not only full full-time workers, but also temporary workers, vendors and contractors. These workers are actually in majority, 135,000

[1] The concept organisational slack was introduced in organisation theory by Cyert and March (e g. 1956, 1963).

against 115,000 full-time workers, and there have been reactions from the workforce for the way the temporary workers and contractors have been treated (Paul, 2021).

Argyris' and Schön's Theory About Organisational Learning

Chris Argyris and Donald Schön are probably the most influential authors on organisational learning and learning organisations. They argue that organisations need to learn how to change themselves in order to survive. The members of the organisation need to learn to reflect over their operations, what is happening outside the organisation and what changes they need to make. With reference to Gregory Bateson this is labelled deutero learning; to learn how to learn.

People have, during life, learned how to act and behave in different situations. A skilled observer (A) can observe and analyse what underlying theories are guiding the actions of person B. These theories are labelled theory-in-use. If observer A asks person B how he/she would act in different situations he/she would say the espoused theory, which often differs from the theory-in-use. Organisations also have espoused theories and theories-in-use. The latter are values and assumptions, which govern how people actually act as a collective, that is the culture of the group or the organisation. The members of the organisation have developed and spread these values and assumptions. The organisational theories-in-use determine how work is divided and coordinated, how people communicate, what control mechanisms are used and what criteria are used for promotions. These values and assumptions are not always explicitly stated in the organisation.

The espoused theories are explicit and stated in strategy documents, policies, organisation charts and job descriptions. The explicit espoused theories and the more or less implicit and tacit theories-in-use often differ and are in conflict with each other. The members of the organisation create, individually and collective, images and maps of the theories-in-use. The organisational maps are partly explicit, for example documented routines, work processes or blueprints of buildings and premises. These images and maps are always incomplete and the members of the organisation are gradually adjusting their images, which has an effect on the theories-in-use.

From Argyris' and Schön's perspective, organisational learning is about reflecting over and changing organisational theories-in-use, which they label double loop learning. When problems of some kind arise in the organisation, people act to solve the problems with the help of the shared images and maps of the existing theories-in-use. This is labelled single-loop-learning which solves problems in order to go back to normal procedures. In single-loop-learning the values and assumptions governing the theories-in-use are not changed. The changing of methods and strategies are taking place within the existing mind-set, the existing way of acting and understanding organisational activities.

Double loop learning however, changes the governing values and assumptions in the organisation which in turn affect methods and strategies. In order for organisational learning to take place, the members of the organisation need to change the images and maps they have on values and assumptions, that is the theories-in-use. The organisation scans the environment and make changes due to competition, demands from customers, laws and regulations. If, for example, new technology is developed' which totally changes the conditions for the products or service the organisation deliver, the top management needs to fundamentally change how they view their business and mission. It is not always however that the top management can manage that process. They might end up in conflicts or make changes only on the single loop level. Double loop learning can take place on different levels in the organisation, for example how to do quality control, or more overall, what business mission should the organisation have. Argyris and Schön, however, point out that it sometimes can be difficult to decide if a change is single or double loop (Argyris & Schön, 1978, pp. 10–29).

Model II Theory-In-Use

In mechanistic organisation models people tend to use model I theory-in-use (see Chapter 3). Model I theory-in-use hinders both individual and organisational learning. According to Argyris and Schön model II theory-in-use is beneficial for learning. In model II people argue and put forward their views, but at the same time they give other people opportunities to question and discuss them. People are prepared to change their opinions when confronted with good arguments. Decisions about objectives and work methods are taken together in order to promote intrinsic motivation. Power is shared with people who have competence in the matter. Open discussions are strived for, where both emotions and factual arguments are put forward and given honest feedback to, in order to prevent defensive positions. In a discussion the norms and values behind opinion are highlighted and reflected upon in order to make double loop learning possible on the individual level (Argyris & Schön, 1978, pp. 136–139).

In an organisation where people are using model II theory-in-use there are more discussions about problems. Conflicts are also more common and are accepted by members of the organisation. Conflicts are used as a collective reflection and search process. Another structure is probably needed in Model II according to the authors. Organisations who are situated in a turbulent and changing environment need a decentralised organisation where responsibility and authority are delegated downwards in the organisation. Also, there need to be forums for collective reflection on theories-in-use and changes of these (Argyris & Schön, 1978, pp. 311–316).

Critical Reflections on the Learning Organisation

Literature about learning organisations take a harmony view of organisations. It is assumed that all people in organisations have the same interests and want to work together towards a common goal. Issues such as power, ideology and politics are ignored in the learning organisation literature. Participation and democratic decision-making are features of learning organisations. However, the literature does not give any clear answers how workers can take part in decision-making. The fact that workers and management often have different interest, is also ignored. It is assumed that all people in the organisation should have the same vision and identity. The power of management is not covered either. The management has power over resources such as money, knowledge and technology. There is a high probability that there would be power struggles over these resources, even in a learning organisation, for example experts in an organisation not seldom use their expert knowledge as a power tool to gain influence in the organisation. The top management initiate, design and control the learning organisation. It is likely that they are aiming at creating intrinsic motivation and organisational commitment, in order to tie workers tighter to the organisation. The higher degree of organisational commitment tends to have negative effects on other parts of life, such as family and friends. Workers are sucked into the organisation with interesting tasks, a creative learning environment and high demands. The rhetoric about participation, development and learning can thereby be used by management as manipulative control mechanisms to exploit workers (Coopey, 1995).

Managers and workers in an organic organisation (the learning organisation has this structure) often experience uncertainty because there is a lack of structure and rules for the work. The ambiguous structure can, for some people, be experienced as confusing and annoying. Some people would ask for a more structured work situation (Burns & Stalker, 1961, pp. 119–125). Stress research report, in line with above, that managers who have many and difficult decisions (unstructured work) have an increased probability to develop stress related problems (Karasek & Theorell, 1990, p. 44). Creative work with high decision authority and high cognitive demands can result in too high demands, which can have negative stress related effects (Waldenström & Härenstam, 2008). However, learning organisation has some features in line with a good work environment, like the sociotechnical work organisation: Social support through cooperation with colleagues, decision authority to take initiatives and how to carry work, and opportunities for using skills and learning new skills. These job features are related to less risk for depression, back pain and cardiac deceases (Bowling et al., 2015; Karasek & Theorell, 1990; Lang et al., 2012; Nixon et al., 2011; Theorell et al., 2016). Workers and their managers need to find a balance between creative, demanding work and work tasks that are not so demanding, but of course also time to rest and wind down.

Project Organisation and Agile Management

A work organisation model often used to change or develop something new is the project organisation. Project organisation, as well as learning organisation, is often contrasted with the rigid bureaucracy. The project organisation is often described as more adoptable to new situations where experimenting, learning and renewal are emphasised. In order to understand what a project is, it can be compared with the every-day activity of routinised production of goods and service, which is ongoing without having a specific end. Definitions of a project emphasises that it is limited in time, have specific objectives and resources. It is however hard to define project, as it is used to describe many different activities. Project can be used to describe routine work or more or less standardised work carried out by consultants. The building construction sector is one example of a relatively standardised work. When a building has been constructed, which can be seen as a project, the company starts a new similar project. In spite of having a lot of possible ways to change the construction of a building, constructors most often use the same methods and well-rehearsed routines. Even earlier mistakes are repeated. Lundin (1998) labels this the renewal paradox. In spite of having possibilities to change methods, the construction project stick to old, well-known methods and routines.

A project is associated with developing something new. It can be development of a new product or service, organisational change or solving a problem. The literature on project organisation describe the second world war and the need to rapidly develop new innovative weapon systems as the breakthrough for project organising. The war started a race on as quickly as possible construct and build efficient weapon systems. Practitioners and researchers worked together in groups to solve specific problems. The individuals had different competences and worked together to create military innovations. The project organisation can be successful for creating innovations, but the knowledge then needs to be diffused in the permanent organisation (Edvik, 2008; Lundin, 1998).

Agile Project Management

Agile project management is a project methodology used by many software companies and the concept has also spread to other sectors. Agile management is primarily used when innovation is needed in a short time, like in software development companies operating on a highly competitive market. According to Rigby et al., (2016, p. 41) Agile methods have "greatly increased success rates in software development, improved quality and speed to market, and boosted the motivation and productivity of IT teams."

The starting point of Agile management was a meeting in Snowbird, Utah, USA 2001. 17 people from software companies met to discuss ways to shorten software development time, and move away from the command-control, preplanned project management where each function did a separate activity. They came up with "The Agile Manifesto" (Beck et al., 2001), which is built around a self-managed multidisciplinary team. The team and the way they work is labelled "Scrum". The team is made up of three to nine people which together have all the skills necessary to carry out the task. Initially a plan is made up, only with the necessary steps to complete the task and then divide work tasks between members and time to finish them. Their work is facilitated by a "Scrum master", who help with the work process and group processes, such as dealing with conflicts. The team develops a working prototype of the product and then invites customers to try the product and give feedback of their experience. Based on customer feedback decisions are made about changes to the product. The project evolves in an organic way rather than in a programmed way. Emphasis in Agile is on face-to-face communication between colleagues. The team has standing up meetings, with inspiration from lean management, several times a week where each person says what has been done and what to do next. The other team members ask questions rather than give advice or instructions. The team often carry out experiments to try out new ideas rather than have lengthy argumentations. The work process is visualised using sticky notes on a whiteboard in columns—planned, doing, and done. This is called a Kanban board, which is taken from the visualisation principle in lean management. Managers and other employees can then follow the process and see if progress being made. Other lean principles are shortening lead times, reduce slack and eliminate waste (see Chapter 5).

Reflecting on the principles of Agile management, it is made up principles from somewhat disparate schools of thought. On one hand, the self-managed working group is in line with the sociotechnical school. Also the facilitator, the Scrum master, resembles the teamleader in the sociotechnical autonomous group based on a democratic leadership style. On the other hand, lean principles such as speeding up processes by eliminating waste (e g. time for breaks?) could potentially lead to high pressure and high demands for output. Also, the lean principle visualisation of the work process and individuals is built upon the motivation principle shame, for instance when workers have caused a stop on the assembly line, it is visualised by lamps starting to blink (see Chapter 5). In the Agile project everyone is aware of their work being observed through the Kanban board, but also through the stand-up meetings. Any individual causing delays will be visualised and shamed (at least this is the aim in lean management). So Agile project management is built up both by principles based on trust, and principle based on mistrust (See McGregor's theory X and Y, Chapter 1).

Very little research has been conducted on effects from Agile work on health and well-being. However, a recent survey study from Germany, including 260 people working in Agile development teams, indicated positive effects. The study indicated that autonomy and taking part in team decision-making can act as stress reducers of high demands on output and time pressure. After all, the teams are deciding themselves how much time should be given to each step in the work process, although the aim is to speed up the development process (Rietze & Zacher, 2022).

Hinders and Prerequisites for Development

Most organisations need both an efficient routinised running production and a development function. In the routinised production, of goods or service, the logic of production dominates where activities are characterised by rules, routine and well-known patterns. Problem solving is here carried out by using well-known rules and methods. The focus here is a stable, efficient and reliable production. Learning is here about mastering procedures and routines. In this adaptation focused learning objectives, means and result are specified beforehand. The routinised production comprises the major part of the activities in most organisations. However, the organisation must have capacity for adapting to new situations and keep being successful. The logic of development is focused on questioning the given, experimenting, risk taking, tolerance for insecurity and diversity. Here, a developmental learning is active (Ellström, 2001).[2] However, if the organisation culture is based on rules, routines and security, this can hinder innovation. This might be a possible explanation for Lundin's aforementioned renewal paradox. This kind of routine and security culture can also develop learned passivity for workers. People who have spent a long time in an organisation characterised by routine and rule-based activities, and who have not been given opportunities for thinking in new ways, might develop a passive approach (Gardell, 1986).

One trend, especially in manufacturing industry, is that workers in lean production or TQM-inspired work organisations are expected to take responsibility for productivity, quality and development of the production. To work with planning and problem solving when for example taking part in kaizen groups, could potentially be beneficial for competence development. There are also potential advantages for the organisation such as cost reduction, improvement of quality and productivity, as mentioned in Chapter 5.

There are however several examples of dissatisfaction and resistance against participating in kaizen activities when workers find that they are not threated in a decent way, as shown in Chapter 5. At the Mazda factory in the US workers found that kaizen work resulted in intensifying work (Fucini & Fucini, 1990, p. 161), and the workers were also not satisfied with the company policies (Kenney & Florida, 1995), which resulted in workers resisted taking part in kaizen activites. At Subaru-Isuzu Automotive (Graham, 1995, p. 43) workers were dissatisfied because they did not get any feedback on the suggestions they handed in. The repetitive and monotonous work, lack of influence at the workplace and hard control tend to be demotivating. These lean working conditions tend to result in workers not engaging in kaizen activities (Börnfelt, 2006).

[2] Ellström's concepts adaptation focused learning and development focused learning build among others on Argryris' and Schöns' (1978) theory about single- and double-loop-learning.

The opposite to passivity can be labelled change competence, which means an individual or a group has the ability to take initiatives and carry through changes at the workplace. High division of work, repetitive and monotonous tasks tend to have a passifying and demotivating effect on people, as we saw in Chapters 2 and 5. Also, as mentioned above, when people feel they are not treated in a respectful way at the workplace they tend to withdraw their engagement. Change competence, on the other hand, is fostered by a low division of labour (see Chapter 4) where it is possible for workers develop understanding of wholes, for example a production system, authority to carry through changes, social support from colleagues and/or managers and where interaction is characterised by dialogue and respect (Aronsson, 1995; Börnfelt, 2006).

Knowledge Management

Many authors in management and related social sciences argue we nowadays live in a knowledge society. Several management scholars argue organisations need to control knowledge in a more efficient way (E g. Davenport et al., 1998; Drucker, 1993; Nonaka, 1994). The economy has moved away from producing products to produce information and knowledge they argue. People in working life are working with their brain instead of their hands. According to researchers it is true that more people work with skilled work than before. This up-skilling trend has been going on for a few decades in the western world. However, from the 1990s a polarisation was observed in the US, where both low-skilled job, low income and high-skilled job, high income jobs increased in numbers. This polarisation has also later been discovered in Europe. The polarisation is distinct in Netherlands, Germany, France, Ireland and Cyprus, but also to a certain extent in the UK and Sweden (Åberg, 2015).

Knowledge has been put forward to be one of the most important factors for organisations to be competitive in the long run (Drucker, 1993; Nonaka, 1994). From the mid 1990s several management authors have therefore emphasised that knowledge needs to be controlled more efficiently and for this purpose introduced the concept knowledge management (KM). Knowledge management focus on creating, storing, diffusing and using knowledge in the most efficient way. The concept is based on a technical view on organising and different IT-tools are used as aids (Easterby-Smith & Lyles, 2003b).

With the help of the KM advocate Stewart (1997) a background is presented about the KM school of thought. In old days unskilled routine workers who quit could easily be replaced. In knowledge companies it is different. What creates value resides in the head of the knowledge workers. In knowledge intensive companies it is not clear who owns the knowledge according to Stewart. The companies therefore need to control or take ownership of the knowledge workers have and control what knowledge they should acquire. In Ford's car factories the owner owned the whole production system and the cars being produced. The workers only had simple, physical tasks.

In knowledge intensive companies, workers carry around valuable knowledge and this knowledge must be spread to the organisation. The diffusion of the knowledge to the organisation results in the company to a higher degree will take ownership of the knowledge. If one person quits the knowledge is, partly, still in the organisation through the remaining workers.

Taylorism and KM share the same theory X (McGregor, 1960/1987) view on organisations but the means are different. In Taylorism the management more or less completely took control over the work process and the knowledge. In knowledge intensive organisations this is not possible because here workers need to be able to act independently in complex situations. In KM the aim instead is to control the knowledge by diffusing it in the organisation and to document it in databases and other IT-systems.

Explaining Knowledge Management

In summary KM focus on creating, storing, diffusing and valuing knowledge in organisations.

1. Creating knowledge. Knowledge is created by making tacit knowledge explicit. Nonaka is an often-cited author in the KM literature. In Nonaka (1994) a model is presented to transform tacit knowledge to explicit knowledge. Explicit knowledge is expressed in words and numbers. Tacit knowledge is based in action and participation in specific contexts. It is based in the human body and conscience together. People have learned skills to act in a specific context, often over a longer period of time, but cannot explain how they act to other people, because the knowledge is tacit. The tacit knowledge is supposed to be made explicit in self organised groups through dialogue in Nonaka's model. This result from the dialogue is both diffusion and storage of knowledge in other people.
2. Storing knowledge. As mentioned above, storage of knowledge is taking place through dialogue with other people, but IT-technology is also used. One example is that the most experienced workers document what they know and this knowledge is stored in a data base. The documentation makes the knowledge explicit and through the databases the knowledge can be shared to the organisation (Gibbert et al., 2011; Huseman & Goodman, 1999).
3. Diffusion of knowledge. As mentioned above diffusion of knowledge is taking place though dialogue between people and by using data bases and other IT-tools. To promote sharing of knowledge different incentives are sometimes used, such as shares, increased pay if workers participate in knowledge sharing networks or share knowledge in It-systems. Culture change projects and creating a sense of trust in the organisation are other methods to promote knowledge sharing (Davenport et al., 1998, Gibbert et al., 2011).

4. Valuing knowledge. Knowledge is valued in financial terms in order to make more valid valuations of companies for business accounting. Knowledge is in this context named intellectual capital (Edvinsson, 1997). Also, national intellectual capital is measured and countries are compared with each other (Lin & Edvinsson, 2008).

Critique of KM

As mentioned above the theory X approach (McGregor, 1960/1987), based on suspicion and control, is pre-dominant in KM. When knowledge only is in possession of the employee, tacitly or explicitly it is seen as a problem in knowledge management. The company should therefore do what it can to tie their employees to the company according to Stewart (1997). 'If the community's heart is in your shop, they'll want to stay. But if their professional satisfaction comes from learning about cheese, you won't keep them if you offer only the chance to build a better mousetrap.' (Stewart, 1997, p. 109). Much effort should be made to tie employees emotionally to the company. Even Stewart believes it sounds too manipulatively and control focused. He tries to calm the reader; 'Community … belonging … If it sounds like Dr. Spock, don't worry. Organizations can help create bonds of ownership in both implicit and explicit ways that are thoroughly adult' (Stewart, 1997, p. 109).

KM is to a large extent technology oriented and there is an emphasis on documenting standardised 'best practice' knowledge in databases. Knowledge is thereby seen as possible to standardise, and then to diffuse to the organisation for workers to use. There is a risk that professional knowledge is reduced in the strive to find optimal theoretical knowledge. All knowledge cannot be transformed to explicit knowledge. For example Rolf (1995) points out that knowledge cannot always easily be transferred to a person, because skilled actions requires experience. Skilled practise is composed by a complicated interplay between abstract theories and situated problems with a high degree of uncertainty. Brown and Duguid (1991) describe communities of practise, which capture this complicated practise well. They use an example of service technicians who solve problems together by telling stories about earlier repair work and working, discussing together in a joint problem-solving process. They make sense of complex situations and find the way to a solution. The company they work for provide documentation for problem solving. The documentation is organised as a predetermined route with no alternatives. It is a decision tree for diagnosis and repair that assumes predictable machines and an unproblematic problem-solving process. These instructions very soon fall short in the real practise and complex situations. One important aspect of the service technician's work is to learn how to be a part of a community of practise. They acquire the special ways of thinking and learn to speak its language. They thereby learn to behave as community members (Brown & Duguid, 1991).

Most large-scale IT knowledge management change projects do not deliver the expected benefits. According to studies around 70% of, often very expensive, KM transformation initiatives fail to achieve their objectives (Gibbert et al., 2011). In most KM literature the assumption is that the knowledge transfer from IT-system to user is easy and friction free. However, studies show that people often prefer human interaction, to share other peoples' experiences and discuss with others. Knowledge sharing is often taking place in dialogue between people even if there are databases with information which have been costly to develop (Brown & Duguid, 1991; Stymne, 2001).

Furthermore, the existence of an informal organisation is often disregarded in knowledge management. The presence of informal organisation was presented by Roetlishberger and Dickson (1939) in their Hawthorne study (see Chapter 1). They showed that people in organisations act very differently against other people, depending on what formal position, status, power they have and how relations have been built up over time. Brown and Duguid (1991) also point out that information flows in different ways in different socio-economic groups. They argue that information is exchanged freely for example among working class people, but not so easily between socio economic groups. There are however some KM authors who mention the importance of creating mutual trust in groups (Gibbert et al., 2011; Nonaka, 1994) but they have little to say how to achieve it. Davenport et al. (1998) and Stewart (1997) have realised that people often resist handing over their competence because they are afraid of losing their job. The authors see this as a problem and express that people do not often want to tell others about their mistakes, even if the company could learn from it.

Summary

Theories about learning organisations have been inspired by the sociotechnical school where dialogue, participation and empowerment are emphasised. Focus in theories about learning organisations is on enhancing learning both for individuals and the organisation. In the learning organisation division of labour and coordination are carried out in an organic way. Workers have a lot of influence how to define and carry out work. Work roles are often changing due to changed circumstances and there are no formal assignments. People make contact and interact in an informal way. In the learning organisation people need to be social, skilled in argumentation, but at the same time they also need good listening skills. From around mid 1990s another management trend emerged—knowledge management (KM), which focus on control of knowledge. In KM theory workers' knowledge is being put forward to be very valuable for the organisation. According to advocates of knowledge management, the organisation must take ownership of that knowledge and maximise its value for the organisation.

In learning organisations open communication, empowerment and worker participation is emphasised. LO is therefore grounded in a theory Y view on the organisation which is built upon trust in the ability of workers. KM, however, is based on a protectionist theory X view of workers and the organisation based on distrust, where control of knowledge is emphasised. In LO, the high worker control/decision authority, opportunities for learning and potentially high social support may have positive effects on health. However, a creative, unstructured work environment with high demands for intellectual work can result in too high demands, leading to stress related health problems. A similar concern probably also is valid for project organising, see next section.

Project work has become more common the last two to three decades in many organisations. Workers, however, have their ordinary everyday work activities to carry out as well as taking part in projects, which can be demanding. All in all, these new organisation models put higher demand on learning, people taking initiative and knowledge sharing compared to classical organisation models. At the same time, these models can support competence development for people working in the organisation.

Reflection Questions

1. Would you like to work in a learning organisation or in an organisation based on knowledge management?
2. Which type of organisations are maybe not suited for being organised as organic, or learning organisations?
3. Why might it be difficult to diffuse knowledge in the organisation through knowledge management?
4. What are the pit holes for emphasising continuous learning and innovations in organisations for workers and for organisations?

Bibliography

Åberg, R. (2015). Svensk arbetsmarknad mot polarisering efter millenieskiftet. *Arbetsmarknad och Arbetsliv, 21*(4).

Argyris, C., & Schön, D. A. (1978). *Organizational learning: A theory of action perspective*. Addison-Wesley.

Aronsson, G. (1995). *Förändringskompetens: Projektledares erfarenheter från 300 Arbetslivsfondsprojekt*. Arbetslivsinstitutet.

BBC. (2018, November 1). *Google staff walk out over women's treatment*. https://www.bbc.co.uk/news/technology-46054202

BBC. (2020, December 3). *Google fired employees for union activity, says US agency*. https://www.bbc.co.uk/news/technology-55173063

Beck, K., Beedle, M., van Bennekum, A., Cockburn, A., Cunningham, W., Fowler, M., et al. (2001). *Manifesto for Agile Software Development*. https://agilemanifesto.org

Bowling, N. A., Alarcon, G. M., Bragg, C. B., & Hartman, M. J. (2015). A meta-analytic examination of the potential correlates and consequences of workload. *Work & Stress, 29*(2), 95–113.

Brown, J. S., & Duguid, P. (1991, February 1). Organizational learning and communities-of-practise: Toward a unified view of working, learning and innovation. *Organization Science, 2*(1).

Burns, T., & Stalker, G. M. (1961). *The management of innovation.* Tavistock.

Börnfelt, P.-O. (2006). *Förändringskompetens på industrigolvet: Kontinuerligt förändringsarbete i gränslandet mellan lean production och socioteknisk arbetsorganisation.* Arbetslivsinstitutet.

Coopey, J. (1995). The learning organization, power, politics and ideology. *Management Learning, 26*(2), 193–213.

Cyert, R. M., & March, J. G. (1956). Organizational factors in the theory of oligopoly. *The Quarterly Journal of Economics, 70*(1), 44–64.

Cyert, R. M., & March, J. G. (1963/1992). *A behavioral theory of the firm* (2nd ed.). Blackwell.

Davenport, T. H., Long, D., & David, W. (1998). Successful knowledge management projects. *Sloan Management Review, 39*(2).

Dierkes, M., Antal, B. A., Child, J., & Nonaka, I. (2001). *Handbook of organizational learning and knowledge.* Oxford University Press.

Drucker, P. F. (1993). *Post-capitalist society.* Harper Business.

Easterby-Smith, M., & Lyles, M. A. (2003a). *The Blackwell handbook of organizational learning and knowledge management.* Blackwell.

Easterby-Smith, M., & Lyles, M. A. (2003b). Introduction: Watersheds of organizational learning and knowledge management. In M. Easterby-Smith & M. A. Lyles (Eds.), *The Blackwell handbook of organizational learning and knowledge management* (pp. xx, 676). Blackwell.

Edvik, A. (2008). *Projektformen och det industriella arvet: Med exempel från sjukvården.* Malmö högskola, Institutionen för urbana studier; Göteborgs universitet. Institutionen för arbetsvetenskap.

Edvinsson, L. (1997). Developing intellectual capital at Skandia. *Long Range Planning, 30*(3).

Ellström, P.-E. (2001). Integrating learning and work: Problems and prospects. *Human Resource Development Quarterly, 12*(4), 421–435.

Finkle, T. A. (2012). Corporate entrepreneurship and innovation in silicon valley: The case of Google, Inc. *Entrepreneurship Theory and Practice, 36*(4), 863–887.

Friedman, V. J., Forslin, J., & Reinhardt, R. (2001). Pratices and tools of organizational learning. In M. Dierkes, B. A. Antal, J. Child, & I. Nonaka (Eds.), *Handbook of organizational learning and knowledge.* Oxford University Press.

Fucini, J. J., & Fucini, S. (1990). *Working for the Japanese.* The Free Press.

Gardell, B. (1986). *Arbetets organisation och människans natur: En forskningsöversikt om människans behov av att behärska tekniken.* Arbetsmiljöfonden.

Garratt, B. (1995, September). An old idea that has come of age. *People Management, 21,* 25–28.

Gibbert, M., Probst, G. J. B., & Davenport, T. H. (2011). Sidestepping implementation traps when implementing knowledge management: Lessons learned from Siemens. *Behaviour & Information Technology, 30*(1), 63–75.

Graham, L. (1995). *On the line at Subaru-Isuzu: The Japanese model and the American worker.* ILR Press.

Huseman, R., & Goodman, J. P. (1999). *Leading with knowledge. The nature of competition in the 21st century*. Sage.

Karasek, R., & Theorell, T. (1990). *Healthy work: Stress, productivity and the reconstruction of working life*. Basic Books.

Kenney, M., & Florida, R. (1995). The transfer of Japanese management styles in two US transplant industries: Autos and electronics. *Journal of Management Studies, 32*(6), 89–102.

Lang, J., Ochsmann, E., Kraus, T., & Lang, J. W. B. (2012). Psychosocial work stressors as antecedents of musculoskeletal problems: A systematic review and meta-analysis of stability-adjusted longitudinal studies. *Social Science & Medicine, 75*, 1163–1174.

Lin, C. Y. Y., & Edvinsson, L. (2008). National intellectual capital: A comparison of the Nordic countries. *Journal of Intellectual Capital, 9*(4), 525–545.

Lundin, R. A. (1998). Temporära organisationer – några perspektivbyten. In B. Czarniawska (Ed.), *Organisationsteori på svenska*. Liber ekonomi.

Maier, G. W., Prange, C., & von Rosenstiel, L. (2001). Psychological perspectives on organizational learning. In M. Dierkes, B. A. Antal, J. Child, & I. Nonaka (Eds.), *Handbook of organizational learning and knowledge*. Oxford University Press.

McGregor, D. (1987/1960). *The human side of enterprise*. Penguin Books Ltd.

Nixon, A. E., Mazzola, J. J., Bauer, J., Krueger, J. R., & Spector, P. E. (2011). Can work make you sick? A meta-analysis of the relationships between job stressors and physical symptoms. *Work & Stress, 25*(1), 1–22.

Nonaka, I. (1994, February). A dynamic theory of organizational knowledge creation. *Organization Science, 5*(1).

Nonås, K. (2005). *Vision verus reality in organizational change*. Arbetslivsinstitutet.

Örtenblad, A. (2004). The learning organization: Towards an integrated model. *The Learning Organization, 11*(2), 129–144.

Paul, K. (2021, January 4). More than 200 US Google employees form a workers' union. *The Guardian*.

Pawlowsky, P., Forslin, J., & Reinhardt, R. (2001). Pratices and tools of organizational learning. In M. Dierkes, B. A. Antal, J. Child, & I. Nonaka (Eds.), *Handbook of organizational learning and knowledge*. Oxford University Press.

Pedler, M., Burgoyne, J., & Boydell, T. (1991). *The learning company*. McGraw-Hill.

Rietze, S., & Zacher, H. (2022). Relationships between Agile work practices and occupational well-being: The role of job demands and resources. *International Journal of Environmental Research and Public Health, 19*(1258), 1–24.

Rigby, D. K., Sutherland, J., & Takeuchi, H. (2016, May). Embracing Agile. *Harvard Business Review*, pp. 41–50.

Roethlisberger, F. J., & Dickson, W. J. (1939). *Management and the worker*. Wiley.

Rolf, B. (1995). *Profession, tradition och tyst kunskap: En studie i Michael Polanyis teori om den professionella kunskapens tysta dimension*. Nya Doxa.

Scarbrough, H., & Swan, J. (2003). Discourses of knowledge management and the learning organization: Their production and consumption. In M. Easterby-Smith & M. A. Lyles (Eds.), *The Blackwell handbook of organizational learning and knowledge management*. Blackwell.

Steiber, A., & Alänge, S. (2013). A corporate system for continuous innovation: the case of Google Inc. *European Journal of Innovation Management, 16*(2), 243–264.

Stewart, T. (1997). Brain power: Who owns it...How they profit from it. *Fortune, 135*(5).

Stymne, B. (2001). Kunskapsåtervinning eller lärande. In T. Backlund, H. Hansson, & C. Thunborg (Eds.), *Lärdilemman i arbetslivet: Teoretiska och praktiska perspektiv på lärande i organisationer*. Studentlitteratur.

Theorell, T., Jood, K., Slunga Järvholm, L., Vingård, E., Perk, J., Östergren, P. O., & Hall, C. (2016). A systematic review of studies in the contributions of the work environment to ischaemic heart disease development. *The European Journal of Public Health, 26*(3), 470–477.

Waldenström, K., & Härenstam, A. (2008). Does the job demand-control model correspond to externally assessed demands and control for both women and men? *Scandinavian Journal of Public Health, 36*(3), 242–249.

CHAPTER 7

Professional Organisation and New Public Management—Conflicting Organisation Models in the Public Sector

Learning Objectives

This chapter should provide you with knowledge about:

- The main differences between three conflicting organisation models in the public sector: The bureaucracy (Chapter 3), the professional organisation and new public management.
- The main arguments for introducing new public management in the public sector and that critical studies point out that these arguments are largely hollow.
- The threat to one of the fundamental principles in the welfare state, of treating cases equally and fairly in the Weberian sense, through the introduction of new public management.

Introduction

Several organisation researchers (E g. Sahlin, 2010 with reference to Scott) describe three organisation models, which have had influence over how the public sector is organised. For a long time, the traditional model, the bureaucracy was the main model for organising public authorities (see Chapter 3). In this classical model administration is supposed to be carried out according to laws, rules and guidelines set out by politicians. Administration is carried out by using a system of rules. To treat all people equally is the governing principle. Employees in an administrative unit are expected to carry out their duties in the same way regardless where the unit is situated geographically, and handle errands based on the same system of rules (E g. Hood, 1995). A second organisation model is professional organisation which is based on collegiality.

P-O Börnfelt, *Work Organisation in Practice*,
https://doi.org/10.1007/978-3-031-21667-1_7

Medical doctors, architects and accountants are examples of professions which have had a strong position for a long time based on professional monopoly by law. When these professions moved into larger organisations, they kept their autonomous positions. From the 1980s onwards a third organisation model, new public management (NPM) is the most influential one (Hood, 1995; Hood & Dixon, 2016). The private company is seen as an ideal for organising in the public sector. The professional organisation and NPM are presented in this chapter. The diffusion of NPM is a global phenomenon. Examples from the UK and Sweden are presented to highlight these changes.

The Professional Organisation

Professions like medical doctors, architects, accountants, lawyers and teachers have a long vocational training. The work is to a large extent coordinated through their common training. According to Henry Mintzberg (1983, chapter 10) skills are standardised in, what he labels, the professional bureaucracy as a result of the long training for the profession. One example Mintzberg uses is an operation team performing a heart surgery. The team members do not need to talk a lot during the operation. Doctors, nurses and other staff know exactly what to do and in what order.

In professional bureaucracies, or as I chose to label them, professional organisations, the main value creating work is carried out by professionals. Examples are hospitals, architect bureaus, accountant bureaus, schools and universities. Coordination mechanisms are, as previously mentioned, the common training, but also mutual adjustment as the professional organisation is decentralised and based on collegiality. Collegiality is here understood as collective decision-making by professional peers in an organisation, department or work group. A professional organisation is a democratic, decentralised organisation where decisions are taken together. Auditing and evaluation of competence are carried out by colleagues. For example, literature written by researchers in a university are evaluated by other researchers, so-called peer review. Seminars and conferences are organised where research results, methods, theory and analysis are critically discussed and examined. These seminars and conferences are both learning forums and serve as evaluation of quality and qualification level. Training and competence development are taking place continuously.

The professionals work autonomously and close to their clients, for example teachers work individually in the classroom with their pupils. In the healthcare sector medical doctors have traditionally managed and controlled healthcare organisations based on the norms and skills of their profession. Professionals, such as medical doctors, tend predominantly have work commitment, that is their profession is what they are interested in and not so much what employer they have. The professionals' work is also focused to promote the common good, for example to cure deceases and promoting well-being. The powerful positions, which the professionals have, or maybe more accurately have had, is set against the traditional, hierarchical view of organisations where the top management take the decisions and control the organisation. As a consequence, politicians and managers have often viewed professionals as difficult to control (Mintzberg, 1983, chapter 10). There seem to be a trend of increased management control, in the last 2–3 decades, over budgets and objectives. For example, in the healthcare sector, there is an increased tension and conflicts between medical priorities and managerial priorities. Medical doctors are experiencing their medical expertise being questioned and overrun (Burnes et al., 2014).

Collegiality in the university sector has a long tradition. Collegiality can have different meanings and have varied between universities. Collegiality, in line with above, is here understood as collective decision-making by academic staff in a university, department or work group. The first university in Europe, Bologna, was founded 1088 and was funded by its students. Then followed Oxford (1167), Cambridge (1209) and Paris (1231). The universities, which were autonomous organisations, developed a tradition of pursuing knowledge, development and truth for its own sake. Wilhelm Humboldt, which founded the University of Berlin in 1810, continued in this liberal tradition and emphasised that research and teaching was inseparable. Humboldt supported the idea that the university was a community of students and scholars based on critical inquiry and search for knowledge. Many of the universities, especially the older ones such as Oxford and Cambridge, were autonomous organisations run by scholars. Decision-making was a collective process where academic staff decided what to teach, which student to admit and what to research about. This is often referred to as the academic freedom (Burnes et al., 2014).

However, the academic freedom and collegiality have lost ground in the western world over the last three, four decades. Decision-making has been centralised and collegial decision-making bodies have lost power or been removed completely in some universities. Governments and top management in universities have increased the control of what courses to run, what kind of research to conduct and where scholars should publish. The decline of collegiality has been reported from many countries such as the UK, the US, Oceania, France, Germany, Netherlands, Spain, Italy and Sweden (Burnes et al., 2014; Sahlin, 2010). The power and influence professionals have in their organisations have been seen as a problem by politicians and administrators. Also, universities have expanded taking in more students. This is a consequence of political decisions about more people, from different social backgrounds should benefit from university educations. In the UK, the economic crises in the 1970s and the shift to the Thatcher government in 1979 started a major cut in public funding to universities (Burnes et al., 2014).

New Public Management

From the 1980s onwards a business-like public management emerged as a model for organising the public sector, which is based on individualism and competition. The main arguments for introducing this new model are to decrease bureaucracy, improve efficiency, cutting costs, and decrease the power of professionals. The development of the new model is often associated with neoliberal ideas,[1] the Ronald Reagan government in the US and the Margaret Thatcher government in the UK during the 1980s (Hood & Dixon, 2016; Pollitt & Bouckaert, 2017, chapter 1), but also with the labour government in New Zealand from 1984. The governments in these Anglophone countries were striving towards a more "business-like" management of the public sector. In the US the movement was labelled Re-inventing Government, and in the UK Christopher Hood (1991) introduced the label New Public Management in a seminal article (Pollitt & Bouckaert, 2017, chapter 1).

NPM strives to reduce government spending and staffing. There is also a shift to privatisation of public organisations, the use of tendering and contracting out services. Central themes in NPM are competition on a market and traditional management principles taken from the private sector, such as hierarchies and line of command. There is a strong belief in competition as a driving force to create more efficient organisations to a lower cost and better quality. Competition is created between public organisations and private companies for example in the healthcare sector. Also, in organisations competition is created through internal markets. Decentralised cost centres are organised and these units are supposed to function as an internal market where the units are customers and suppliers to each other. The internal customers can also buy service and products outside the organisation, often focusing on lower costs, even if there are internal suppliers for the same service or product. The hierarchy is strengthened, inspired by a traditional view of organisation. As a result, the head of departments gain more power for example in universities and collegial decision-making is weakened, as mentioned before. Managers receive more discretion to manage, contrary to the rule-based management in bureaucratic organisations, which was intended to protect the autonomy of civil servants to prevent favouritism and harassment. NPM put emphasis on labour discipline and resisting union activities (Hood, 1991, 1995). Managers are then in NPM given an important role. Christopher Pollitt has coined the term managerialism which is part of NPM but also is a broader term: 'Managerialism is an ideology which positions better management as transformative…It is *management* which that will direct and channel professional skills so as to focus on the highest priority goals. It is *management* that will turn broad

[1] People are in neoliberalism seen as rational actors striving to maximise their own egoistic goals. The distribution of welfare services is expected to be carried out through an unregulated market, where customers can choose between different alternatives (E g. Harvey, 2007).

political aspirations into measurable outputs and outcomes' (Pollitt, 2016, p. 431).

Other characteristic features of NPM are individual pay based on job performance.

As an example, performance based contracts have been used in New Zealand and Australia for top managers. The idea is to let the market forces decide the level of pay. Top managers are hired on fixed term contracts and rewarded according to their performance—measured by performance standards. There has, however, been problems with specifying performance standards, and the prescribed performance standards tend to promote inflexible and rigid management—"to go by the book" (Christensen & Lægreid, 2002; Lægreid, 2002).

TQM is integrated in NPM by defining citizens as customers and also by measuring performance and quality by key performance indicators. Quality is measured by using customer satisfaction surveys. Systematic evaluations of performance and quality are made to compare providers. The customers should be provided with alternatives, for example healthcare or schools and make choices by for example comparing the quality of different providers (Hood, 1991, 1995; Pollitt & Bouckaert, 2017, chapter 1).

The core NPM countries are of course The US and the UK where NPM originated, but also New Zealand and Australia were early adopters. There have been debates about the diffusion om NPM, if NPM is a global model adopted by most developed countries in the world, or if there are variations in countries (Pollitt & Bouckaert, 2017, chapter 1). According to Hood (1995), high adopters of NPM among OECD countries are Sweden, Canada, France, Denmark, Norway, Netherlands and Ireland. A number of countries have not moved, or have just made a few modest changes, towards the NPM model. According to Hood, the low adopters are Greece, Spain, Germany, Switzerland, Japan and Turkey.

In Sweden the reforms inspired from NPM were introduced somewhat later than in the US and the UK. However, a large part of the public sector in Sweden is exposed to competition today, for example schools and the healthcare sector. The reformation in Sweden started in the beginning of the 1990s. The centre-right government 1991–1994 introduced legislation, which made it possible for municipalities to expose welfare services to competition. 1992 the government carried through a school reform, which made it possible for private companies to run schools on elementary and high school levels for profit, however they are still funded by the public in the same way as schools run by the municipalities. The social democratic (centre left) government 1994–2006 continued the NPM development (Hartman, 2011; Szebehely, 2011; Vlachos, 2011). Studies of the public sector being exposed to competition show that cost can be reduced between 10 and 30% (Almqvist, 2006). However, other studies point in the opposite direction, that costs are increasing, see below.

Critical Reflections on the Professional Organisation and NPM

The autonomy of the professionals can have negative effects on cooperation with, and influence from other interest groups. Mintzberg (1983) argues that professionals prefer to pursue their work without interference from colleagues, managers, administrators or politicians. Coordination with other actors can thereby be a problem. The loyalty to the organisation is week and the workplace is seen as a comfortable place to practise their profession. The autonomy and power of the professionals tend also to result in lengthy change processes, which are characterised by conflicts with managers and administrators (Mintzberg, 1983, chapter 10).

The critique of NPM is structured following the aforementioned arguments for implementing NPM in the public sector, but also the negative effects on treating cases equally and fairly according to 'the Weberian' rules of law, and finally negative effects of abandoning collegiality. Advocates of NPM have argued NPM would (1) decrease bureaucracy, (2) lead to higher efficiency and decreasing costs, and (3) decrease the power of professionals. Research indicates opposite effects regarding arguments 1, mixed results for argument 2, but support for argument 3. However, regarding argument 3, the effects are not necessarily positive for clients and for democratic decision-making.

Advocates of NPM have often criticised the traditional Weberian bureaucratic model for beeing too bureaucratic, in the sense of overly complicated, resource demanding and costly processes. They argue NPM is leading to less bureaucracy. On the contrary, research indicate the opposite, NPM is leading to increased administration, which result in civil servants need to spend more time on indirect, non-value adding tasks. The professional then have less time to treating patients, teaching and developing their professional skills. NPM, quality certification (ISO 9000 etc.), evaluations, balanced score cards and lean management have, according to several researchers, led to increased administration for civil servants. The political scientist Patrik Hall (2012), who summarise this research, uses the term management bureaucracy, which comprises administrative tasks such as coordination, planning, control, accountancy, documentation and information. This neobureaucracy, as some scholars label it, lacks the Weberian aspects of a bureaucracy—equal treatment and rule of law (ibid., chapter 3). If more work processes, as a result of these new management concept, are controlled, evaluated and documented it leads to increased administration. Accordingly, for example medical doctors, police officers, teachers, and home care workers report increased administrative tasks (Hall, 2012, chapter 1; Parding et al., 2020, chapter 2). Home care workers in Scandinavian countries are also more controlled in detail using digital technology, in line with digital Taylorism (Brown et al., 2011). Work tasks are prescribed and the number of minutes to perform them. According to Nordic studies, the care workers experience a role conflict, as they feel there is a clash between their own ideas how to care for the elderly, based on human dignity, and manager's instructions based on digital Taylorism. The workers also experience an intensification of their work. The higher work demand, combined with the dissatisfaction with not being able to give the right care to care takers based on dignity, tend to create stress reactions (Parding et al., 2020, chapter 2). A survey study of job centre workers in Germany also shows stressful working conditions and role conflicts. Worker performance is measured against targets and workers are made to put pressure on vulnerable job seekers to take low-income jobs. The results from the survey indicate considerably higher stress related working conditions compared to the average German worker (Olejniczak & Salmon, 2014).

Another method to capture the change in public bureaucracy is to count the change in the number of employees with administrative roles. New Zealand is considered to be a country that more or less fully has adopted the NPM model. The public sector in New Zealand has seen a growth in the number of employees with administrative roles, especially the number of managers has increased. Between 2006 and 2018 administrative employees grew by 59%, compared to 50% for employees in core functions, such as nurses, police officers or social workers. Examples of occupations that increased in the administrative group are customer service representatives, information professionals, specialist managers, office managers and general managers (Löfgren et al., 2022).

The research results are mixed regarding the main argument for introducing NPM, that competition and privatisation should improve efficiency, save costs and increase quality. Pollitt and Dan (2011) have made a meta-analysis of the impact on efficiency and quality in the EU from NPM. A large part of cases saw improvements in efficiency (54%) and quality (43%), but a substantial number of cases registered negative effects or no change. Unfortunately Pollitt and Dan's report does not give much details of what has been evaluated. However they provide one example, an evaluation of a campaign in the UK National Health Service. The aim of the campaign, which started 2003, was that 98% of patients arriving to accident and emergency (A and E) departments should be treated within four hours after arrival. The objective was part of a system of rating all hospitals with stars, from zero to three. In 2007 59% of the surveyed 155 hospitals reached the target, compared to 1% in 2002. The campaign offered hospitals cash incentives to reach the target. Severe dysfunctional effects from the campaign were found at Mid Staffordshire hospital in an inquiry by the Healthcare Commission in 2009. The hospital had extraordinarily high death rates. It was found the hospital favoured the patients with minor ailments at the expense of patients who were seriously ill in order not to breach the four-hour target (Pollitt & Dan, 2011). Bevan and Hood (2006) provide other examples of dysfunctional effects such as deliberate misreporting from hospitals, and letting patients wait in ambulances outside hospitals in order to not to breach the four-hour target.

The anthology Konkurrensens konsekvenser (Consequences from competition, Hartman, 2011) presents an overview of studies in Sweden about effects from competition in the public sector. Overall, no positive effects on efficiency and quality have been found. Private companies often have lower costs, but the savings (of tax-payers money) are often used as profit to the owners. Cutting down on staff is a way to save costs. A comparison between elementary schools run by municipalities and private companies shows that the municipality schools have somewhat higher staff level (year 2009): 8.3 compared to 7.6 teachers per 100 pupils (Vlachos, 2011). In elderly care homes there is a similar pattern. Both Swedish and international studies show that staff density is around 10% higher in municipality care homes or non-for-profit care homes compared to care homes run by private companies (Szebehly, 2011). Lower staff density is likely to have negative effects on the work environment and for caretakers.

Also, in the school sector competition has resulted in non-desirable effects. In Sweden the number of private schools has risen considerably from the 1990s. Thus, parents can choose between municipal and private schools. The private schools are also publicly funded and they are allowed to make a profit to their owners (Varjo & Kalalahti, 2015). Studies show that competition between schools has resulted in grade inflation in elementary- and high schools. From 1995 to 2010 the grades have more or less increased constantly. However, pupils' knowledge levels, on the contrary, have decreased overtime. The schools are using grades to compete for pupils (Vlachos, 2011). While Sweden's result in the PISA study (2003–2012), which measure 15-year-old' ability in reading, mathematics and science, has fallen year by year, Finland's result is among the top countries (Samuelsson & Lindblad, 2015).

Sweden's result has improved in the 2018 study but, more importantly, Finland is maintaining its position among the top countries (OECD, 2020). The elementary school in Finland is run by the municipalities and the pupils normally go to their neighbourhood school. Less than two percent of the schools are run by private providers or the state (Finnish Ministry of Education & Culture, 2020). Finnish schools perform very well in spite of lack of competition it seems. Furthermore, there are other institutional differences between the Swedish and the Finnish schools according to the study by Samuelsson and Lindblad (2015). Finnish schools more strongly resemble the professional organisation. The teachers have longer education (most teachers have an MA), stronger professional autonomy and the organisation is based on collegiality; the teachers take part in joint decision-making, share knowledge and cooperate more with each other compared to Swedish teachers (ibid., 2015). There is a long tradition of high trust between school principals and teachers, and teachers experience considerable empowerment in their profession (Paulsen, 2018). Moreover, the differences between pupils and between schools in the PISA study are considerably smaller in Finland compared to other OECD countries. This is due to the fact that Finland actively promotes equality, in line with a Weberian bureaucracy ethos. Finnish civil servants monitor possible schools with difficult socio-economic compositions and take measures to support these schools. There is also a substantial cooperation between schools in a non-competitive manner (Varjo & Kalalahti, 2015).

Exposition to competition can also result in employees keeping silent about wrongdoing and problems at the workplace, because the organisation needs to protect its brand. An interview study in Sweden including 126 workers and union representatives in the education- and the healthcare sector highlighted this effect. Protecting the brand on a market is counteracting the freedom of expression public employees have in Sweden.[2] Both managers and workers are aware of the importance of protecting the brand in order to stay competitive on the market. Some workers in schools for instance, use self-censorship to conceal problems at the workplace. There are examples of managers telling teachers not to talk about lack of resources or other problems at their school to parents, politicians or media. Also, some schools do not report criminal offences to the police in order to conceal problems. If the school or care centre receive bad publicity, customers, that is parents or patients, will probably choose other alternatives (Börnfelt, 2015, 2021).

From the UK, Hood and Dixon (2016) report that NPM has failed to deliver decreased costs in the public sector. They show that costs in central and local governments have increased considerably since 1980 and the introduction of NPM in the public sector. They have been studying running costs or operational costs '...broadly, the costs of employment, office infrastructure, equipment, and related overhead costs in central government, as opposed to spending on programmes or transfers' (p. 419). The running costs in central government have increased over three decades, even during Margret Thatcher's government, which is highly associated with slashing bureaucracy. The number of civil servants has been cut by a third since 1980, but it has not saved any money. The authors explain the increase of costs for consultancy have risen considerably and services, like IT, have been outsourced to subcontractors. Outsourcing can be explained as the transfer of carrying out production or services to an external provider. An organisation can outsource to a provider within the country or to a provider in another country (Dekker & Koster, 2018).

Internal markets can also result in lower efficiency because of suboptimization. The cost centre tends to see their own unit as more important than the organisation as a whole or to deliver good service to citizens. The units calculate costs and revenues in comparison with other units, which can contribute to an instrumental/economical attitude. Organisational members sell their services rather than giving help to colleagues. NPM with competition and cost cutting is also difficult to combine with equality, professional and ethical judgements. Economic arguments like cutting costs and keeping the

[2] Employees in the Swedish public sector have freedom of expression and a right to anonymously inform media protected by the constitution. There is also a prohibition for the organisation to investigate who is the source and against retaliation, if a person has used his/her right to inform media (Fransson, 2013).

budget collide with the need for care and helping people (Hasselbladh, 2008a, 2008b). Management by objectives through the use of key performance indicators (KPI) to measure and compare efficiency can have dysfunctional effects also in Sweden. In the healthcare sector a common KPI is to measure patient throughput time, which reward quick treatments. This can lead to healthcare managers sift out patients with complicated diagnosis that are difficult and time consuming to treat (Dellve et al., 2013).

Hood and Dixon (2016) report, in line with the argumentation above, that previous studies have highlighted cutting costs in the public sector can have negative effects on good administration in the Weberian sense, that is treating cases equally and fairly according to rules of law. In their own study Hood and Dixon investigated the number of formal complaints to the parliamentary ombudsman about allegations for maladministration, which they define as 'perceptions of poor categorization, careless case-handling or unfair or inconsistent application of rules to cases, as well as other features such as delay and rudeness.' During the period there was a huge rice in the number of complaints, especially in departments dealing with welfare benefits, such as social security. The sharpest rise took place in the 1990s. They also investigated the number of applications for 'permission to apply' (p. 415), which is the first stage in judicial reviews in England and Wales. Also, here the authors found a rise, most notably in the 1990s. The most common cases concerned the criminal justice system, community care, benefits, housing and education. Hood and Dixon conclude that for consistency and fair treatment over the period, since the introduction of NPM, 'the judgement has to be placed somewhere on a spectrum from 'just a bit worse' to 'quite a lot worse.'

Abandoning collegiality, that is joint decision-making by professionals for example by scholars in universities also tend to have negative effects on motivation, job satisfaction and tend to lead to inferior decision-making. Change processes also tend to go slower and are less successful. Accordingly, universities that have kept collegiality at the department level such as Oxford and Cambridge in the UK, are associated with more success. In line with the above joint decision-making tend to improve trust and job satisfaction and increase commitment to decisions (Burnes et al., 2014). These results confirm studies about change processes in organisations in general (see Chapter 6). Academics are also trained to question and critically examine statements, methods, decisions and argumentation, so an open discussion is important for this process to be successful. Therefore, maybe even more than in other organisations, a joint decision-making and collegiality is essential, because it is the very foundation universities are built upon, with the main focus on a collective pursue of knowledge for its own sake (Burnes et al., 2014).

Summary

For a long time, bureaucracy was the main model for organising public authorities. All cases are administered equally and consistently by using a system of rules. In professional organisations like hospitals, courts and schools the professional organisation medel has also been influential. The professionals like medical doctors, university lecturers and teachers have had a lot of power in these organisations. The professionals have a long education and their work is characterised by a low division of labour. Their work is coordinated through standardisation of skills and knowledge, which the professionals develop through their common education and training. Work is also coordinated by mutual adjustment, often labelled collegiality, in a democratic decision-making process. Peer review is used for auditing and quality assurance.

Since the 1980s however, politicians and public administrators have increasingly started to question the power of the professionals. New public management (NPM) was put forward as the new management model with the arguments higher efficiency and cost cutting. The private company competing on a market is seen as an ideal model in NPM. Customers, for example patients, should have the opportunity to choose between different alternatives. As a help to choose, units are compared by key performance indicators and customer satisfaction surveys. The division of labour and coordination are to some extent affected for the professionals by NPM. The line of command and top-down decision-making is emphasised. The collegial decision-making tends to be diminished, which for example has taken place in universities. The professionals also get more administrative tasks.

The research results are mixed regarding the main argument for introducing NPM –improved efficiency, saving costs and increasing quality. However, a number of studies indicate increased costs overall, and lower quality, in the Weberian sense of treating cases equally and fairly. Also, several undesirable side effects are reported, such as grade inflation in Sweden. The schools are competing with grades to attract students. Several studies also point out stressful working conditions in organisations using NPM principles.

Reflection Questions

1. What are possible drawbacks to the peer review system, for instance when university colleagues evaluate each other's research articles?
2. Is it possible to combine the two models: Bureaucracy in the Weberian sense of equal treatment, and competition between welfare organisations introduced through NPM?
3. If you are given the task to specify key performance indicators for primary schools (competing with each other) what indicators would you chose? What are possible side-effects from these indicators?

4. What kind of functions in the public sector is appropriate to expose to competition, and what is not? Some examples: Schools, healthcare centres, the police, the military, legal courts, job centres.

Bibliography

Almqvist, R. M. (2006). *New public management: NPM: Om konkurrensutsättning, kontrakt och kontroll*. Liber.

Bevan, G., & Hood, C. (2006). What's measured is what matters: Targets and gaming in the English public health care system. *Public Administration, 84*(3), 517–538.

Brown, P., Lauder, H., & Ashton, D. (2011). Chapter 5. Digital taylorism. In *The global auction: The broken promises of education, jobs and incomes*. Oxford University Press.

Börnfelt, P.-O. (2015). Kritik på arbetsplatsen – efterfrågas och motarbetas. *Arbetsmarknad Och Arbetsliv, 21*(2), 26–41.

Börnfelt, P.-O. (2021, November 17). Raising concerns at work in the Swedish healthcare and educational sectors: Silence and voice climates. *Employee Responsibilities and Rights Journal*. https://doi.org/10.1007/s10672-021-09396-w

Burnes, B., Wend, P., & Todnem By, R. (2014). The changing face of English universities: Reinventing collegiality for the twenty-first century. *Studies in Higher Education, 39*(6).

Christensen, T., & Lægreid, P. (2002). 1. Introduction. In T. Christensen, & P. Lægreid (Eds.), *New public management: The transformation of ideas and practice*. Ashgate.

Dekker, F., & Koster, F. (2018). Outsourcing in 18 European countries: The role of worker power. *Economic and Industrial Democracy, 39*(3), 481–499.

Dellve, L., Eriksson, A., Fredman, M., & Kullén Engström, A. (2013). Lean i hälso- och sjukvården. In P. Sederblad (Ed.), *Lean i arbetslivet*. Liber.

Finnish Ministry of Education and Culture. (2020). https://minedu.fi/en/basic-education, https://minedu.fi/en/education-system. Accessed September 19, 2022.

Fransson, S. (2013). *Yttrandefrihet och whistleblowing: Om gränserna för anställdas kritikrätt*. Premiss förlag.

Hall, P. (2012). *Managementbyråkrati: Organisationspolitisk makt i svensk offentlig förvaltning*. Liber.

Harvey, D. (2007, March). Neoliberalism as creative destruction. *The Annals of the American Academy, 610*, 21–44.

Hartman, L. (2011). Inledning. In L. Hartman (Ed.), *Konkurrensens konsekvenser: Vad händer med svensk välfärd?* SNS Förlag.

Hasselbladh, H. (2008a). Kapitel 3. Problematiseringens jordmån. In H. Hasselbladh & E. Bejerot (Eds.), *Bortom new public management*. Academia Adacta.

Hasselbladh, H. (2008b). Chapter 4. Kritisk analys av NPM—Bortom koloniseringstesen. In H. Hasselbladh, E. Bejerot, & R. Å. Gustafsson (Eds.), *Bortom new public management*. Academia Adacta.

Hood, C. (1991). A public management for all seasons. *Public Administration, 69*(Spring), 3–19.

Hood, C. (1995). The "new public management" in the 1980s: Variations on a theme. *Accounting, Organizations and Society, 20*(2/3), 93–109.

Hood, C., & Dixon, R. (2016, November). Not what it said on the tin? Reflections on three decades of UK public management reform. *Financial Accountability & Management, 32*(4).

Lægreid, P. (2002). 7. Transforming top civil servant systems. In T. Christensen & P. Lægreid (Eds.), *New public management: The transformation of ideas and practice*. Ashgate.

Löfgren, K., Darrah-Morgan, B., Hall, P., & Alamaa, L. (2022). The rise of a new public bureaucracy in New Zealand. *Administration and Society, 54*(1), 57–86.

Mintzberg, H. (1983). *Structure in fives: Designing effective organizations*. Prentice-Hall.

OECD. (2020). https://www.oecd.org/pisa/. Accessed September 19, 2022.

Olejniczak, M., & Salmon, D. (2014). Workers in German UB II job centers—Stress caused by new public management? *Journal of Workplace Rights, 17*(3–4), 255–282.

Parding, K., Sjögren, F., Petersson, C., & Pekkari, N. (2020). *Organisering av arbete och dess betydelse för hälsa och välbefinnande*. Kunskapssammanställning 2020: 7.

Paulsen, J. M. (2018). Conceptualizing professional commitment-based school strategy: A Finnish perspective. *Nordic Journal of Comparative and International Education, 2*(2–3), 72–85.

Pollitt, C. (2016). Managerialism redux. *Financial Accountability & Management, 32*(4), 429–447.

Pollitt, C., & Bouckaert, G. (2017). *Public management reform: A comparative analysis—Into the age of austerity*. Oxford University Press.

Pollitt, C., & Dan, S. (2011). *The impacts of the new public management in Europe: A meta-analysis*. European Union: COCOPS Deliverable 1.1.

Sahlin, K. (2010). Den svåra konsten att leda universitet och högskolor. In M. Lindh & J. Sundeen (Eds.), *Vetenskap för profession. Rapport nr 15. Från Högskolan i Borås till Humboldt* (Vol. 1, pp. 37–56). Högskolan i Borås.

Samuelsson, K., & Lindblad, S. (2015). School management, cultures of teaching and student outcomes: Comparing the cases of Finland and Sweden. *Teaching and Teacher Education, 49*, 168–177.

Schnall, P., Dobson, M., & Landsbergis, P. (2016). Globalization, work and cardiovascular disease. *International Journal of Health Services, 46*(4), 656–692.

Szebehely, M. (2011). Insatser för äldre och funktionshindrade i privat regi. In L. Hartman (Ed.), *Konkurrensens konsekvenser: Vad händer med svensk välfärd?* SNS förlag.

Varjo, J., & Kalalahti, M. (2015). The conceivable benefits of being comprehensive – Finnish Local Education Authorities on recognising and controlling the social costs of school choice. *European Educational Research Journal, 14*(3–4), 312–330.

Vlachos, J. (2011). Friskolor i förändring. In L. Hartman (Ed.), *Konkurrensens konsekvener: Vad händer med svensk välfärd?* SNS.

CHAPTER 8

Network Organising

Learning Objectives

This chapter should provide you with knowledge about:

- Different ways organisations are using networks for coordination and creating value in the global economy.
- Some of the downsides of global supply chains for workers.
- The concept of open innovation, and how networks of actors can cooperate to create innovations.
- What the gig economy and platform organisations are.
- What consequences the gig economy has for gig workers.

The Network Society and Global Supply Chains

Today it is said that we live in a network society where internet makes it possible to communicate globally (Castells, 2000). This, so-called *new economy*, is based on information, which means creating value using information and knowledge. The network society is global. Production, consumption, capital, work, raw material and management is taking place globally through a network of organisations. The economy has however been global for a long time, as was mentioned in Chapter 1. People have traded with other parts of the world for thousands of years. The new is that activities and communication is taking place globally in real time with the aid of internet. Business projects take place in a network of financial transactions, information, production sites, labour pools, markets and companies. 'The network enterprise, as a new form of business organization, is made of networks of firms or subunits

P-O Börnfelt, *Work Organisation in Practice*,
https://doi.org/10.1007/978-3-031-21667-1_8

of firms organized around the performance of a business project.' (Castells, 2000, p. 695).

It is very common nowadays for companies to use subcontractors for a range of services and parts of the production. This is often labelled outsourcing, which can be explained as the transfer of carrying out production or services to an external provider. If the subcontractor is in another country the term offshored is often used. Examples of activities that often are outsourced, within a country or to other countries, are manufacturing, product development, marketing, IT and sales. Outsourcing occurs both in the private and in the public sector and has increased substantially all over the world. Outsourcing increased by nearly 30% from 1970 to 1990 in ten OECD countries. Outsourcing of manufacturing activities grew by around 30% in Euro countries between 1995 and 2004 (Dekker & Koster, 2018).

These networks of suppliers form global supply chains, and at the top of the chains there are lead companies, often large and powerful multinational companies. The lead companies coordinate production and decide the terms for the companies in the supply chain. Due to their powerful position, the lead companies often have a major impact on the suppliers' work organisation and working conditions (Anner et al., 2020; Wright & Caine, 2015). There are companies that do not have any own production at all. One example is Nike which has split their brand from the actual production of their sport gear. All production of Nike's sport shoes and other gear is taking place in their global supply chain, thereby avoiding direct responsibility for workers' health and well-being (Anner et al., 2020). Nike has received extensive critique over the years for using suppliers which breach human rights. One example is reported by Washington Post (Fifield, 2020): One of Nike´s suppliers in China since 30 years, Quingdao Taekwang Shoes Co., is using forced labour. Hundreds of Uighurs from the Xinjiang region have been sent to the factory against their will to produce Nike's shoes. Nike is however not the only company that use suppliers which break human rights. According to a coalition of more than 180 human watch groups, many of the leading fashion brands use cotton from the Xinjiang region in China. China has a forced labour system in Xinjiang where Uighurs, and other Muslim people are forced to work in cotton farms and factories. China is the largest producer of cotton in the world and over 80% of the cotton in China is produced in Xinjiang (Kelly, 2020).

The increasing global competition and demands from the financial market for higher profits drive outsourcing of production and service to low wage countries and so-called Free Trade Zones (FTZ). For example, FTZs in Mexico, Latin America, Philippines, China and India companies do not need to pay tax on their profits (Schnall et al., 2016). These zones are also-called Export Processing Zones or Free Ports. Tax benefits are given, sometimes tax freedom as mentioned above, and health and safety regulations are eased or not enforced in order to attract foreign investments. FTZs have increased substantially over the last decades. In 1975 there were 79 FTZs in 25 countries. In 2004 the number of FTZs had exceeded 5000 in over 100 countries.

Around three quarters of the workers in FTZs work in China (Kjellström et al., 2007). Thus, one reason for outsourcing is to decrease labour costs. Other reasons for outsourcing are that the organisation lacks competence in a specific area, a desire to avoid legal obligations for employees, greater numerical flexibility for fluctuation in demand. Also, large powerful companies can select suppliers and locations which offer low taxes, lower labour standards, where there is no collective bargaining, and none or weak unions. In the public sector outsourcing has been driven by ideas from new public management (Anner et al., 2020; Dekker & Koster, 2018; Donaghey et al., 2014; Wright & Caine, 2015).

Workers and unions are also increasingly using networks to defend human rights and improve working conditions. Global networks of unions have been formed, for instance the International Trade Union Confederation. There are also non-union networks, such as Self-Employed Womens' Association in India and Ubers' drivers strikes in many countries over pay and conditions 2019, prior to Uber's public offering. Furthermore, a number of different autonomous groups can form a loosely connected network around common objectives. Such networks can consist of unions, members of the public, civil society organisation, governments and informal groups of workers. The network can for instance highlight breaches of labour rights and bring them to public attention, and connect with each other in the network, using digital communication and media (Anner et al., 2020). One example of such a network is the Accord for Fire and Building Safety in Bangladesh, which was formed after the Rana Plaza garment factory collapse in Bangladesh 2013 where over 1000 workers were killed and more than 2500 were wounded. Bangladeshi unions, international unions, and labour rights NGOs cooperated in negotiation with over 200 garment buyers from North America, Europe and Asia. The negotiations led to a collective agreement, the Accord programme, where the purchasers promised to buy from Bangladesh for at least two years, which made it easier for garment employers in Bangladesh to invest in workplace safety as they had a steady stream of orders coming in. Furthermore, the buyers are bound to pay for some safety improvement and the suppliers have to include workers and union representatives in health and safety committees. A committee of unions, companies and the International Labour Organization (ILO) as a neutral chair overseas that the participants follow the Accord program (Anner et al., 2020; Donaghey & Reineke, 2018; Papadakis, 2021).

Open Innovation

Companies can connect suppliers, customers and their own employees in a network in order to develop products or services. The network can be beneficial for innovation and cut develop times considerably. This kind of innovation process in a network, often labelled open innovation, can therefore be profitable for companies (Lakemond & Tell, 2016). Henry Chesbrough is often mentioned as the father of open innovation, see for instance a review of the field by Bigliardi et al. (2020). Since the publication of his book in 2003 there has been considerable attention for the concept both from scholars and practitioners. The main argument for the use of open innovation, according scholars active in the field, it is not enough for companies any longer to innovate within its own borders. Companies need to collaborate with external actors, to exchange ideas, knowledge, and technologies in order to stay competitive in a global fast-moving economy. Examples of external actors to network with are competitors, customers, suppliers, universities and research centres. The first use of open innovation was first reported from high tech industries like software, telecommunications, and electronics followed by more low-tech companies. According to some scholars open innovation is driven by competition intensity, globalisation and the speed of technology development within the business segment. Some studies have focused effects from open innovations and the results are mixed. Some results point towards increased innovative performance, but other studies highlight that too much open innovation can be negative for firm performance (Bigliardi et al., 2020).

Open innovation is mostly used in connection to organisations systematically searching for knowledge from external actors. However, organisations might also allow internal knowledge to transfer to actors outside the organisation for others to use. Research about open innovation differs between inflow and outflow of knowledge, monetary and non-monetary transactions. An example of non-monetary inflow of knowledge is when companies ask their customers for help to develop their products and services (Brunswicker & Chesbrough, 2018; Lakemond & Tell, 2016). Some companies are investing substantially in open innovation, for instance having several employees working full-time managing open innovation (Brunswicker & Chesbrough, 2018).

One perspective is made up of a totally open innovation process where no one owns the innovation. This perspective is based on democracy and public good. Anyone can use the knowledge and it is free to use. Well-known examples are the encyclopedia Wikipedia and software with open-source code such as Linux (Lakemond & Tell, 2016). The label crowdsourcing is used to describe outsourcing work to a large number of people, which will be explored further in the gig economy section below. Crowdsourcing is also used in open innovation. As mentioned above, in the totally open innovation perspective, a large number of users cooperate to develop for instance Wikipedia. Crowdsourcing is also used for the purpose of social innovation, which aims is to solve social problems and finding novel solutions benefitting the society rather than commercial interests. In any crowdsourcing there are three actors, an organisation that provide a digital platform and the rules for interaction, creators and consumers. The creators are people outside the organisation who bring in suggestions for innovations and they sometimes are encouraged to cooperate with each other by the organisation. The consumers are the people who buy or use the new service or product. The organisation can be for-profit on non-profit. An example of a social innovation platform (non-profit) is OpenIDEO, where people cooperate to innovate in order to tackle social challenges (Kohler & Chesbrough, 2019).

However, in the commercial perspective the innovation process is partially open where companies charge users to use their knowledge and sometimes also pay for bringing in knowledge to the organisation (Lakemond & Tell, 2016). An example of for-profit crowdsourcing is the platform InnoCentive where companies present problems they want to find solutions to. A cash reward is given for the best solution in an open call to a large group of unknown people (Kohler & Chesbrough, 2019).

Another example how open innovation can be organised is the road safety competence and research centre SAFER in Gothenburg, Sweden. 30 organisations from universities, private companies and the public sector work together on research and development of road safety. SAFER, which works with both inflow and outflow of knowledge, is a competence centre at Chalmers Technical University. The participating organisations have a common interest to develop knowledge about road safety and they contribute with resources to the centre. Most of the people working at the centre are employed by the participating organisations (Elmquist, Ollila & Yström, 2016).

The Gig Economy: Platform Organisations

A new kind of network organising is the so-called platform economy, also labelled gig economy where digital platforms are used by "employers" or clients to advertise work tasks and where workers can find work tasks (Wood et al., 2019). "The gig economy consists both of work that is transacted via platforms but delivered locally and thus requires the worker to be physically present, and work that is transacted and delivered remotely via platforms" (Ibid., p. 57). Most workers who receive work through these platforms are independent contractors (De Stefano, 2016). The first category, where the worker is physically present; "…is a form of work in which the execution of traditional working activities such as transport, cleaning and running errands, but also forms of clerical work, is channelled through apps managed by firms that also intervene in setting minimum quality standards of service and in the selection and management of the workforce…" The second category can be understood as"working activities that imply completing a series of tasks through online platforms…Typically, these platforms put in contact an indefinite number of organisations and individuals through the internet, potentially allowing connecting clients and workers on a global basis." (Ibid., p. 1). From an employer perspective this can be labelled online outsourcing. This online work is often referred to as crowdwork. Companies have, via the digital platforms access to a large number of workers (a crowd) all over the globe. Crowdwork arose in the beginning of 2000 as web-based companies needed help with digital work tasks. In the beginning the platforms merely used Internet as a way to find workers who could perform work tasks from home instead of a workplace. An early example was the company LiveOps in the US which used home workers for call centre tasks instead of having employees in an office, thereby saving costs for running an office (Berg et al., 2018, Chapter 1). Combining the words outsourcing and crowd Jeff Howe, a Wired magazine writer, 2005 coined the term crowdsourcing which refers to: "The act of taking a job once performed by a designated agent (an employee, free-lancer or a separate firm) and outsourcing it to an undefined, generally large group of people through the form of an open call, which usually takes place over the Internet." (Berg et al., 2018, p. 3).

Crowdwork, following Heeks (2017), can be labelled the digital gig economy. Examples of digital platforms are Upwork, Amazon Mechanical Turk, CloudFlower, and Freelancer. The first category hence can be labelled the physical gig economy and examples of platforms are Uber, Airbnb and TaskRabbit (Ibid.; Wood et al., 2019).

The workers in the platform economy have no formal job security. Their job can be terminated without notice. The worker can easily be replaced by someone else and their income is uncertain. The work can thus be categorised as precarious. Arne Kalleberg (2009, p. 1) defines precarious work as "...employment that is uncertain, unpredictable, and risky from the point of view of the worker". Precarious work has become more common the last few decades. Guy Standing (2011) has categorised the growing group of people without any employment security competing for low paid, short-term jobs as a new class; the precariat.[1]

The reasons for the growth of precarious work are, according to Kalleberg (2009), neoliberal principles such as deregulation of the labour market towards a more flexible workforce and market driven solutions, declining trade union power, a global economy, and development of new technology.

As the workers in the gig economy to a large extent are independent contractors the "employer" avoids laws and regulations that otherwise regulates the labour market such as minimum wage laws, sick pay, holidays, social security contribution and insurance. Costs for technical infrastructure, for instance computers or a car are shifted to the worker (De Stefano, 2016; Heeks, 2017). According to Heeks (2017) the benefits for employers from the digital platform economy are lower costs, greater flexibility and access to a wider (global) skills pool. The first two factors should also apply for the physical gig economy. Although the number of workers in the gig economy is relatively few, it is growing fast. The annual growth rate is estimated to be 26% (Wood et al., 2019).

[1] In his book; *The precariat. The new dangerous class*, Guy Standing argues that the growing number of people with precarious low paid work competing with other people for short-term jobs tend to feel worried, frustrated and angry. Therefore, the precariat is an easy target for new fascist populistic partied that blame immigrants for unemployment and other problems in the society which in reality have more structural causes; neoliberal politics and practices.

Division of Labour, Coordination and Control of Work in the Platform Organisation

At digital crowdwork platforms simple work tasks are advertised by requesters to a large number of people in many parts of the world, work tasks are retrieved and evaluated by requesters, and workers are paid for their work. Conversely, these crowd platforms provide an infrastructure for workers to get an overview of work tasks provided by requesters, deliver work when completed and receive payment for the work (Berg et al., 2018).

There is both low and high skilled job in the digital gig economy. I am using the term platform organisation for the kind of work organisation the platform economy is built upon. Examples of platforms for fragmented low skilled work, sometimes called microwork are Amazon Mechanical Turk (AMT), CloudFlower, Clickworker, and Microworkers. These digital platforms are referred to as microwork platforms in this text.

Examples of work tasks on microwork platforms are:

- Finding information, like addresses or Email-addresses.
- Categorisation, for instance selecting all images that have traffic lights in them.
- Creating fake traffic on websites and "liking" them or advertised products and services.
- Rating products or services such as video quality, restaurants, and hotels.
- Machine learning. Helping algorithms to learn, for instance by recording short videos with everyday objects.
- Transcribe information from audio, video or photos.
- Completion of surveys, product and app testing, market research, and participating in experiments.

Initially microwork platforms, like one of the oldest microwork platforms AMT, emerged due to failure by artificial intelligence. Customers at Amazon's online marketplace where irritated by finding the same product, but from different vendors, when they did a product search. Amazon could not solve this through artificial intelligence. Human intelligence was needed to classify the nuances of images, texts and sounds. In early 2000 Amazon started using their employees for identifying and filter out duplicates of products at their marketplace. Also, Amazon soon opened up this platform, with a number of different simple tasks, to external workers (Berg et al., 2018; Heeks, 2017, Chapter 1–2). At the digital platform Upwork both microwork and more skilled tasks are distributed (Wood et al., 2019) and at Freelancer skilled work is channelled, like developing software, web design, translation, data analytics, marketing, and administrative support (Heeks, 2017).

Work on crowdwork platforms is coordinated and controlled by algorithmic management, monitoring workers, and in some cases by bidding for jobs. Digital technologies are built on algorithms, "…sets of defined steps structured to process instructions/data to produce an output... (Kitchin, 2017, p. 14). Algorithms are used in automated decision-making processes. Following Rosenblat and Stark (2016), algorithmic management can be understood as automated control mechanisms which aim to influence workers' behaviour and practises.

Managers are not directly coordinating and controlling work in the platform organisation, instead algorithmic management is used for coordination and control. The workers need to interact with a system. Furthermore, the algorithms have very low transparency—it is rarely possible for the worker to find out which criteria the algorithms are basing their automated decisions on. The platform companies tend to keep these criteria secret. The algorithm on crowd platforms controls the work process, evaluates the worker's submissions and calculates the payment. Workers often complain about unfair rejections of completed work, with the consequence of no payment. Rejected work can also lead to that the worker is deactivated, as there often is a threshold for approval rate. There is no way for the worker to find out about the reason for the rejection, due to the "black box" nature of algorithms. It is also often very difficult for workers to contact the platform management about any concerns (Berg et al., 2018).

Platforms use algorithm generated ranking of workers, based on rating from clients, in order to channel work away from those who underscore. At Uber workers can even be deactivated from the platform if they do not reach a certain level of customer satisfaction or ride acceptance rate (Ravenelle, 2017; Rosenblat & Stark, 2016; Wood et al., 2019). Furthermore, some digital platforms are monitoring number of keystrokes, mouse clicks and also take shots of the computer screen. Also, platforms like Upwork, uses a bidding system to channel work. All workers can see each other's bids which result in a downward pressure on pay levels (Wood et al., 2019).

Consequences for Platform Workers and Initiatives for Fairer Work

Most crowd workers (microwork) seem to be satisfied with their work according to an ILO report. Above all, the reasons people state are flexibility and the opportunity to work from home (Berg et al., 2018). Studies have reported some benefits from a worker perspective in development countries. The work is typically outsourced from the northern hemisphere to development countries. Heeks (2017) who has conducted a literature review on the digital gig economy, also concludes that workers from development countries are on the whole happy with their work. In general, they earn more compared to the local labour market. There are more opportunities for employment as work locally tend to be in short supply, and the location and timing of work is flexible. However, studies also report many negative effects. Workers in the northern hemisphere complain about low pay, not seldom under the minimum wage. Jobs are unsecure as there is no guarantee for getting work and as the workers are not formally employed, they lack social security benefits and are not covered by labour laws (Berg et al., 2018; Heeks, 2017). Workers not seldom need to work long hours and/or to tight deadlines, leading to work intensification. As a result, workers often report exhaustion and pain in the body. In order to earn a decent income, workers need to have several jobs, and promise to meet tighter deadlines than their competitors. They also need to do unpaid work, like bidding for work, and learning new skills in order to get payed work. In order to get jobs workers are dependent on a good reputation, as the algorithmic control mechanisms channel away work from workers with less good customer satisfaction. Also, there is often an oversupply of workers. Many digital platform workers therefore struggle to get an income they can live on. Furthermore, working from home can lead to social isolation, as you do not have any colleagues. Platform workers from development countries often have clients in the US, Europe and Australia, so they need to adapt to theses time zones. For this reason, workers often need to work at night leading to sleep deprivation (Wood et al., 2019). Furthermore, workers have to bear all the cost for technical infrastructure (E.g. computer and internet), competence development, sick leave, holidays, pensions and insurance (Heeks, 2017).

There are some recent initiatives to regulate digital platforms. In 2021 the European Commission made a proposal for improving the working conditions for workers on digital platforms in EU. One of the aims is that more workers on digital platforms should be classified as employed, thus have social and labour rights such as minimum wage, collective bargaining, health protection, sick leave and paid holiday. Another aim of the legal framework is to increase transparency in algorithm management and to give workers right to contest automatic decisions (European Commission, 2021).

There are also a number of initiatives from platform workers to improve their conditions. Gig drivers and delivery workers have been striking in many countries demanding better pay and working conditions. Groups of workers, their advocates and unions in different parts of the world have made lawsuits concerning classification as contractor, rather than employed, failures to pay minimum wage, and lack of transparency on management decisions hidden by algorithms. In the UK the Supreme Court in the beginning of 2021 issued a judgement that Uber drivers are to be categorised as workers, not as self-employed. It could mean that Uber drivers in the UK are intitled to minimum wage and holiday pay. Uber appealed to the highest level, the Supreme Court, after having lost in previous courts. It took a number of drivers and App Drivers & Couriers Union over four years to reach this final verdict (BBC, 2021). Trade unions have been negotiating with platform companies in different parts of the world regarding worker's rights. An example is from Sweden, where the food delivery platform Foodora recently signed a collective agreement with Transportarbetareförbundet (the Transport workers union) after one year of negotiations (Lag & Avtal, February 25, 2021). Furthermore, there are several online worker discussion forums and initiatives that allow workers to rate requesters such as Turkopticon for workers at AMT, run by a third party. A number of unions are also working for improvements on workers' rights. FairCrowdWork.org is run by IG Metall in Germany, The Austrian Chamber of Labour and the Swedish white-collar union Unionen. FairCrowdWork.org provide information about legal rights and has ratings of larger crowd platforms. There is also a Code of Conduct for crowd sourcing launched by the German testing platform Testbirds, and an Ombuds Office initiated by IG Metall and a number of German crowd platforms. The Ombuds Office resolves disputes between platforms and workers by consensus (Berg et al., 2018; FairCrowdWork, 2021; Bacchi & Asher-Schapiro, 2020).

The authors of the ILO report, Digital labour platforms and the future of work: Towards decent work in the online world, suggest a number of criteria for fairer crowd work, such as:

- Workers should be classified as employees if they are employees in practise.
- Workers should have freedom of association and thus the right to be a member of a union, and for collective bargaining.
- Platform employees should at least receive the minimum wage in the worker's location. For self-employed workers the pay must be higher as they have additional costs, for instance for infrastructure and social benefits such as holiday, sick leave and pension.
- If workers are self-employed, they should be free to choose work tasks and when to work.
- Clients and platforms should reply to workers communication promptly and politely.
- Workers should get information about who the clients are and the purpose of the work.
- Find a way to adapt the social security system so all kinds of "employees" are covered, such as self-employed platform workers (Berg et al., 2018, chapter 6).

Summary

The society of today is sometimes called a network society. The internet makes it possible to communicate globally. This network based *new economy*, is based on information, which means creating value using information and knowledge. The management of work, raw material, capital, production, development of new product and services, and consumption, is taking place globally through a network of people and organisations.

Different organisations can cooperate, perform different part of a business and work together in value adding processes. This structure is sometimes called a network organisation. In the concept open innovation, organisations cooperate with suppliers, competitors, universities, research centres, customers, and other people outside the organisation to develop products and service. Open innovation builds upon open communication and knowledge sharing between organisations and between organisations and people.

The platform economy, a variant of network organising, uses online platforms to coordinate and control contract workers. The platforms tend to use algorithmic management, based on customer rating and other performance indicators to channel away work for the workers who underscore. The work tasks in the platform economy vary a lot, from very narrow and simple tasks, so-called microwork, e g. finding addresses on internet and completing surveys, to broader high-skilled tasks such as developing software or other new product and services.

All platform work is however considered as precarious work, as the self-employed contractors can lose their job without notice, the workers lack social security benefits, and have to cover cost for insurances, technical infrastructure such as computers or vehicles.

Reflection Questions

1. Why are a lot of companies using outsourcing?
2. What can you, unions and people in general do to prevent or decrease the use of forced labour and hazardous working conditions in global supply chains?
3. What are pros and cons for companies to use open innovation?
4. How would you feel if you would be a gig worker?
5. What criteria should you use to categorise someone as employed versos self-employed?

Bibliography

Anner, M., Fischer-Daly, M., & Maffie, M. (2020). Fissured employment and network bargaining: Emerging employment relations dynamics in a contingent world of work. *Industrial and Labor Relations Review*, Published online October 14: https://journals.sagepub.com/doi/full/10.1177/0019793920964180

BBC. (2021). https://www.bbc.com/news/business-56123668. Accessed April 19, 2023.

Bacchi, U., & Asher-Schapiro, A. (2020). The gig workers taking legal action to regain control of their data. *Reuters*. https://www.reuters.com/article/global-workers-data-idUSKBN28Q0OY

Berg, J., Furrer, M., Harmon, E., Rani, U., & Silberman, M. S. (2018). *Digital labour platforms and the future of work: Towards decent work in the online world*. International Labour Organization.

Bigliardi, B., Ferraro, G., Filippelli, S., & Galati, F. (2020). The past, present and future of open innovation. *European Journal of Innovation Management*.

Brunswicker, S., & Chesbrough, H. (2018). The adoption of open innovation in large firms. *Research-Technology Management, 61*(1), 35–45.

Castells, M. (2000). Toward a sociology of the network society. *Contemporary Sociology, 29*(5), 693–699.
Dekker, F., & Koster, F. (2018). Outsourcing in 18 European countries: The role of worker power. *Economic and Industrial Democracy, 39*(3), 481–499.
De Stefano, V. (2016). The rise of the just-in-time workforce: On-demand work, crowdwork and labour protection in the gig-economy. *Conditions of Work and Employment Series* (Vol. 71). ILO.
Donaghey, J., Reinecke, J., Niforou, C., & Lawson, B. (2014). From employment relations to consumption relations: Balancing labor governance in global supply chains. *Human Resource Management, 53*(2), 229–252.
Donaghey, J., & Reinecke, J. (2018). When industrial democracy meets corporate social responsibility: A comparison of the Bangladesh Accord and Alliance as responses to the Rana Plaza Disaster. *British Journal of Industrial Relations, 56*(1), 14–42.
Elmquist, M., Ollila, S., & Yström, A. (2016). Arenor för öppen innovation: organisering av gemensamt kunskapsskapande. In N. Lakemond & F. Tell (Eds.), *Öppen innovation – i teori och praktik*. Studentlitteratur.
European Commission. (2021). Commission proposals to improve the working conditions of people working through digital labour platforms. https://ec.europa.eu/commission/presscorner/detail/en/ip_21_6605. Accessed September 19, 2022.
FairCrowdWork. (2021). http://faircrowd.work. Accessed September 19, 2022.
Fifield, A. (2020, February 29). China compels Uighurs to work in shoe factory that supplies Nike. *Washington Post*.
Heeks, R. (2017). Decent work and the digital gig economy: A developing country perspective on employment impacts and standards in online outsourcing, crowdwork, etc. *Development Informatics Working Paper Series* (Vol. 71). Centre for Development Informatics, University of Manchester.
Kalleberg, A. L. (2009, February). Precarious work, insecure workers: Employment relations in transition. *American Sociological Review, 74*, 1–22.
Kelly, A. (2020, July 23). 'Virtually entire' fashion industry complicit in Uighur forced labour, say rights groups. *The Guardian*.
Kitchin, R. (2017). Thinking critically about and researching algorithms. *Information, Communication & Society, 20*(1), 14–29.
Kjellström, T., Håkansta, C., & Hogstedt, C. (2007). Globalisation and public health. *Scandinavian Journal of Public Health, 35*(Suppl 70), 7–13.
Kohler, T., & Chesbrough, H. (2019). From collaborative community to competitive market: The quest to build a crowdsourcing platform.
Lag, & Avtal. (2021). https://www.lag-avtal.se/nyheter/foodora-och-transport-tecknar-kollektivavtal/1472769. Accessed April 19, 2023.
Lakemond, N., & Tell, F. (2016). Öppen innovation i teori och praktik: en kort introduktion. In N. Lakemond & F. Tell (Eds.), *Öppen innovation – i teori och praktik*. Studentlitteratur.
Papadakis, K. (2021). 4. A short history and future prospects of cross-border social dialogue and global industrial relations agreements. In G. Delautre, E. Echeverría Manrique, & C. Fenwick (Eds.), *Decent work in a globalized economy: Lessons from public and private initiatives*. International Labour Office.
Ravenelle, A. (2017, July). Sharing economy workers: Selling, not sharing. *Cambridge Journal of Regions Economy and Society*, 1–15.

Rosenblat, A., & Stark, L. (2016). Algorithmic labor and information asymmetries: A case study of uber's drivers. *International Journal of Communication, 10*, 3758–3784.

Schnall, P., Dobson, M., & Landsbergis, P. (2016). Globalization, work and cardiovascular desease. *International Journal of Health Services, 46*(4), 656–692.

Standing, G. (2011). *The precariat: The new dangerous class*. Bloomsbury Academic.

Wood, A. J., Graham, M., Lehdonvirta, V., & Hjorth, I. (2019). Good gig, bad gig: Autonomy and algorithmic control in the global gig economy. *Work, Employment and Society, 33*(1), 56–75.

Wright, C. F., & Kaine, S. (2015). Supply chains, production networks and the employment relationship. *Journal of Industrial Relations, 57*(4), 483–501.

CHAPTER 9

A Changing Working Life—Both Up-Skilling and Down-Skilling, More Pressure and Control

Learning Objectives

This chapter should provide you with knowledge about:

- The changes that have taken place the last decades regarding the introduction of new work organisation models and management concepts, and the effects on working life.
- The increase of sophisticated coordination and control mechanisms, often in combination, to control and monitor workers.
- How dominant contemporary management concepts increase demands and pressure on workers, leading to increased stress related ill-health.

Introduction

This is a concluding chapter on a macro (society) level following the main structure of the book—the division of work and coordination/control methods. It is often said that we nowadays live in a knowledge society, where work has been up-skilled, that is a decreased division of labour. However, there is also, during the last few decades signs of polarisation, both increased up-skilling for some people and down-skilling for others. Deregulations, part of the neoliberal agenda, and a more global economy have led to a substantial growth of financial markets, which in turn has resulted in increased demand from investors for higher and faster return of investment. These changes have laid the ground for new management models such as lean production, time based management, business process reengineering, new public management, internal markets, high commitment workplaces and corporate culture. There are many indications that these models have resulted in increased demands and

P-O Börnfelt, *Work Organisation in Practice*,
https://doi.org/10.1007/978-3-031-21667-1_9

pressure on workers with the aid of an elaborate arsenal of coordination and control mechanisms.

Polarisation—Both Up-Skilling and Down-Skilling

Working life researchers agree that there have been substantial changes in the society the last decades and that these changes have affected working life in several ways. The international trade of products and services has increased, which is often labelled globalisation. One consequence of globalisation is that un-skilled manufacturing work often is outsourced to low wage countries. Technological development has also resulted in automatization of simple and repetitive tasks. Especially IT-technology has led to higher efficiency and also to more skilled work. These changes have decreased demand for low-skilled labour in the western world manufacturing industry. People are generally also nowadays more educated and less inclined to take monotonous and hazardous work. Several authors have stated that we now live in a knowledge society and/or a post-industrial society. They argue that we have left the Fordistic repetitive work behind us and that it has been replaced by more skilled work. This conclusion is however somewhat exaggerated, but studies show that production work have decreased and high-skilled jobs have increased substantially. For example, Sweden had 1.2 million production workers in 1965, compared to half that number today. Higher skilled jobs have risen in the Anglo-Saxon, Continental and Nordic countries from 7–15% in the 1950s to 32–40% in 2009. However, since the 1990s a trend of polarisation can be seen in several countries, where both low-skilled and high-skilled work are increasing. In the US the number of low paid jobs in the service industry, such as restaurants and retail, have increased. A similar trend can be seen in Europe. Polarisation is especially evident in Germany, the Netherlands, France, Ireland and Cyprus, and to some extent in the UK. Also in Sweden there is a polarisation tendency after the millennium shift (Åberg, 2015; Gallie, 2017).

More Sophisticated Control Mechanisms

In the classical Tayloristic and Fordistic manufacturing work the management was solely interested in workers performing their simple and repetitive tasks in an orderly and disciplined way. The workers were controlled by foremen and in Ford's factories the work pace was also controlled by the assembly line. People were in this organisation more or less reduced to a cog in a machine. Many new management concepts however, emphasize that organisations need to use the whole capacity of people, not only hands, but also mind and heart (Warhurst & Thompson, 1998). With this perspective, control mechanisms have also become more sophisticated in today's work organisations. Managerial knowledge has also grown about different methods and approaches to control and coordinate workers in order to increase efficiency and profits.

Control and power can however also be analysed from an ethical perspective. How much can or should organisations control workers? What choices should be made between individual freedom and taking part in collective contexts (Kunda, 1992, pp. 14–15)? What rights for privacy should workers have in order to maintain human dignity? When is surveillance getting abusive?

When comparing coordination and control mechanisms, used in the six whole work organisation models[1] presented in this book, substantial differences are highlighted. In Taylorism and Fordism work is coordinated and controlled by foremen giving instructions and orders (direct supervision), but also standardised tasks and formal work assignments. Furthermore, in Fordism control of the work pace is added through the assembly line. Coordination and control mechanisms in bureaucracy is mainly a system of rules and formal work assignments. In the sociotechnical work organisation work is coordinated through mutual adjustment in self-directed working groups, but also management by objectives where the groups to a large extent set their own objectives. Professional organisations use standardisation of skills as coordination, which medical doctors and teachers acquire through their common education and training. The professionals also use mutual adjustment, for example in evaluation of work accomplishments, such as research articles which are peer reviewed. In lean production an extensive arsenal of coordination and control mechanisms is used. Lean production is based on the coordination and control principles of Fordism. Other methods are added such as more technological control mechanisms, internal markets, management by objectives, visualisation (visualising workers and work processes), motivation and control through emotions (competition, shame and pride). Lean production seems to aim at total control of workers behaviour, work pace, norms, attitudes and feelings. This type of organisation has been referred to as 'The high-surveillance firm' (Procter, 2005). Another label could be total control management (TCM). As lean production is one of the most used work organisation models today one can therefore assume that control systems in working life have become more elaborate and sophisticated. In Table 9.1 we can see that the number of coordination and control mechanisms are seven in lean production compared with for example two in the bureaucracy and the sociotechnical (ST) model.

Management by Objectives (MBO), Cultural Engineering, Digital Taylorism, Algorithmic Management and the Introduction of Competition in the Public Sector.

Some management authors claim that organisations have left the era of control and instead workplaces are characterised by high commitment, thus taking a harmony perspective on organisations. According to this perspective managers and workers develop relations based on trust, a shared vision and objectives.

[1] Whole work organisation models refer to theories that cover how work is divided, coordinated and controlled.

Table 9.1 Coordination and control mechanisms in six work organisation models

Coordination/ control	*Taylorism*	*Fordism*	*ST*	*Bureau-cracy*	*Prof org*	*Lean production*
Direct supervision	x	x				x
Mutual adjustment			x		x	
Standardised tasks	x	x				x
Formal assignments	x	x		x		
Standardised skills				x[2]	x	
System of rules				x		
Technology		x				x
Management by objectives			x			x
Internal market						x
Visualisation						x
Emotions						x

In these, so-called, high commitment workplaces some authors argue that workers and managers share the same interest, so control is not needed (E g. Walton, 1985). A more critical analysis might however reveal that for example so-called high commitment workplaces have not ended control, but rather control mechanisms have changed in character in many organisations, from direct supervision to other forms of control, like influencing the organisational culture. Furthermore, digital surveillance, algorithmic management, and other forms of monitoring are getting increasingly popular in many organisations.

Management by objectives (MBO) is an example of a management concept which is based on shared objectives between management and workers and intrinsic motivation, thus focused on organisational commitment. MBO is a very common coordination method in modern organisations. It is for example used in the sociotechnical model and in lean production. Peter Drucker (E g. 1976) is often mentioned as a prominent author on MBO. Drucker wanted to solve two organisational problems: (1) The work of the individual is isolated from the overall goals of the organisation (as for example in the

[2] Like in the professional organisation work is coordinated by standardisation of skills in some bureaucratic organisations such as law courts. Judges and lawyers have long education and training where they acquire shared knowledge. However, standardised skills is not a coordinating mechanism in all bureaucratic organisations. For example in most private owned organisations with a bureaucratic structure workers have often different background and education.

bureaucracy). (2) Managers spent far too much time managing by direct supervision (as in Taylorism). Using MBO, departments and people have more freedom to take initiatives and set their own goals. According to Drucker MBO should result in worker commitment and responsibility, in order to make self-responsibility possible. People work toward the overall objectives and use self-control. Workers decide themselves how to achieve the objectives. MBO starts with top management formulating distinct organisational objectives. Then the different departments break down the objectives and decide what strategies to use to reach their objectives. The department have more specific objectives, but they must relate to the overall objectives. Each department can decide what objectives and strategies to focus more on than other organisational objectives. The objectives should be measurable and the departments should evaluate to what extent the objectives are reached. Evaluation of the objectives is also a learning process where the departments can change their objectives and strategies (Drucker, 1976; Røvik, 1998, pp. 51–53).

Management can also try to create commitment with the help of organisational culture. In management literature about organisational culture the assumption is made that the culture is possible to change by management. There are many different definitions of organisational culture, but several definitions share the following characteristics: '...shared rules governing cognitive and affective aspects of membership in an organization...shared meanings, assumptions, norms, and values that govern work-related behaviour...' (Kunda, 1992, p. 8). It can however be questioned if an organisation has one coherent culture. An organisation, especially if it is a large one, have many different groups with different interests, norms and identities. There are for example different occupations, positions in the hierarchy, blue-collar, and white-collar workers (Alvesson, 2003).

Gideon Kunda (1992, Chapter 1) uses the concept cultural engineering from a critical perspective. He describes different measures the 'Tech company' takes to tie employees emotionally to the organisation. The Tech company develops and manufactures high technology products. Workers should not primarily be interested in their tasks, but instead be committed to the company and identify with the goals of the company. The Tech company uses different methods to influence the culture such as career paths, video recordings of the CEOs talks, bonus system, training and taking part in decision-making. The culture is also spread by colleagues communicating and influencing each other. Workers are expected to take initiatives, be entrepreneurs, make connections and cooperate with each other. The management has deliberately designed a flexible organisation with no specific work assignments. At Tech there is an informal climate where workers take initiatives and cooperate in different informal constellations. Workers are expected to be creative, take risks, have fun, work hard, be committed to the company and identify with it. Kunda describes how the culture sucks people into the corporation and gives examples of people's commitment leading to burnout (Kunda, 1992).

MBO and managing organisational culture are thus concepts management use to create organisational commitment. Steven Lukes (2008) is a political and social theorist and has written about the exercise of power through ideology, which can be used to interpret the power dimension on organisational culture. If person A can have influence on person B's will, thoughts and wishes without B being aware of this manipulation, power is exercised and B's obedience can be obtained without any conflict. This is an 'efficient' way of exercising power. If perceptions, attitudes and values are changed without people are aware of it, people accept their place in the society or the organisation. Control is always exercised in organisation in some way. It can be very concrete as in direct supervision, but it can also be more subtle as in culture manipulation. In the latter case people might not always be aware of this kind of 'culture management' aim to create organisational commitment. Information technology in the form of internet, lap-tops and mobile phones make it possible for people to work around the clock. It is not always easy for people to set boundaries for work themselves, especially when the culture is signalling demands for high commitment. One possible consequence can be workers take on too much work, work excessive overtime and take work home, which in turn can lead to different kinds of stress related health problems. The use of internal markets in organisations can also be seen as a way to manage the organisational culture. The idea is that the internal customers should control quality and time of delivery of products and service from the internal suppliers. Thereby the relations between colleagues tend to change from cooperation and helpfulness between peers to more instrumental attitudes and the use of pressure from the internal customers on the internal suppliers.

As we saw in Chapter 5, organisations are increasingly using IT for surveillance, part of what is sometimes labelled digital Taylorism (Brown et al., 2011). Digital Taylorism has several features in common with Lean production such as standardisation of work tasks, increased division of labour and the control mechanism visualisation. A related concept is algorithmic management which can be understood as automated control mechanisms that aim to influence workers' behaviour and practises (Rosenblat & Stark, 2017). One example of algorithmic management is used in Amazon's warehouses. Workers use a bar code scanner which is assigning tasks, communicating orders, gives instruction to the worker where to go, monitor work and workers (Delfanti, 2019). Platform organisations extensively use algorithmic management. They e g. use algorithm generated ranking of workers based on customer rating, in order to channel work away from those who receive low rating. Uber drivers can even be automatically deactivated from the Uber platform if they do not reach a certain level of customer rating or ride acceptance rate (Ravenelle, 2017; Rosenblat & Stark, 2017; Wood et al., 2019).

With the huge increase of people working from home because of the COVID-19 pandemic, companies who provide software for remote monitoring and surveillance have seen demand surge (Harwell, 2020; Hern, 2020).

However, as ILO (2020) point out, worker surveillance can have counter-productive effects. ILO has published a practical guide for homework during the pandemic. They advise that employers should restrain from using worker surveillance tools, as it can have negative effects on motivation and reduce trust between workers and their employer.

From the USA Ajunwa et al. (2017) report that digital surveillance of workers has increased substantially due to lack of federal laws limiting employer surveillance, development in technology, lower cost for surveillance tools, and decreased power of trade unions. Union density in the USA has fallen from a low 20% in the 1980s to 11% in 2016. Therefore, unions have not much negotiation power to defend personal integrity against excessive surveillance. For instance, it is common for employers to monitor internet browser history, e-mail and number of keystrokes. Employers also track the location of workers using the GPS in employer provided mobile phones. Another example is the delivery company UPS, which in 2009 fitted their trucks with around two hundred sensors tracking data like driving speed and stopping times. UPS used this information to find out how many deliveries could be carried out in a day, and, as a result, increased the number of deliveries with fewer drivers. However, the constant monitoring and pressure result in drivers breaking safety rules and thereby increases the risk for accidents. Another example is employee ID-badges with a microphone and a location sensor developed by a firm called Sociometric Solutions in Boston. The company claims it tracks employee interaction, which employees are talking to each other and how this affect employee performance. Furthermore, in order to monitor remote workers, who for instance work from home, some companies take photos of workers computer screens, count mouse clicks and keystrokes, and taking photos of workers. Some companies are using technology which use these sources of information to monitor emotions from facial expression, raised voices or children crying in the background when workers are on the phone (Ajunwa et al., 2017).

In some call centres cameras and voice recording are used to monitor operators' performance; how many calls they answer and how they deal with customers. Employers are increasingly using software tools that measure customer satisfaction and other performance indicators (see also the platform economy in Chapter 6). Individual workers are compared with each other and their results are not seldom put up on displays. Also, in other parts of the world the same trend can be seen. An International bank in India has developed staff league tables to measure performance such as sales result, how many times their staff had met with customers and customer satisfaction (Brown et al., 2011).

Another trend is wellness programs initiated by organisations, often with the focus to stop smoking and losing weight. Many wellness programs use wearable fitness trackers such as Fitbit or Jawbone to measure workers health status.[3] Employers in the USA can also obtain information, from so-called employee wellness firms, which medicine prescription workers have, if they have voted in elections, and when they stop ordering birth control prescriptions (Ajunwa et al., 2017). The wellness programs can be more or less voluntary to participate in. In some companies there are incentives like higher pay. However, many employees report that wellness programs create guilt and anxiety. Employees feel that in order to stay employable, they not only need to be productive at the workplace, but also lose weight by exercising and eat special diets (Manokha, 2019).

Also, in other parts of the world surveillance is increasing. A study from the trade union organisation Trade Union Congress (TUC, 2018) in the UK used an online survey, focus groups and interviews with their members. A similar surveillance pattern can be seen in the UK as was reported from the USA. According to the TUC report, a whole range of surveillance methods are used by some employers in the UK:

- monitoring worker's e-mails and internet browser history.
- monitoring workers using webcams on work computers.
- recording phone calls.
- using keystroke-logging to monitor how much and when workers are typing.
- tracking the location of for instance company vehicles, computers and phones.
- monitoring the mood of workers using facial recognition software.
- using wearable devices to monitor the location and movements of workers within the workplace.
- monitoring and limiting the time workers spend going to the toilet.
- monitoring workers on Facebook and other social media outside working hours.

In the TUC report there is an example of standardisation and performance measurement which is part of digital Taylorism. It is a quote from a gas technician in a large energy company in the UK. His performance is measured by how long time he is spending on each job:

'I get 18 minutes to fit a length of pipe. If I go over, the system tells my boss, who then asks why I'm taking too long. But sometimes, you have to move a sofa or lift a carpet to get to the pipe. There's no room for error.' (TUC, 2018, p. 18).

A rather extreme variant of digital surveillance can be found in Sweden. In a Swedish innovation hub, Epicenter, a microchip the size of a rice grain has been developed which is injected in your hand. The chip tracks the location of employees and can be used for instance as a key to open doors, and to pay

[3] As the authors point out, the data from these devices are often unreliable and need to be interpreted by medical experts.

with at the companies vending machines (Manokha, 2019). The ethical problems are commented by the microbiologist Ben Libberton from the Karolinska Institute in Stockholm:

'Conceptually you could get data about your health, you could get data about your whereabouts, how often you're working, how long you're working, if you're taking toilet breaks and things like that.' (Brooks, 2017).

The Market as the Governing Principle in New Public Management

Also, in the public sector we have seen changing coordination and control mechanisms, which were presented in Chapter 7. The bureaucratic organisation was a management ideal during the major part on the twentieth century, which used fairly concrete coordination mechanisms; governing by a system of rules and formal assignments. Since the 1980s new public management (NPM) is however the most influential concept. The ***private company*** competing on a ***market*** is seen as the ideal to strive for. Competition from private companies and internal markets are used in the public sector with the aim of increasing efficiency and cutting costs. Competition between organisation is achieved in two ways: (1). Contract provision. For example, a municipality invites tenders for offer to run their home-help service. The tenders need to offer low bids if they want to be accepted by the municipality.

Several studies (Härenstam, 2005) show that contractors in general have less good working conditions than normal. As the contractor which delivers the lowest offer gets the commission, there is less scope for creating good working conditions. (2). Competition is also achieved by allowing private companies to compete with public organisations. For example, private schools compete with public schools for pupils. Both public and private schools in Sweden are funded by tax revenues. The surplus in the private schools generates profit for the owners. The private schools are therefore interested in cutting costs, which tend to result in less staff in private schools than in public ones, as was shown in Chapter 7 (Hartman, 2011; Hood, 1995). When there are less workers the effect is often higher demands on the remaining workers, which might lead to work intensification.

To conclude, the general picture points to an increasing number of control methods deployed by organisations. Consequently, the surveillance and control of workers behaviour, minds and performance seem to have increased over time since roughly the 1980s. The 1960s, 1970s, and is some countries into the 1980s, saw growth in alternative work organisations such as the sociotechnical school and quality of working life. These models emphasized participation, empowerment and democracy at the workplace. The main focus was to empower people to take decisions independently as individuals and in autonomous working groups. To use McGregor (1960/1987) theoretical framework, these schools of thought were based in Theory Y, to trust people, and give them resources to change things themselves in a decentralised organisation. Taylorism and other top-down models, with their theory

X approach, were heavily criticised during this period, both by researchers and by many managers in working life. The last decades the pendulum has swayed back again towards the theory X view of organisations and workers. The trend is more power to employers, in line with the neoliberal wave in society, which emphasizes a traditional hierarchical view of organisations and an unregulated labour market where trade unions do not have a place. The employers are again aiming at centralising power at the top and strive to control the organisation in a machine-like way.

In knowledge management we have seen the strive to control knowledge and in digital Taylorism to break down knowledge work in smaller components and standardise them. In lean production a whole arsenal of control mechanisms is used. Both in lean production and in new public management internal markets are deployed to create internal suppliers and customers, thus creating pressure on internal customers to deliver in the right time and to the specified quality. Management by objectives and cultural engineering aim to create internal commitment, which aims at making employees to feel more responsible and engaged in the organisation. Other control mechanisms use external commitment. In for instance digital Taylorism and NPM performance is measured in many ways and compared to targets. Performance, behaviour, social interaction, health status, mood and mindset are measured for each individual in digital Taylorism. All in all, if all these control mechanisms are used by an organisation, it is not farfetched to use the term total control management (TCM).

Increased Demands, Intensification of Work and Stress Related Unhealth

A number of contemporary work organisation models lead to intensification of work and as a result contribute to stress related unhealth. Several of the new work organisation models have in common that they in different ways strive to solve problems associated with the classical models, such as sub optimization, inflexibility, inefficiency, demotivating work, lack of learning and innovation for people and organisations. Contemporary work organisation models tend to emphasise process organisation, intrinsic motivation, learning, flexible teams and work in projects. Workers in such organisations are expected to be flexible, work independently, be able to cooperate with many different people, and continuously work to develop their own competence, contribute to organisational knowledge and development. The expectations and demands on workers are thus high. Furthermore, the demands are also increasing through time reductions in work processes and thus speeding up these. To organise by processes (Chapter 5) rather than functions is a strong trend in contemporary management models. Process organisation is a significant feature in lean production, time based management (TBM) and business process engineering (BPR). In these concepts focus is on cutting lead times, for example the time from customer order to delivery of a product to the customer. Also, the lead time to develop new products and services are shortened. For example, car manufacturers, which can present new models at a faster rate than their competitors have a competitive advantage. After reorganising work processes can often run ten times faster according to the BPR authors Hammer and Champy (1995). In lean production work is intensified and stressful and the tasks are narrow and repetitive. The higher demand for performance makes it harder for example elderly and people who have not perfect health to cope with work (Landsbergis et al., 1999; Toivonen & Landsbergis, 2013). In this kind of work, where workers have low control and demands are high is related to higher risk for stress related unhealth such as sleeping problems, stomach problems, sleeping problems, back pain, headache and cardiac deceases (E g. Bowling et al., 2015).

The introduction of NPM in the public sector has several principles that lead to increased demands and pressure on workers. Competition between organisations and between units within organisations is one of these principles. Some public service in outsourced to contractors. According to studies (Härenstam, 2005) show that contractors often have less good working conditions than normal, because the contractor which delivers the lowest offer often are chosen. Then there is less scope for creating good working conditions. Also within the organisation NPM (and lean) postulates the use of internal markers, where internal customers are expected to demand service in time and at the specified quality, thus pressure is built into the internal market.

As presented above, NPM also strives to reduce government spending in the public welfare sector, which results in cutting down on staff (Schnall et al., 2016). For example, the number of civil servants in the UK was cut by a third from 1980 to 2010 (Hood & Dixon, 2016). In Sweden, during the 1990s, there was also substantial downsizing in the public sector. In Swedish hospitals the staff was cut by 20% on average. It is among workers in county councils, where most of the healthcare workers are employed, the sharpest rise in work demands has been seen in Sweden. In 1991 45% of women and 43% of men reported too high demands at work. In 1999 this share had risen to 69% for women and 67% for men. Also, possibility to control one's work decreased in the Swedish public sector (Theorell, 2006, Chapter 1). Furthermore, NPM endorses a top-down decision model, giving more power to managers, thus less decision authority for workers. NPM also leads to increase in administrative tasks, which in turn results in further intensification of work. As a result, studies report high stress levels in organisations using NPM principles (Olejniczak & Salmon, 2014; Parding et al., 2020; Chapter 2).

To work in projects is also more common in contemporary working life. Workers are expected to participate in projects, cooperate with others and contribute with their competence. At the same time, they often have their regular tasks to handle. Process- and project organisations place demand on knowledge sharing and learning. Workers are also often expected to take part in changing and improving work systems. Several work organisation models emphasise this. In TQM and lean production workers are involved in kaizen—continuous improvements of the production system. In the learning organisation and in the boundaryless organisation, workers are expected to question routines and work methods, communicate with people in and outside the organisation, take initiatives to their own and the organisation's development. According to some studies this kind of flexible work, which can be characterised by high autonomy about how to perform work and how much work should be carried out, can result in unhealth. In such flexible and boundaryless workplaces people also often have responsibility for their own competence development. Certainly, they have a large discretion, but the freedom can be experienced as high demands because there are no limits in work and what a reasonable workload should be (Håkansson & Isidorsson, 2006, p. 4; Waldenström & Härenstam, 2008).

Flexibility is a buzz word in working life of today. Workers are expected to be flexible in different ways, for example to be able to perform and change between different tasks, which is labelled functional flexibility. Organisations can also choose to have temporary employees; hourly employed or hire staff from an agency. These workers have to be available to work at short notice. This kind of flexibility is labelled numerical flexibility (Pinfield & Atkinson, 1988). An extreme form of numerical flexibility is found in platform organisations (Chapter 8), as the platform organisation potentially has access to a large crowd of gig workers, without having any employer responsibility for them. All the risk is transferred to the gig workers, as they need to carry all the costs for infrastructure, sick-leave and holiday as they are self-employed. The gig worker is controlled by algorithm management where customer rating and job acceptance rate automatically channel away work from those who underscore. Precarious work in the gig economy is growing rapidly. Work is often low paid and workers often need to have several jobs to make a living. Gig workers often need to work long hours and/or to tight deadlines, leading to work intensification. Therefore, they often report exhaustion and pain in the body (Wood et al., 2019).

The location of work is also often flexible in contemporary working life, especially for office workers. Remote working or teleworking increased already before the COVID-19 pandemic, but has surged since the outbreak of the pandemic. A lot of workers are required to telework full-time in order to prevent the spread of the virus. In Europe around 40% of workers are teleworking during the COVID-19 pandemic (ILO, 2020).

There are a number of advantages with teleworking. Employers save a lot of money on office rent if workers do not have regular places. Workers can for example work from home part of the time and when at the workplace use any available work desk, sometimes called hot desking. According to several studies teleworking can be beneficial for productivity, or at least not having a negative effect on productivity. Most workers are satisfied with teleworking and want to continue doing it, especially if they have the autonomy to choose to when and where to telework. The flexible work arrangement makes it easier for people to combine family life with work. It is also reducing commuting time for people. On the downside is the risk of social isolation when not meeting colleagues. Studies also show that teleworking tends to lead to longer working hours and intensification of work. This boundaryless work, with opportunity to be constantly online, can colonise people's lives, decrease leisure and resting time and lead to stress related problems. A constant inflow of E-mails, online meetings, and phone calls can also make it difficult for people to concentrate on work in longer periods (Standing, 2011; Chapter 2 and 5; Messenger et al., 2017; Felstead & Reuschke, 2020; DeFilippis et al., 2020).

People who mainly work from home during the COVID-19 pandemic or because of other reasons tend to report lower mood and lower levels of mental health (ILO, 2020). A study in the UK (Felstead & Reuschke, 2020) showed that those who only worked from home during the three month COVID-19 lockdown reported lower levels of mental health than those who worked in the workplace. In general, according to an overview of telework, partial teleworking, when workers can decide when to work at the workplace or from home, tend to result in better health and work-life balance (Messenger et al., 2017).

Surveillance and monitoring are increasingly used to control workers, especially regarding remote work/teleworking, for instance by using webcams to take pictures of workers, taking screen pictures, tracking movements, and monitoring keystrokes (Ajunwa et al., 2017). According to an overview of teleworkers' experiences of electronic monitoring during Covid 19, common reactions are tension, anxiety and stress, but also negative attitudes and resistance towards management (Jeske, 2022). Monitoring is a visualisation principle, which is also used in lean production and in algorithm management.

To sum up, studies of new work organisation models indicate higher demands and pressure on workers. Demands are high to perform routine- and development tasks fast in process-oriented concepts such as lean production, digital Taylorism, TBM and BPR. Workers are expected to be functionally flexible, that is to be able to perform and change between different tasks. Various coordination and control mechanisms, such as visualisation through monitoring and algorithm management reinforce demands and pressure. Precarious low paid work is increasing which make it difficult for people to earn a living and leads to long working hours. Competition in the public sector introduced through NPM, and pressure from the financial market in the private sector, often result in downsizing of the work force to keep costs down, which results in higher work intensity for the remaining staff.

Studies on the macro level (society) of working life are in line with the picture presented above. Studies report above all that demands on workers have increased, but also to some extent that control have decreased for parts of the work force, which will be the focus below.

The number of working hours in advanced societies during the twentieth century has fallen according to Gallie (2017). A Eurofound report (Parent-Thirion et al., 2017) came to the same conclusion covering EU states between 2005 and 2015. However, the authors point out that the decline in working hours can largely be explained by more people working part time and fewer people are working 48 hours or more per week (Parent-Thirion et al., 2017). The general trend however, is that workers report increased work intensity and tighter deadlines in the last 3–4 decades. In some countries, like the UK, France and the US the trend started in the 1980s, but from the 1990s it seems to be a general trend. Workers report that they find it harder and harder to finish work within the time available. The sharpest rise in work intensity during the 1990s has been reported from the UK, France and Ireland. Other countries, such as Spain, Luxembourg, Denmark, Greece and Germany have seen less dramatic increase in work intensity. From the end of the 1990s to 2008 work intensity levelled off, but increased again with the economic crises in 2008 (Gallie, 2017). Green et al. (2021) report a continuing increase of work intensification in the UK from 2006 to 2017 across most industries and occupations. Green et al. find a positive correlation between rising requirements to learn at work and work intensification. The same goes for the rising number of self-employed, and workers who perceive a high degree of competitive environment for the organisation they work for. According to a global overview from ILO and Eurofound (Aleksynska et al., 2019), 33% of workers in the EU and 46% in the US work at high speed three-quarters of the time or more. 37% of workers in the EU and 48% in the US work to tight deadlines three-quarters of the time or more.

However, studies differ about changes in job control between countries and also within countries. The general pattern however, is that the Nordic countries stand out, where workers have the highest level of control over how to carry out work. The lowest levels of control are found in south and eastern Europe (Gallie, 2017). According to Gallie (2017), job control declined in the 1990s in Spain and the UK, and increased in Germany and Sweden. Other studies however show that job control, to some extent, decreased in Sweden during the 1990s, see below.

There were some improvements in working life during the 1970s and 1980s in Sweden. The physical work environment improved. Occupational healthcare received extensive government funding and the unemployment rates were very low (Theorell et al., 2002). An inquiry by Le Grand et al. (2001) provide us with an overview of studies about changes in skills, job demands and control in Sweden. In the 1980s work demands increased but control over work was stable (Le Grand et al., 2001, p. 102). In the beginning of the 1990s however, Sweden was hit by a recession. Unemployment rose from 3 to 10% and there were demands for increased efficiency in both the public and the private sector. Decision-makers focused on new organisation models, which could improve efficiency fast. Substantial downsizing in organisation and diffusion of lean management and NPM followed, which in turn resulted in impaired working conditions, increased work-related un-health and sick leave. The social security system was weakened and funding to occupational healthcare was withdrawn (Theorell et al., 2002; Theorell, 2006, Chapter 1). In line with these changes several studies indicate that job demand in Sweden continued to increase in the 1990s. In contrast to the 1980s also job control, to some extent, declined in the 1990s, contrary to what Gallie argues. It is however important to point out that the decrease of control is only about work pace and not about choices of work methods and how to carry out work. The decline in control was concentrated to the healthcare sector, the education sector, parts of the retail and parts of the manufacturing industry (Le Grand et al., 2001, pp. 101–108).

The health risks of an intensified working life have been highlighted by stress research. High demand on work output combined with lack of control over work increase the risk for developing stress ill-health (Bowling et al., 2015; Lang et al., 2012; Nixon et al., 2011; Theorell et al., 2016). Burnout is one example of stress related ill-health. Aronsson et al. (2017) carried out a meta-analysis about effects from the work environment on burnout. They found that high demands and high workload, low control, low reward and job insecurity increases the risk for developing burnout. Burnout definitions (there are several) pinpoint overall exhaustion from work overload leading to cognitive weariness, depression and reduced resilience (Aumayr-Pintar et al., 2018, pp. 3–4). An EU report indicates an increase in burnout in two out of three countries that have studies covering changes of the prevalence of burnout over time. The Netherland Working Condition Survey 2007–2016, using a sample of over 40 000 employees, showed a rise in burnout from 11.3% in 2007 to 14.6 in 2016. A Portuguese study using a sample of over 38 000 professionals in four sectors; education, health, distribution and service saw an increase in burnout from 8% in 2008 to 15% 2013. A Swedish study using a sample of 1000 people in the northern part of the country showed no change over a five-year period; 12.9% in 2004 and 13.1% in 2009 (Aumayr-Pintar et al., 2018, pp. 5–6). There are however other studies from Sweden, which indicate that negative effects on health from work have increased, see below.

Another EU report (Milczarek et al., 2009), based on the European Working Conditions Survey 2005 reports levels of stress and stress related health problems in the EU. In the 15 EU states, prior to the accession in 2005, 23% of workers reported that work had caused them fatigue, 15% reported headache from work, and 8% sleeping problems (p. 21). In the UK, an estimation based on the labour force survey 2019, there were 602,000 cases of stress related ill-health caused or made worse by work. Stress related mental ill-health from work has increased slightly during the last few years. In 2019 stress related ill-health from work accounted for 44% of all cases of ill-health in the UK (HSE, 2019).

The increasing job demands and to some extent the decreased control of work pace in the 1990s resulted in a rise in stress related mental illness in Sweden. SCB (the Swedish official statistics) have since 1989 studied the number of people in the work force that work in high strained jobs (using Karasek and Theorell's demand/control model). The share that work in high strain jobs have increased between 1989 to 2015 from 15 to 20% for men and for women from 20 to 35%. The increase took place largely during the 1990s and then levelled out. In 2021 there is a slight decline for women—29% work in high strain jobs. For men there is no change in 2021 (Arbetsmiljöverket (Swedish work environment authority), 2022, Chapter 6).

There are large differences between sectors and also between occupations. In the healthcare- and in the education sector between 35 and 65% of workers have high strain jobs 2015. In line with this negative trend, the number of people who report that they every week when coming home from work have pain in back, shoulders or arms, legs, knees and feet have increased since the beginning of the 1990s.[4] In 2015 about a third of workers reported any of these problems. Women are also here overrepresented (Arbetsmiljöverket (Swedish work environment authority), 2016, Chapter 4 and 11).

Also mental illness caused by work has increased in Sweden. In 1996 6% of women and 3% of men had job related mental illness. In 2003 the shares had risen to 14% for women and 8% for men. Long-term sick leave caused by job related mental illness increased substantially from 1997 especially for women (Theorell, 2006). A few years from 2004 onwards there was a slight decline in job related mental illness, but from 2012 the share started to rise again. In 2016 the number of job-related mental illness cases were back on the 2003 level. The share of sick leave cases related to job related illness rose from 30 to 48% of the total number of sick leave cases from 2010 to 2018 (Hartman & Odmark, 2019). There was a decline in stress related mental illness during the pandemic, but the numbers of people on sick leave with stress related illness, such as burnout, started to rise again after the pandemic, and account for almost half of sick leave cases 2022. 79% of these sick leave cases are women (Försäkringskassan (the Swedish Social Insurance Agency), 2022).

Summary

There is support to the idea that the western world is a knowledge society. The number of white-collar workers has increased at the expense of blue-collar workers. More people also have higher education. However, since the 1990s there is a trend of polarisation in several countries, where both low-skilled and high-skilled work are increasing.

Since the 1990s we have seen increased demands and pressure in the working life. As a consequence, work-related ill-health has increased. The organisation models that have had a major impact on working life, since the 1990s, are mainly lean production and new public management (NPM), but also rising rapidly, platform organisations. In lean production the focus is to create fast and efficient processes with less resources. This tends to intensify work for the remaining work force. Exposition to competition in the public sector, based on NPM, put pressure on organisations to decrease

[4] According to stress research an inadequate psycho-social work environment, more specifically high job demands, low job control, low support from colleagues and managers increase the risk for musculo skeletal problems like back pain and shoulder pain etc. (Lang et al., 2012). There is also an increased risk for emotional exhaustion, a symptom which is related to burnout (Aronsson et al., 2017).

costs. Private companies compete with public companies, for example in the healthcare sector. This competition often results in less staff and intensified work. A coordination and control mechanism in lean production and NPM is internal markets or pseudo markets, where workers are defined as suppliers and customers. Internal customers are supposed to control that the internal suppliers deliver products or service in time and with the specified quality. Other control mechanisms are management by objectives and organisation culture. Workers should, from this perspective, be committed to the organisation and take responsibility for the work.

At the same time many organisations today are more organic and boundaryless. Workers have to structure work themselves and also have the technical possibilities, such as mobile phones and laptops, to take work home. Also, employers are increasingly using digital surveillance to control workers, for instance using webcams to take pictures of workers, taking screen pictures, tracking movements, and monitoring keystrokes.

Precarious gig work in platform organisations is increasing. All the risk is transferred to the gig workers, as they are self-employed. The gig worker is controlled by algorithm management where for instance low customer rating automatically channel away work. Gig workers are typically low paid and often need to work long hours and/or to tight deadlines, leading to work intensification. Therefore, they often report exhaustion and pain in the body.

Contemporary work organisation trends have resulted in higher demands and pressure on workers which has led to intensification of work for many. Probably, because of these new trends, there are higher levels of stress-related ill-health like burnout, pain in back, shoulders, legs, knees and feet.

Gruop Exercise—Health Problems at a Hospital As organisation consultants, you have been asked by the management of a hospital to analyse problems in the organisation and come up with suggestions for improvement.

Due to budget cuts, the staff has been downsized at the hospital, but the number of patients has increased. Staff turnover is high at the hospital. Many nurses and assistant nurses are on sick leave, some for burnout, others have back pain, headaches, stomach problems and sleeping problems.

Also, the relation between management and the union is bad. The union representatives have complained about a lack of understanding from managers of the health problems and other issues. They feel they are not listened to. Many employees have also complained about communication problems and conflicts with managers and doctors, but also IT-systems that are not working well, too many rigid routines and too much administration. The management on the other hand, feel that their instructions are not followed, and employees are not following the line of command by talking to the union instead of raising issues directly to their unit supervisor.

1. In your analysis phase, what questions would you ask managers, staff and union representatives in order to analyse the work organisation, and possible causes for the problems?
2. Think of possible typical answers to your questions from managers, staff and union representatives. What are the main themes (imaginary) that arise from your interviews with these three groups?
3. Based on the result of your analysis, what remedies would you recommend to the hospital?

Reflection Questions

1. Do you think we will see an up-skilling trend in the future, or will we see more of down-skilling, or will the polarisation trend maybe continue in working life?
2. Why do you think some organisations apply extensive control and surveillance on workers?
3. From an ethical perspective, what control and/or surveillance methods would you say is okay and what is not in working life?
4. Why do we see a trend of intensified work in many organisations during the last few decades?
5. What are the remedies to create a more sustainable working life for good health and well-being?

Bibliography

Åberg, R. (2015). Svensk arbetsmarknad mot polarisering efter millenieskiftet. *Arbetsmarknad och Arbetsliv, 21*(4).

Ajunwa, I., Crawford, K., & Schultz, J. (2017). Limitless worker surveillance. *California Law Review, 105*(3), 101–142.

Aleksynska, M., Berg, J., Foden, D., Johnston, H., Parent-Thirion, A., & Vanderleyden, J. (2019). *Working conditions in a global perspective*. Luxembourg and Geneva: Eurofound and International Labour Organization.

Alvesson, M. (2003). Att synkronisera föreställningar—Företagskultur och ledarskap. In Å. Sandberg (Ed.), *Ledning för alla?: perspektivbrytningar i arbetsliv och företagsledning*. SNS.

Arbetsmiljöverket. (2016). Arbetsmiljön 2015. *Arbetsmiljöstatistik. Rapport, 2016*, 2.

Arbetsmiljöverket. (2022). Arbetsmiljön 2021. *Arbetsmiljöstatistik. Rapport, 2022*, 2.

Aronsson, G., Theorell, T., Grape, T., Hammarström, A., Hogstedt, C., Marteinsdottir, I., Skoog, I., & Hall, C. (2017). A systematic review including meta-analysis of work environment and burnout symptoms. *BMC Public Health, 17*(264).

Aumayr-Pintar, C., Cerf, C. & Parent-Thirion, A. (2018). *Burnout in the workplace: A review of data and policy responses in the EU*. link/ef18047. Accessed September 19, 2022.

Bowling, N. A., Alarcon, G. M., Bragg, C. B., & Hartman, M. J. (2015). A meta-analytic examination of the potential correlates and consequences of workload. *Work & Stress, 29*(2), 95–113.

Brooks, J. (2017). Swedish workers implanted with microchips to replace cash cards and ID passes. *Independent, April 6.*

Brown, P., Lauder, H., & Ashton, D. (2011). Chapter 5. Digital taylorism. In *The global auction: The broken promises of education, jobs and incomes* Oxford University Press.

DeFilippis, E., Impink, S. M., Singell, M., Polzer, J. T., & Sadun, R. (2020). *Collaborating during coronavirus: The impact of COVID-19 on the nature of work.* NBER Working Paper Series: National Bureau of Economic Research.

Delfanti, A. (2019). Machinic dispossession and augmented despotism: Digital work in an Amazon warehouse. *New Media and Society, 12*, 1–17.

Drucker, P. F. (1976). What results should you expect? A users' guide to MBO. *Public Administration Rewiew, 36*(1), 12–19.

Felstead, A., & Reuschke, D. (2020). *Homeworking in the UK: before and during the 2020 lockdown.* Cardiff: Wales Institute of Social and Economic Research.

Försäkringskassan (2022). Stressrelaterade sjukskrivningar ökar igen efter pandemin. https://www.forsakringskassan.se/nyhetsarkiv/nyheter-press/2022-10-24-stressrelaterade-sjukskrivningar-okar-igen-efter-pandemin. Accessed March 1, 2023.

Gallie, D. (2017). The quality of work in a changing labour market. *Social Policy & Administration, 51*(2 March), 226–243.

Green, F., Felstead, A., Gallie, D., & Henseke, G. (2022). *Working Still Harder. ILR Review, 75*(2), 458–487.

Håkansson, K., & Isidorsson, T. (2006). *Arbetsmiljöarbete och långsiktigt hållbara arbetsorganisationer: Ett delprojekt inom Arbetslivsinstitutets tema Strategier, metoder och arbetssätt för fungerande arbetsmiljöarbete SMARTA.* Arbetslivsinstitutet förlagstjänst.

Hammer, M., & Champy, J. (1995). *Reengineering the corporation: A manifesto for business revolution.* Brealey.

Härenstam, A. (2005). Different development trends in working life and increasing occupational illness requires new working environment strategies. *WORK. A Journal of Prevention, Assessment and Rehabilitation, 24*(39), 261–277.

Hartman, L. (2011). Inledning. In L. Hartman (Ed.), *Konkurrensens konsekvenser: Vad händer med svensk välfärd?* SNS Förlag.

Hartman, L., & Odmark, P. (2019). Arbetsmiljö, organisation och hälsa—hur hänger det ihop och varför? *Hälsan och arbetsmiljön.* veriges företagshälsor.

Harwell, D. (2020, Managers turn to surveillance software, always-on webcams to ensure employees are (really) working from home. *The Washington Post. (April 30).*

Hern, A. (2020, Shirking from home? Staff feel the heat as bosses ramp up remote surveillance. *The Guardian, (September 27).*

Hood, C., & Dixon, R. (2016). Not what it said on the tin? reflections on three decades of UK public management reform. *Financial Accountability & Management, 32*(4, November).

Hood, C. (1995). The "new public management" in the 1980s: Variations on a theme. *Accounting, Organizations and Society, 20*(2/3), 93–109.

HSE (2019). Work-related stress, anxiety or depression statistics in Great Britain, 2019. *Health and Safety Executive,* www.hse.gov.uk/statistics/. Accessed September 19, 2022.

ILO (2020). *Teleworking during the COVID-19 pandemic and beyond: A practical guide*. International Labour Office.

Jeske, D. (2022). Remote workers' experiences with electronic monitoring during Covid-19: Implications and recommendations. *International Journal of Workplace Health Management, 15*(3), 393–409.

Kunda, G. (1992). *Engineering culture: Control and commitment in a high-tech corporation*. Temple University Press.

Landsbergis, P. A., Cahill, J., & Schnall, P. (1999). The impact of lean production and related new systems of work organization on worker health. *Journal of Occupational Health Psychology, 4*(2), 108–130.

Lang, J., Ochsmann, E., Kraus, T., & Lang, J. W. B. (2012). Psychosocial work stressors as antecedents of musculoskeletal problems: A systematic review and meta-analysis of stability-adjusted longitudinal studies. *Social Science & Medicine, 75*, 1163–1174.

Le Grand, C., Szulkin, R., & Tåhlin, M. (2001). Har jobben blivit bättre?: En analys av arbetsinnehållet under tre decennier. In *SOU 2001: 53. Välfärd och arbete i arbetslöshetens årtionde*: Statens offentliga utredningar.

Lukes, S. (1974). *Power: A radical view*. MacMillan Press Ltd.

Manokha, I. (2019). New means of workplace surveillance: From the gaze of the supervisor to the digitalization of employees. *Monthly Review, 70*(9), 25–39.

McGregor, D. (1987/1960). *The human side of enterprise*. Penguin Books Ltd.

Messenger, J., Vargas Llave, O., Gschwind, L., Boehmer, S., Vermeylen, G., & Wilkens, M. (2017). Working anytime, anywhere: The effects on the world of work. Eurofound and the International Labour Office.

Milczarek, M., Schneider, E., & Rial González, E. (2009). *OSH in figures: stress at work—facts and figures*. European Agency for Safety and Health at Work.

Nixon, A. E., Mazzola, J. J., Bauer, J., Krueger, J. R., & Spector, P. E. (2011). Can work make you sick? A meta-analysis of the relationships between job stressors and physical symptoms. *Work & Stress, 25*(1), 1–22.

Olejniczak, M., & Salmon, D. (2014). Workers in German UB II job centers—stress caused by new public management? *Journal of Workplace Rights, 17*(3–4), 255–282.

Parding, K., Sjögren, F., Petersson, C., & Pekkari, N. (2020). *Organisering av arbete och dess betydelse för hälsa och välbefinnande*. Kunskapssammanställning 2020: 7. Gävle.

Parent-Thirion, A., Biletta, I., Cabrita, J., Vargas, O., Vermeylen, G., Wilczynska, A., et al. (2017). *Sixth European Working Conditions Survey—Overview report (2017 update)*. Luxembourg: Eurofound.

Pinfield, L. T., & Atkinson, J. S. (1988). The flexible firm. *Canadian Business Review, 15*(4), 17–19.

Procter, S. (2005). Organizations and organized systems: From direct control to flexibility. In S. Ackroyd, R. Batt, P. Thompson, & P. S. Tolbert (Eds.), *The Oxford handbook of work and organization*. Oxford University Press.

Ravenelle, A. (2017). Sharing economy workers: Selling, not sharing. *Cambridge Journal of Regions Economy and Society, July*, 1–15.

Rosenblat, A., & Stark, L. (2016). Algorithmic labor and information asymmetries: A case study of uber's drivers. *International Journal of Communication, 10*, 3758–3784.

Røvik, K. A. (1998). *Moderne organisasjoner: Trender i organisasjonstenkningen ved tusenårsskiftet*. Fagbokforlaget.

Schnall, P., Dobson, M., & Landsbergis, P. (2016). Globalization, work and cardiovascular desease. *International Journal of Health Services, 46*(4), 656–692.

Standing, G. (2011). *The precariat: The new dangerous class*. Bloomsbury Academic.

Theorell, T., Weingarten, A. M., & Westerlund, H. (2002). Psychosomatic perspectives on job stress in a changing world—individual and structural perspectives. *International Congress Series, 1241.*

Theorell, T. (2006). *I spåren av 90-talet*. Karolinska institutet, University Press.

Theorell, T., Jood, K., Slunga Järvholm, L., Vingård, E., Perk, J., Östergren, P. O., et al. (2016). A systematic review of studies in the contributions of the work environment to ischaemic heart disease development. *The European Journal of Public Health, 26*(3), 470–477.

Toivanen, S., & Landsbergis, P. (2013). Lean och arbetstagarnas hälsa. In P. Sederblad (Ed.), *Lean i arbetslivet*. Stockholm: Liber.

TUC. (2018). *I'll be watching you*. https://www.tuc.org.uk/research-analysis/reports/i'll-be-watching-you. Accessed September 19, 2022.

Waldenström, K., & Härenstam, A. (2008). Does the job demand-control model correspond to externally assessed demands and control for both women and men? *Scandinavian Journal of Public Health, 36*(3), 242–249.

Walton, R. E. (1985). From control to commitment in the workplace. *Harvard Business Review, 63*(2), 77–84.

Warhurst, C., & Thompson, P. (1998). Hands, hearts and minds: Changing work and workers at the end of the century. In P. Thompson & C. Warhurst (Eds.), *Workplaces of the future*. Macmillan.

Wood, A. J., Graham, M., Lehdonvirta, V., & Hjorth, I. (2019). Good gig, bad gig: Autonomy and algorithmic control in the global gig economy. *Work, Employment and Society, 33*(1), 56–75.

CHAPTER 10

Sustainable Work Organisations

Learning Objectives

This chapter should provide you with knowledge about:

- The meaning of sustainable work organisations and what constitutes them.
- Actors, agreements and frameworks supporting a sustainable working life.
- Some of the challenges to develop a sustainable working life globally.

Throughout the book negative effects from several work organisation models have been reported such as intensification of work, high surveillance and control of workers, which in turn have had negative consequences for health and well-being. We have also seen negative effects from some work organisation models on organisational performance, that is productivity, quality and innovation.

Furthermore, increased competition between companies creates pressure on companies to cut costs. Multinational companies (MNC) are using complicated chains of subcontractors in low wage countries in order to reduce costs. MNCs not seldom 'regime shop', playing off governments against each other in order to ease labour regulations and to get tax benefits. This ugly side of globalisation has led to a 'race to the bottom' through lowering wages, the use of child labour, long hours of work and other unhealthy working conditions (Donaghey et al., 2014; Doellgast et al., 2021, pp. 373–374).

There are however alternatives to this short-term 'low road' to efficient organisations. As Wilkinson et al. (2001, p. 1) argue, for human sustainability there needs to be: '…a shift in focus from short-term corporate survival to long-term business success.' A long-term 'high road' aims to combine

P-O Börnfelt, *Work Organisation in Practice*,
https://doi.org/10.1007/978-3-031-21667-1_10

efficiency with healthy working conditions, sometimes named sustainable organisations. This section has two parts. The first part deals with what factors research has highlighted as benefitting sustainable work organisations, thus taking a meso perspective. The second part takes a societal perspective (macro), where actors, frameworks and agreements in the society are presented, which support the development of a more sustainable working life.

There has been a long debate in society how to create sustainable development in the world. Originally sustainable development referred to the question of our short-term use of natural resources in the world and that they might end in the future. The UN has organised many conferences and publications over the years about sustainability. The importance of protecting the environment and public health is emphasised (Kjellström et al., 2007). Sustainable development was defined in the UN Brundtland report from 1987 as 'development that meets the needs of the present without compromising the ability of future generations to meet their own needs' (Purvis et al., 2019, p. 684).

The concept of sustainability, on a macro level, has often been described in three pillars or circles: Environmental, social and economic sustainability. These three sustainability categories have rather unclear origins and are not very well theoretically grounded, especially how they relate to each other. Economic sustainability is controversial and has attracted a lot of critique from radical authors. The UN vague concept of sustainability can be seen as a compromise that many institutional actors and nations can accept, where economic sustainability is placed on equal footing with environmental and social sustainability (Purvis et al., 2019, p. 692).

Ecological sustainability has attracted a lot of attention in society overall, in media, in research and in organisations. Oddly enough social sustainability has not been given nowhere near the same coverage (Pfeffer, 2010). This chapter however, will focus on social sustainability in a working life context. Several sustainability concepts have been put forward, such as sustainable work, sustainable working life, sustainable work organisations, sustainable HRM and healthy workplaces. The definitions regarding working life follow along the same lines as the more general concept sustainable development defined in the UN Brundtland report.

Sustainable work and sustainable working life can be understood as 'to meet today's needs without jeopardising future resources…activities and processes should create and re-create human resources rather than consume them' (Svensson et al., 2008, p. 13, author's translation). This definition, I would argue, also includes the society and the supply chain. For instance among authors on sustainable human resource management (HRM) it is becoming more and more common to include human rights in supply chains as the responsibility of corporations (Aust et al., 2020). Sustainable work organisations and healthy workplaces can be understood as the combination of a good working environment and high organisational efficiency. A good work environment, according to this view, results in healthier workers who develop and contribute to an efficient and successful organisation. Furthermore, a good work environment is seen as a precondition to an efficient, effective and competitive organisation (Docherty et al., 2002; Chapter 1[1]; Lindberg & Vingård, 2012, p. 40).

However, a good work environment does not automatically lead to long-term survival for the organisation. If the organisation is not effective, that is provides products or services that there is a demand for by customers, the organisation will not survive for long.

There is no self-evident definition of a good work environment. However, the Swedish work environment act can provide some guidance. 'The purpose of this act is to prevent occupational illness and accidents and to otherwise ensure a good work environment.' (AML, Chapter 1, 1 §). 'Furthermore, efforts must be made to ensure that working conditions provide opportunities for personal and professional development, as well as for independence and professional responsibility.' (AML, Chapter 2, 1 §).

Healthy Working Conditions

From overviews of work environment research, a number of factors which supports health and well-being can be derived. Regarding the physical work environment, a varied physical activity is healthy. The body needs varied activity but also rest, time to recover and repair damages in tissues. Too little strain, for example from sitting still in long periods, and too much strain increases the risk for damages. When it comes to the psycho-social work environment a number of factors support health and well-being at the workplace. The factors are not ranked.

1. Influence through participation, that is that workers have opportunity to take part in decision-making processes.
2. Autonomy/delegation. Workers can, to a large extent, decide how to carry out their work.
3. Not excessive high work pace and other work demands.
4. Sufficient resources at the workplace such as staff, equipment and financial resources.
5. Accessible and fair managers who treat people with respect and dignity.
6. Good communication and cooperation at the workplace. Openness from managers for critical viewpoints and discussion with workers.
7. A positive, open and social climate with opportunities for social interaction with colleagues.
8. Opportunities for learning and competence development.
9. Related to number 1 (influence) and 8 (learning) is that workers participate in continuous change work where they can contribute with their ideas. If the workplace has got an open and supportive discussion climate the change work can result in a more efficient running of operations

[1] Docherty et al. use the concept sustainable work systems.

> but also to development of products and services (effectiveness). Participation in change work can contribute to the competitiveness of the organisation (Aronsson et al., 2017; Lindberg & Vingård, 2012; Nyberg, 2008; Stenfors et al., 2013).

The organisation models that have the highest degree of correspondence with the factors above are sociotechnical work organisation and the learning organisation. There are also definite similarities with prerequisites for successful organisational change and change competence which were presented in Chapter 6. These models can provide a foundation to design sustainable work organisations. Point 3, not excessive work demands, is of course not guaranteed in any work organisation model. Furthermore, holistic understanding, which is put forward in the sociotechnical school, facilitates taking part in development and change work, which in turn contributes to a sustainable work organisation. The low division of work and the enrichment of work through indirect tasks in the sociotechnical model, provide opportunities for workers to create holistic understanding of for example a production system, economy and customer expectations. If workers have an overview of a production system, it makes it easier to spot problems and see where improvements can be made.

Knowledge, learning and investing in people have been put forward to be of central importance to sustained corporate success (Wilkinson et al., 2001). The concepts workplace innovation and innovative workplaces are based in the sociotechnical tradition. The idea is, in line with a sustainable work organisation, that skilled and empowered workers contribute to workplace innovation which in turn leads to good work and high organisational performance. A definition of workplace innovation used by several of the scholars in this field is: "a developed and implemented practice or combination of practices that structurally (division of labour) and/or culturally (empowerment) enable employees to participate in organisational change and renewal to improve quality of working life and organisational performance" (E g. Oeij et al., 2017, p. 150).

Central factors promoting workplace innovation are said to be democratic relations at the workplace, workers using their skills and participating in improvement and innovation of technology and how work is organised (Pot et al., 2016). Furthermore, a culture based on fairness, trust, and where it is allowed to make mistakes and learning from mistakes is emphasized. It is natural in this culture for workers, and managers, to raise concerns and openly discuss solutions to problems in the organisation, also across and between organisational units. Other enablers to support workplace innovation are supporting diversity, help and training for elderly workers, promoting environmental sustainability, work-life balance practices and health programmes. The role of managers is sharing information, supporting and cooperating with workers on a mutual basis of trust (Hansen et al., 2017; Kesselring et al., 2014).

Also, beneficial for creating innovations is organisational slack, which is to have surplus resources such as time away from routinised work activities to develop new ideas. For instance, at Google 20% of their time, employees are free to explore and develop their own ideas, which has led to several innovations (Finkle, 2012, see Chapter 6). The principle organisational slack totally contradicts the popular lean philosophy which aims to eliminate all surplus resources. As we saw in Chapter 5, using lean management in product development processes is detrimental to the innovation process (Lovén, 2013). Moreover, another feature from theories about learning organisations (Chapter 6) is learning forums where people meet and reflect over the often taken-for-granted organisational structures, routines and activities, which might lead to double loop learning—bigger loops where the new activities and structures are based a new set of assumptions and values. For single loop learning, that is small adjustments in the existing organisational system, quality circles or kaizen groups used in TQM and lean production (Chapter 5) can be beneficial.

However, as mentioned in Chapter 1, there is no single optimal work organisation model and the same goes when designing a sustainable work organisation. There are many aspects to consider, and organisational features might affect various organisational outcomes in different ways. The environment around the organisation has to be taken into account. Is the environment fast moving or more stable (Burns & Stalker, 1961)? Work organisations differ substantially between for instance a law court, a car manufacturing plant, a hospital and an IT-company developing new products and services at a fast rate. Certain work organisation models are more suitable depending on what kind of activities are to be performed in the organisation or the department. If you for example use a lot of time and other resources on learning and innovation by designing a learning organisation, when the organisation really needs more efficient daily operations, the organisation can suffer from low profitability, or if it is a public organisation, use unnecessary large amount of tax-payers money (Ellström, 2001). Also, there might be possible goal conflicts between efficiency and the human side. For instance, if you optimise lead times in order to get maximum speed of processes, with the help of TBM, BPR or lean production, this can have negative effects on health and well-being for workers if work is intensified. Another example could be it the organisation introduce more organic and flexible work to enhance innovation. This kind of job could lead to role ambiguity, uncertainty and increased cognitive demands, which in turn might lead to unsustainable effects such as stress related problems (Aust et al., 2020).

Bureaucracies, such as public authorities, which operate in stable environments can be efficient. Such stable and predictable work organisations, where no major organisational change is taking place, can also be beneficial for health and well-being (Härenstam & Bejerot, 2004). Although it also depends what kind of personality you have. If you prefer structure and objectives and prescribed tasks, this is the work organisation you should work in. If you, on the other hand, like to work in a more innovative atmosphere, like to take initiatives to changes and development, a bureaucratic work organisation would probably not benefit your well-being (E g. Furnham, 2005, Chapter 4).

Trade unions are watch-dogs for healthy working conditions and are thus essential parts of sustainable work organisations. When employers do not have a counterpart, employers have sovereign power to design the organisation and employment conditions at their own will, see for example in Chapter 2 about Taylorism and Chapter 5 about lean production. This can result in exploitative work organisations with hazardous working conditions, a downward pressure on pay, and high surveillance of workers. Trade unions, if they work well, look after their members interest and strive for good working and employment conditions. Unions can provide a counterforce and prevent hazardous employment conditions. They can also be valuable discussion partners, which can contribute with ideas in order to create sustainable organisations. Many countries have institutional frameworks supporting union activity. For instance, in Sweden a lot of concerns from workers regarding working conditions are channelled through unions, and it is mandatory for employers to negotiate with the union about major changes in the organisation. There is an extensive institutional framework in Sweden supporting union activity. Around 70% of the workforce in Sweden are members of a union (Kjellberg, 2017) and most workplaces have union representatives.

Actors, Agreements and Frameworks Supporting a Sustainable Working Life

Trans-National Institution-Led Frameworks and National Legislation

There are a number of agreements, frameworks and actors supporting decent work and a sustainable working life. The majority of countries support freedom of association, that is the right to form and join an association, for example a trade union. The International Labour Organisation (ILO) is a UN agency where governments, employers and trade unions work together to set labour standards with the aim to promote decent work. Freedom of association and the right to collective bargaining are two of the fundamental conventions set down by ILO for securing decent work. ILO (2019) has 'identified eight conventions as "fundamental", covering subjects that are considered as fundamental principles and rights at work: freedom of association and the effective recognition of the right to collective bargaining; the elimination of all forms of forced or compulsory labour; the effective abolition of child labour; and the elimination of discrimination in respect of employment and occupation.'

'The eight fundamental conventions are:

1. Freedom of Association and Protection of the Right to Organise Convention, 1948 (No 87)
2. Right to Organise and Collective Bargaining Convention, 1949 (No 98)

3. Forced Labour Convention, 1930 (No. 29)
4. Abolition of Forced Labour Convention, 1957 (No. 105)
5. Minimum Age Convention, 1973 (No. 138)
6. Worst Forms of Child Labour Convention, 1999 (No. 182)
7. Equal Remuneration Convention, 1951 (No. 100)
8. Discrimination (Employment and Occupation) Convention, 1958 (No. 111)'(ILO, 2019).

A majority of countries, which are members of ILO, have ratified these fundamental conventions, or most of the conventions and incorporated them in their national legislation. Even so, these fundamental rights are often breached by companies. As mentioned above, especially multinational companies, are using long chains of subcontractors, often in different parts of the world. Production are outsourced, which is sometimes called offshored, if the subcontractor is in another country. These global supply chains make it difficult for the traditional labour tripartite governance model to function, that is when labour, the state and employers regulate labour conditions. Also, as mentioned above trade unions have lost power and have had difficulties to develop substantial international cooperation between unions in different parts of the world (Donaghey et al., 2014). However, there are a number of initiatives for international union cooperation. In the EU there is an established industrial relation structure, European Works Councils (EWS), initiated in 1994. MNCs with at least 1000 employees with operations in the EU are obliged to have EWSs where managers and employee representatives communicate certain specified issues (Kjellström et al., 2007). Also, there are a number of so-called international framework agreements (IFA) which are agreements between an MNC and an international workers federation. IFAs can take several different forms, from substantial agreements regulating employment conditions for subcontractors and suppliers, to the specification of rights such as freedom of association and collective bargaining. Ideally IFAs makes it possible for local unions to operate in the supply chains. There are however also 'lighter' forms of IFAs that merely requires MNCs to inform suppliers that there is an IFA in place and recommendations for suppliers (Donaghey et al., 2014; Kjellström et al., 2007).

An example of an international framework agreement (IFA) in the garment industry was mentioned in Chapter 8 about network organisations. After the Rana Plaza garment factory collapse in Bangladesh 2013 the Accord for Fire and Building Safety in Bangladesh was formed. Bangladeshi unions, international unions, and labour rights NGOs cooperated in negotiation with over 200 garment buyers from North America, Europe and Asia. A committee of unions, companies and the International Labour Organization (ILO) as a neutral chair overseas that the participants follow the Accord program (Anner et al., 2020; Donaghey & Reineke, 2018; Papadakis, 2021). IFAs have proven effective solving conflicts between MNCs and unions and improving working conditions. They also often result in increasing number of union members.

These effects have been noted in first-tier suppliers of MNCs. The impact further down in the supply chain is not known due to lack of transparency in these companies (Papadakis, 2021).

Two transnational standards are the UN initiative Global compact and OECDs guidelines for multinational enterprises (GME), which both build upon ILOs fundamental conventions. Global compact, launched in 2000, builds upon ten principles in the areas of human rights, labour standards, the environment and anti-corruption. It is a voluntary framework and it is the worlds' largest initiative for sustainable development for corporations. In 2012 there were over 2000 business participants in 135 countries. The Organisation for Economic Co-operation and Development (OECD) is formed of the 30 richest countries in the world.

GME, developed by OECD, are guidelines for health and safety at work and for consumer safety. GME has been approved by all 30 OECD countries and a number of other countries. The OECD countries have guaranteed to promote GME. However, Global compact and GME are only recommendations and thus non-binding (Kjellström et al., 2007).

In recent years, a number of nations have introduced legislation making it mandatory for large companies to disclose their measures for preventing human rights to be breached in their supply chains (Bright, 2021). The California Transparency in Supply Chains Act of 2010 was first out. Other examples are the UK Modern Slavery Act in 2015, the Australian Modern Slavery Act in 2018, and the Norwegian Draft Act in 2019 regarding larger companies´ impact on human rights and working conditions in their supply chains. However, the UK and Australian legislations merely require companies to report the steps they have taken to prevent slavery or human trafficking in their supply chains. These legislations have been criticised for having little impact on workers right in practise. The laws require companies to report rather than to act. The French Duty of Vigilance Law adopted in 2017 goes further. It requires larger companies to implement a vigilance plan for identifying risks and preventing severe violations of human rights. 'The ***aims of the legislation*** are twofold: (i) to provide access to remedy for individuals and communities whose human rights were adversely affected by the activities of French companies or suppliers in their global supply chains; and (ii) to enhance corporate accountability.' (Bright, 2021, p. 88).

Social Movement Frameworks and Business Driven Initiatives

There are also certification standards initiated by social movements. Social Accountability International (SAI) developed SA 8000 in 1998. SA 8000 is considered one of the most stringent certification standards regarding labour conditions. SA 8000 measures performance in eight areas, which build upon ILOs fundamental principles and UNs declaration of human rights. They carry through regular revisions and monitoring, usually twice a year, using both announced and unannounced visits to organisations. According to SAI they help securing ethical working conditions for over two million workers in over 4000 organisations. The Fairtrade movement is another certification standard, which builds upon product labelling in order to make it easier for consumers to make ethical choices. Fairtrade, established in 1992, supports small scale farming such as coffee and cocoa. Fairtrade sets standards for workers' rights and the environment and monitors that the standards are followed. There are standards in areas such as minimum price and income, democratic leadership, gender equality, decent working conditions, for example the right to join a trade union. According to Fairtrade there are 1.66 million farmers and workers in Fairtrade certified organisations (Donaghey et al., 2014; Fairtrade, 2019; SAI, 2019). A more recent initiative is Economy for the Common Good (ECG) established in 2010. ECG has four values: Human dignity, solidarity and social justice, environmental sustainability, transparency and co-determination. The four values are measured in five areas: Suppliers, owners, equity- and financial service providers, employees, customers and business partners and social environment. Companies can be certified through an auditing process, which is repeated after two years. Around 400 companies are certified (ECG, 2019).

In later years there has been an increased awareness of ethical issues concerning the products and services consumers buy. An increasing number of people want to buy decent or fair products, that is which have been produced without exploiting people and/or the nature. Media and activist groups also work to promote decent work by exposing abusive working conditions in transnational supply chains. Companies have become more aware of their reputation regarding how they are perceived by the public as taking ethical responsibility or not. These trends have spurred companies to adopt codes of conduct in line with corporate social responsibility (CSR). The codes of conduct are policies for suppliers and subcontractors about human rights, employment conditions and environmental concerns. Many multinational companies have created codes on conduct in order to be seen as responsible actors in the society. However, these codes of conducts are voluntary policies adopted by companies and there are no third parties that can verify if policies are followed in the supply chains or not. Therefore CSR-policies have not seldom been associated with paying lip service (Donaghey & Reinecke, 2018; Kuruvilla et al., 2021). Trade unions therefore generally prefer international framework agreements (IFA) covering the supply chains of multinational companies (Donaghey et al., 2014; Kjellström et al., 2007).

Reports of violation of human rights in supply chains are unfortunately not very hard to find. For instance, a report from Oxfam (Zahn et al., 2022) regarding German supermarket chains, sheds light of the working conditions on banana and pineapple farms in Costa Rica and vineyards in South Africa. Many migrant workers, often without work papers, work long hours on these farms on starvation wages. They are afraid to protest because they risk losing their jobs and also to be deported. Four big supermarket chains have 85% of the market in Germany: Rewe with Penny Markt, Aldi, Edeka with Netto and the Schwarz Group owning Lidl and Kaufland. For instance Aldi and Lidl have CSR policies, never the less there are major violations of workers' rights in their supply chains. Due to their bargaining power these German supermarket chains can negotiate very low prices from the suppliers. As a result, the price of wine from South Africa and pineapples from Costa Rica have decreased by around 50% in twenty years. As a comparison, the State owned Swedish Systembolaget pays 50% more, compared with German importers, for South African wine. The low prices paid by the German supermarket chains create a downward pressure on the wages for farm workers. Following up their studies 2016 and 2017 Oxfam found that little had changed in 2021. Migrant workers in Costa Rica earns only 60% of Costa Rica workers. Women earn even less. These migrant workers earn much less than the minimum wage in the country and a living wage. It is estimated that a living wage is 27 Euros per day and the migrant workers earn only 4.50 to 16 Euros per day. They often work long hours, in some cases over 12 hours a day, often without protective clothing against pesticides. As a consequence, the interviewed workers talked about health problems caused by the toxic substances, such as dizziness, pain and breathing problems. The fruit companies also, in many cases, prevent workers from forming unions.

In South Africa, 37% of the interviewed workers on grape farms received wages under the minimum wage (194 Euro per month). Furthermore, migrant women in South Africa often experienced abusive treatment. 45% of the women in the study reported racism, discrimination, violence, or sexual abuse. New legislation is however implemented in Germany to prevent violations of workers' rights. From 2023, according to a new supply chain act, all companies with more than 3000 employees need to take measures to stop human right violations in their supply chains. EU is also on the way to develop a supply chain law (Zahn et al., 2022).

There are also business driven auditing and certification initiatives to help companies to protect human rights in their supply chains. The Business Social Compliance Initiative (BSCI) is one of them, which started in 2003. BSCI has 11 principles covering areas such as the right to join an association and collective bargaining, fair remuneration, no discrimination, occupational health and safety and no child labour. BSCI helps with advice to monitor and audit supply chains, however it is not providing certification. The International Organization for Standardisation (ISO) introduced ISO 26000 (Social responsibility) in 2010. ISO certify in other areas but in ISO 26000 they also, like BSCI, only provide guidance to companies. Their guidance covers seven areas, such as human rights, labour practises, the environment and fair operating practises (BSCI, 2019; Donaghey et al., 2014; ISO, 26000, 2019). These two business driven frameworks officially claim that they are multi stakeholder initiatives in order to get legitimacy. Scholars have however pointed out that MNCs and other actors with more financial resources have had more influence on the agenda in these industry-led frameworks compared to other actors such as trade unions and social movements (Donaghey et al., 2014).

Summary

What are the remedies to counteract the negative trends described in the previous chapter and instead design more sustainable work organisations, so that human resources are not consumed but instead are re-generated? In the sustainable work organisation, a good work environment and efficiency are combined. A healthy work environment is according to this view a necessary condition to have an efficient work organisation. Healthy working conditions are characterised by participation in decision-making, a certain autonomy for the individual to carry out work, learning and competence development, social support from colleagues, open communication between people, and managers who treat people with respect and dignity. By participating in making improvements at the workplace, workers can contribute developing the organisation and thereby improve efficiency. There are a number of transnational institutions and agreements supporting decent work and a sustainable working life. Within the UN the International Labour Organisation (ILO) has identified eight fundamental principles supporting decent and sustainable work, such as the right to form and join an association, for example a trade union. Frameworks that build upon ILOs principles are for example UNs Global compact and OECDs guidelines for multinational enterprises (GME). There are also certification standards initiated by social movements, such as SA 8000 and Fairtrade, which support sustainable and decent work.

Reflection Questions

1. What is the difference between sustainable organisations and sustainable work organisations (think effectiveness and efficiency)?
2. What, would you say, are the main obstacles to create a sustainable working life in your country and globally?
3. What can employers do to create more sustainable organisations?
4. Can unions have a role to play to promote more sustainable working life, and if so, what can they do?

Bibliography

AML. https://www.riksdagen.se/sv/dokument-lagar/dokument/svensk-forfattningssamling/arbetsmiljolag-19771160_sfs-1977-1160#K1. Accessed April 19, 2023.

Anner, M., Fischer-Daly, M., & Maffie, M. (2020). Fissured employment and network bargaining: Emerging employment relations dynamics in a contingent world of work. *Industrial and Labor Relations Review*,https://doi.org/10.1177/0019793920964180. Published online October 14.

Aronsson, G., Theorell, T., Grape, T., Hammarström, A., Hogstedt, C., Marteinsdottir, I. ... Hall, C. (2017). A systematic review including meta-analysis of work environment and burnout symptoms. *BMC Public Health, 17*(264).

Aust, I., Matthews, B., & Muller-Camen, M. (2020). Common good HRM: A paradigm shift in sustainable HRM. *Human Resource Management Review, 30*, 1–11.

Bright, C. (2021). 2. Mapping human rights due diligence regulations and evaluating their contribution in upholding labour standards in global supply chains. In G. Delautre, E. Echeverría Manrique, & C. Fenwick (Eds.), *Decent work in a globalized economy: Lessons from public and private initiatives*. International Labour Office.

BSCI. (2019). *Business Social Compliance Initiative*. https://www.amfori.org/content/amfori-bsci. Accessed September 19, 2022.

Burns, T., & Stalker, G. M. (1961). *The management of innovation*. Tavistock.

Docherty, P., Forslin, J., & Shani, A. B. (2002). *Creating sustainable work systems: Emergent perspectives and practise*. Routledge.

Doellgast, V., Wright, C. F., Lee Cooke, F., & Bamber, G. J. (2021). 15. Conclusions: Globalisation, crises and institutional responses. In G. J. Bamber, F. Lee Cooke, V. Doellgast, & C. F. Wright (Eds.), *International & comparative employment relations*. Sage.

Donaghey, J., & Reinecke, J. (2018). When industrial democracy meets corporate social responsibility: A comparison of the Bangladesh accord and alliance as responses to the Rana Plaza Disaster. *British Journal of Industrial Relations, 56*(1), 14–42.

Donaghey, J., Reinecke, J., Niforou, C., & Lawson, B. (2014). From employment relations to consumption relations: Balancing labor governance in global supply chains. *Human Resource Management, 53*(2), 229–252.

ECG. (2019). *Economy for the Common Good*. https://www.ecogood.org/en/. Accessed September 29, 2022.

Ellström, P.-E. (2001). Integrating learning and work: Problems and prospects. *Human Resource Development Quartely, 12*(4), 421–435.

Fairtrade. (2019). *Fairtrade Foundation*. http://www.fairtrade.org.uk/What-is-Fairtrade. Accessed September 29, 2022.

Finkle, T. A. (2012). Corporate entrepreneurship and innovation in Silicon Valley: The case of google, Inc. *Entrepreneurship theory and practice, 36*(4), 863–887.

Furnham, A. (2005). *The psychology of behaviour at work*. Psychology Press.

Hansen, K., Amundsen, O., Berg Aasen, T. M., & Gressgård, L. J. (2017). 19. Management practices for promoting employee-Driven innovation. In P. R. A. Oeij, D. Rus, & F. D. Pot (Eds.), *Workplace innovation: Theory, research and practice*. Springer.

Härenstam, A., & Bejerot, E. (2004). Multilevel analyses of organizational change and working conditions in public and private sector. *European Journal of Work and Organizational Psychology, 13*(3), 305–343.

ILO. (2019). *International Labour Organization*. https://www.ilo.org/global/standards/introduction-to-international-labour-standards/conventions-and-recommendations/lang--en/index.htm. Accessed September 29, 2022.

ISO26000. (2019). *ISO 26000:2010*. https://www.iso.org/iso-26000-social-responsibility.html. Accessed September 29, 2022.

Kesselring, A., Blasy, C., & Scoppetta, A. (2014). *Workplace innovation: Concepts and indicators*. European Commision.

Kjellberg, A. (2017). Fack, arbetsgivare och industrial relations. In M. Bengtsson & T. Berglund (Eds.), *Arbetslivet*. Studentlitteratur.

Kjellström, T., Håkansta, C., & Hogstedt, C. (2007). Globalisation and public health. *Scandinavian Journal of Public Health, 35*(Suppl 70), 7–13.

Kuruvilla, S., Li, N., & Jackson, J. L. (2021). 6. Private regulation of labour standards in global supply chains: Current status and future directions. In G. Delautre, E. Echeverría Manrique, & C. Fenwick (Eds.), *Decent work in a globalized economy: Lessons from public and private initiatives*. International Labour Office.

Lindberg, P., & Vingård, E. (2012). Den goda arbetsmiljön och dess indikatorer: Kunskapsöversikt. *Arbetsmiljöverket, Rapport, 2012*, 7.

Lovén, E. (2013). Kreativitet, innovation och lean. In P. Sederblad (Ed.), *Lean i arbetslivet*. Stockholm: Liber.

Nyberg, A. (2008). Det goda chefskapet: Organisatorisk effektivitet och anställdas hälsa. En kunskapsöversikt. In M. Döös & K. Waldenström (Eds.), *Chefskapets former och resultat* (Vol. 15). Stockholm: Vinnova.

Oeij, P. R. A., Dhondt, S., Ziauberyte-Jakstiene, R., Corral, A., & Preenen, P. (2017). Implementing workplace innovation across Europe: Why, how and what? In P. R. A. Oeij, D. Rus, & F. D. Pot (Eds.), *Worplace innovation: Theory, research and pratice*. Springer.

Papadakis, K. (2021). 4. A short history and future prospects of cross-border social dialogue and global industrial relations agreements. In G. Delautre, E. Echeverría Manrique, & C. Fenwick (Eds.), *Decent work in a globalized economy: Lessons from public and private initiatives*. International Labour Office.

Pfeffer, J. (2010). Building sustainable organizations: The human factor. *Academy of Management Perspectives, 24*(1), 34–45.

Pot, F., Totterdill, P., & Dhondt, S. (2016). Workplace innovation: European policy and theoretical foundation. *World Review of Entrepreneurship, Management and Sustainable Development, 12*(1), 13–32.

Purvis, B., Mao, Y., & Robinson, D. (2019). Three pillars of sustainability: In search of conceptual origins. *Sustainability Science, 14*, 681–695.

SAI. (2019). *Social Accountability International. SA8000:2014*. http://www.sa-intl.org. Accessed September 19, 2022.

Stenfors, C. U. D., Magnusson Hanson, L., Oxienstierna, G., Theorell, T., & Nilsson, L. -G. (2013). Psychological working conditions and cognitive complaints among Swedish Employees. *PLOS ONE* www.plosone.org, *8*(4).

Svensson, L., Aronsson, G., Randle, H., & Eklund, J. (2008). *Hållbart arbetsliv: Projekt som gästspel eller strategi i hållbar utveckling*. Malmö: Gleerups Utbildning AB.

Wilkinson, A., Hill, M., & Gollan, P. J. (2001). The sustainability debate. *International Journal of Operations & Production Management, 21*(12), 1492–1502.

Zahn, T., Vogel, S., Rötzsch, F., & Knapp, J. (2022). *No limits to exploitation: Migrant laborers in the supply chains of German supermarkets*. Oxfam Deutschland.

Index

P-O Börnfelt, *Work Organisation in Practice*,
https://doi.org/10.1007/978-3-031-21667-1

Printed by Printforce, United Kingdom